Analyzing Wealth Effects for Bondholders

Corporate Finance and Governance

Edited by Dirk Schiereck

Volume 20

Zur Qualitätssicherung und Peer Review der vorliegenden Publikation

Die Qualität der in dieser Reihe erscheinenden Arbeiten wird vor der Publikation durch den Herausgeber der Reihe geprüft.

Notes on the quality assurance and peer review of this publication

Prior to publication, the quality of the work published in this series is reviewed by the editor of the series.

Daniel Maul

Analyzing Wealth Effects for Bondholders

New Insight on Major Corporate Events from the Debtholders' Perspective

PL ACADEMIC RESEARCH

Bibliographic Information published by the Deutsche Nationalbibliothek
The Deutsche Nationalbibliothek lists this publication in the Deutsche Nationalbibliografie; detailed bibliographic data is available in the internet at http://dnb.d-nb.de.

Zugl.: Darmstadt, Techn. Univ., Diss., 2015

Library of Congress Cataloging-in-Publication Data
Names: Maul, Daniel, author.
Title: Analyzing wealth effects for bondholders : new insight on major corporate events from the debtholders' perspective / Daniel Maul.
Description: 1 Edition. | New York : Peter Lang, 2016. | Series: Corporate finance and governance, ISSN 1869-537X ; Volume 20 | Ph. D. Technische Universität Darmstadt 2015
Identifiers: LCCN 2016000978| ISBN 9783631671191 (Print : alk. paper) | ISBN 9783653064261 (E-Book)
Subjects: LCSH: Corporate bonds. | Corporate debt. | Corporations—Finance.
Classification: LCC HG4651 .M378 2016 | DDC 332.63/23—dc23 LC record available at http://lccn.loc.gov/2016000978

D 17
ISSN 1869-537X
ISBN 978-3-631-67119-1 (Print)
E-ISBN 978-3-653-06426-1 (E-Book)
DOI 10.3726/978-3-653-06426-1

PL Academic Research is an Imprint of Peter Lang GmbH.

Peter Lang – Frankfurt am Main · Bern · Bruxelles · New York · Oxford · Warszawa · Wien

This publication has been peer reviewed.

www.peterlang.com

Geleitwort

Während sich die empirische Kapitalmarktforschung seit Jahrzehnten mit den Auswirkungen strategischer Unternehmensentscheidungen auf den Shareholder Value und damit auf die Kursreaktionen bei Aktien auseinandersetzt, fristet die Analyse von Anleihekursreaktionen immer noch ein Schattendasein. Das muss zunächst einmal verwundern, ist doch das alljährlich am Kapitalmarkt platzierte Anleihevolumen viel höher als das bei Aktien. Aber ein näherer Blick zeigt schnell, dass das Analysedefizit in erheblichem Maße sicherlich auch getrieben wird von den zahlreichen und großen methodischen Schwierigkeiten, die solche Analysen bei Anleihen (Bonds) mit sich bringen. Denn im Gegensatz zur Aktie ist jede Anleihe sehr individuell ausgestattet (Laufzeit, Kupon, Besicherung etc.), und einzelne Emittenten haben manchmal mehr als 100 Anleihen gleichzeitig zu bedienen.

Die Analyse von Werteffekten bei Anleihegläubigern bedarf also spezifischer methodischer Kenntnisse und recht komplexer Auswertungsmethoden. Dann aber sind zahlreiche bislang noch offene Forschungsfragen präzise zu adressieren, und neue, innovative Einsichten zu den Konsequenzen strategischer Unternehmensentscheidungen sind möglich. So war bspw. bislang unklar, ob die Aufstockung einer bestehenden Anleihe am Kapitalmarkt anders interpretiert wird als die Begebung einer neuen Anleihe. Und für M&A-Transaktionen ruhte der Fokus nahezu ausschließlich auf der Eigentümerseite, was mit den Gläubigern passiert, war Nebensache.

Die vorliegende Arbeit nimmt sich dieser bedeutenden Forschungslücke mit viel Liebe zum Detail und höchster Sorgfalt in beeindruckender Weise an. Ihr primäres Ziel war es, sowohl über Kapitalmarktdaten als auch Rechnungslegungsinformationen den Erfolg von kritischen Unternehmensentscheidungen auf die Werthaltigkeit des Vermögens von Anleihegläubigern zu ermitteln und wesentliche Determinanten dieses Erfolgs zu bestimmen. So wird ein objektiver Kenntnisstand erreicht, auf dessen Basis sich fundierte Handlungsempfehlungen für die Finanzierungspraxis ableiten lassen.

Herr Maul kann die selbst gesetzten Ziele in seiner Dissertationsschrift bestens erfüllen. Die Arbeit enthält eine Fülle hoch interessanter Resultate und ist so geschrieben, dass es dem Leser große Freude machen wird, sie Seite für Seite bis zum Ende zu lesen. Ich wünsche der Arbeit eine weite Verbreitung.

Prof. Dr. Dirk Schiereck

Acknowledgements

I completed this dissertation while working as a research and teaching assistant at the Chair of Corporate Finance of the Technische Universität Darmstadt. The aim of my thesis is to provide insight into how corporate debt markets respond to new information and how this reaction correlates with the firms' equity securities. I present evidence that proves that adding the "debt perspective" can alter the overall conclusion about the impact of an event on firm value. I would like to take the opportunity and thank all the people who contributed to this work and supported me during the last four years.

Firstly, I want to thank my supervisor Prof. Dr. Dirk Schiereck. His influence on me was the main reason that I decided to stay at the university after my first degree and work on receiving a doctorate. A step I certainly will never regret.

Secondly, I want to thank my colleagues at the Chair of Corporate Finance for their support. The opportunity to discuss one's research, exchange ideas and receive helpful critics, as well as, from time to time, blow of some steam together very much helped to make this dissertation happen. A special thank goes out to Robert Fraunhoffer and Sascha Kolaric with whom I shared an office. Both were great sources of helpful comments and useful recommendations for my research.

Thirdly, I am grateful for the help my twin brother Stefan offered me. Lacking his support and encouragement, I would have gone insane long ago and starting this project would have been impossible. I could not have done this without him!

Finally, my thanks go out to my wonderful girlfriend. While she had her own battles to fight, she always found the time to build me up when times were bleak and help me finish this project. Daniela, for this and for many more reasons I love you!

Daniel Maul

Overview

Table of Contents

List of Tables

List of Figures

List of Abbreviations

a.k.a.	Also known as
AAR	Average Abnormal Return
ABR	Abnormal Bond Return
ACAR	Average Cumulative Abnormal Return
ACMVD	Abnormal Change in the Market Value of Debt
ACMVE	Abnormal Change in the Market Value of Equity
AR	Abnormal Return
ASBR	Abnormal Standardized Bond Return
ASR	Abnormal Stock Return
bps	Basis Points
BQR	Bank Quotation Record
BR	Bond Return
CAAR	Cumulative Average Abnormal Return
CABR	Cumulative Abnormal Bond Return
CAR	Cumulative Abnormal Return
CASR	Cumulative Abnormal Stock Return
CDS	Credit Default Swap
CEO	Chief Executive Officer
CFC	Commercial and Financial Chronicle
CUSIP	Committee on Uniform Security Identification Procedures
DFDB	Deutsche Finanzdatenbank
DRI	Data Resources Inc.
e.g.	for example (exempli gratia)
EBR	Expected Bond Returns
ER	Expected Return
ex.	Excluding
FBR	Firm Bond Return
FIDB	Lehman Brothers Fixed Income Database
FINRA	Financial Industry Regulatory Authority
FISD	(Mergent) Fixed Income Security Database
GDMO	Government's Debt Management Office
GDP	Gross Domestic Product
GNP	Gross National Product
HML	High Minus Low
i.e.	That is (id est)

ICMA	International Capital Market Association
IDC	Interactive Data Corporation
IDD	Investors Dealers Digest
IOSCO	International Organization of Securities Commissions
IPO	Intial Public Offerings
ITCV	Impact Threshold for a Confounding Variable
LBBD	Lehman Brothers Bond Database
LBO	Leveraged Buyout
LREO	Leverage Reducing Exchange Offers
M&A	Merger and Acquisitions
max.	Maximum
MBO	Management Buyout
MBS	Mortgage Backed Securities
Mio.	Million
N	Number of Observations
NA	Not Available
NAIC	National Association of Insurance Commissioners
NASD	National Association of Security Dealers
NYSE	New York Stock Exchange
OBR	Observed Bond Return
OLS	Ordinary Least Squares
OTC	Over the Counter
PR	Premium Return
PBR	Portfolio Bond Return
R	Return
RI	Total Return Index
ROA	Return on Assets
ROE	Return on Equity
S&P	Standard & Poor's
SABR	Standardized Abnormal Bond Return
SBR	Standardized Bond Return
SEO	Seasoned Equity Offerings
SIC	Standard Industrial Classification
SMB	Small Minus Big
SOX	Sarbanes-Oxley Act
SPR	Standardized Portfolio Bond Return
STD	Standard Deviation of Abnormal Returns
TR	Treasury Return
TRACE	Trade Reporting and Compliance Engine

US	United States
USA	United States of America
VIF	Variance Inflation Factors
VPI	Valuation Prediction Error
WSJ	Wall Street Journal

1. Introduction

1.1 The Importance and Economic Relevance of Corporate Bonds

Whenever a company is in need of funds to finance future investments, management is frequently confronted with the question as to which type of capital to choose: equity, debt or a combination of both. Straight equity capital can be gained through initial public offerings (IPO) or, if the company is already publicly listed, seasoned equity offerings (SEO). Basically, buyers of the shares (i.e. share- or stockholders) own a part of the company and obtain the potential to profit or lose from this investment depending on how the company fares. Monetary gains for the investors are realized through dividend payments or stock price appreciation, while the latter requires the shareholders to sell their stocks. Losses for the stockholders occur when the stock price declines. While stockholders in general, have numerous rights and the power to decide about the utilization of a company's earnings, they are not entitled to a steady return on their investment. In a worst case scenario, shareholders obtain no or only negative returns because the company only generates losses and its stock price declines. On the other hand, stockholders have access to, in theory, possibly unlimited returns, as they participate with a certain percentage on a firm's profit.

If equity capital is on the left hand side of the continuum of types of funds, then debt capital represents the right hand side of this continuum. The reason is that debt and debt securities typically have the exact opposite configuration as stocks. For instance, corporate debt, which can be subdivided in corporate loans and corporate debt securities like bonds, usually includes predefined arrangements that contain a payment structure for the interest and principal as well as information about how much interest the borrowing company has to pay to the creditor[1]. Thus, under the assumption of negligible default risk and held to maturity investments, creditors know exactly what return they will receive on their investment. Furthermore, when a company goes bankrupt, creditors, unlike shareholders, have first claim to the assets available, again underlining that debt securities in general are less risky than stocks. Like stocks, debt securities

1 Often, creditors and debt security holders (e.g. bondholders) are viewed as two different groups. Nevertheless, in this context the word "creditors" is used to also address holders of debt securities.

can be sold on the secondary market to realize a profit through increased prices. However, markets for plain corporate debt securities like bonds exhibit a much weaker liquidity compared to stocks, leading to higher liquidity risk.[2] Moreover, debt like loans and bonds usually constitute segregated contracts between debtor and creditor and thus do not represent any ownership of the borrowing company. Therefore, they do not give the investors (e.g. bondholders) the same number of rights that stockholders receive.

The third group of funds contains hybrids of equity and debt financing (e.g mezzanine, convertibles, etc.).[3] One of them are convertible securities, also known as convertible bonds or just convertibles. Typically, they consist of a plain corporate bond and a non-detachable call option on the company's stock, increasing the upside potential of this security compared to the stand-alone bond (Brennan & Schwartz, 1980). This also leads to lower yields demanded by investors, which can be interpreted as the payment from the investors to the issuer for the additional call option. Previous research argues that convertibles are used by management to raise equity capital through the backdoor when regular stock offerings seem to be unattractive (Stein, 1992).

But how are the three types of funds related to each other? A well-known theory in corporate finance that links the three security classes equity, debt, and hybrids together and makes statements about their "attractiveness" for management is the Pecking Order Theory developed by Myers and Majluf (1984). In summary, the theory states that management tries to minimize adverse selection costs when deciding how to finance investments. These adverse costs stem from an asymmetric distribution of information between managers and investors and in order to minimize them managers will follow a pecking order. First they retain earnings, then issue debt, and lastly issue stocks. Therefore, the Pecking Order Theory predicts stronger negative (abnormal) stock returns for the announcement of SEO compared to debt offerings. Convertibles, as a quasi-equity debt instrument, should fit between stocks and bonds. Not surprisingly, previous research found increased negative price responses from plain debt offerings to the announcement of SEO, thereby confirming this hypothesis (Eckbo, Masulis, & Norli, 2007). However, capital markets are transforming. Research by Duca, Dutordoir, Veld, and Verwijmeren (2012) provides evidence that since 2000 negative announcements returns are strongest for convertible bonds, showing that

2 See chapter 2.1.1 for further discussion of the illiquidity of corporate bonds.

3 In this section only convertible bonds are discussed as they are compared to plain equity and debt later on (see Figure 1-1 and Figure 1-2).

capital market players obviously changed their behavior and the Pecking Order Theory does no longer apply universally. This example shows that, from time to time, markets experience systematic changes which, in turn, dramatically affect the conclusions research will draw about investors and their behavior. In such a context, researchers need to adapt to the new situation and acknowledge that rules have changed.

While debt offerings still result in much (economically and statistically) weaker abnormal stock returns compared to stock offerings (Duca et al., 2012), debt markets also present substantial changes in the last two decades. A current report by Rohini Tendulkar and Gigi Hancock from the IOSCO Research Department shows that the importance of bonds as a part of the capital structure for non-financial companies worldwide has increased drastically (Tendulkar & Hancock, 2014). Overall, they reached a size of $49 trillion in 2013 and almost tripled their volume since 2000, while about one third came from non-financial issuers. One reason is that lending by banks is continuously substituted by bonds, in particular in the United States and Europe. Issues grew from $0.9 trillion in 2000 to $3.2 trillion in 2013, and many emerging economies began to issue corporate bonds (from 5% in 2000 to 30% in 2013). The increasing relevance of corporate bond markets for the economy is also confirmed by several other reports (e.g. ICMA, 2013; Kaya, 2013). Thus, it is a known fact that bonds have gained importance for corporations in comparison to stocks, and firms rely heavily on debt capital to fund their venturing.

All the same, the Thomson One Banker database is utilized to check the validity of this statement. Figure 1-1 presents the number of issues (right axis) and sum of proceeds (left axis) for corporate bond and convertible bond issues, as well as SEO and IPO over the last 30 years.

As expected, funds through bonds always played an important role for companies. The black bar is constantly the largest and normally as high as or higher than equity capital through SEO (white bar) and IPO (light gray bar) combined. Especially, from 2011 to 2014 a clear predominance of debt financing over equity financing with a peak in 2013 is shown. In comparison, convertibles play only a minor role (dark gray bar). Surprisingly, higher proceeds are achieved with a smaller number of issues. For the most part, the quantity of corporate bond issues remains between 2,000 and 6,000 issues per year while the number of SEO outperforms the bond issues for the first time in 1999 and reaches over 13,000 issues in 2013. Hence, the average volume in the corporate bond market considerably increased over the last 15 years. Overall, Figure 1-1 confirms the conclusion of recent reports about the growing importance of bond financing for non-financial firms.

Figure 1-1: Corporate Bond Issuance, Convertibles, SEO, and IPO Activity of Non-financial Firms 1985–2014

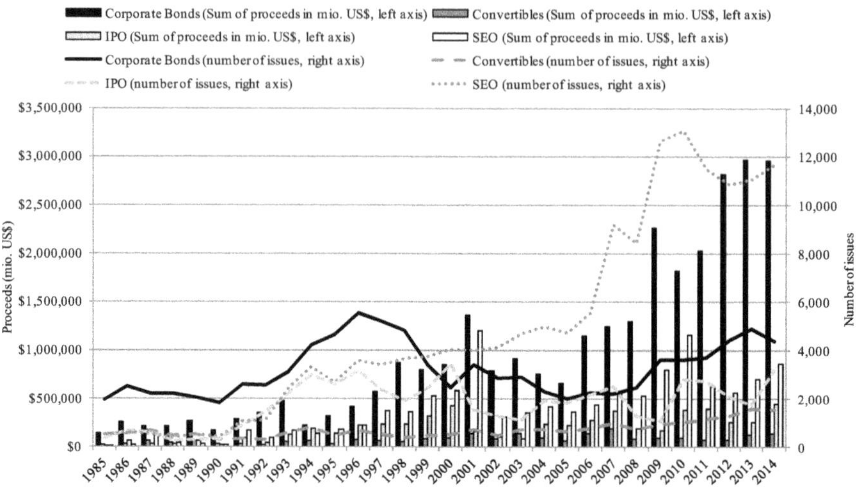

This graphic presents the number and proceeds of all straight corporate bond issues, convertible issues, SEO, and IPO of non-financial firms (indicated by Thomson Financial Macro Description) from Thomson One Banker database between 1985 and 2014.

Figure 1-2 presents the issuing activity separated by six different regions (1. Africa/Middle East/Central Asia; 2. America (ex USA); 3. Asia-Pacific (ex Central Asia); 4. Europe; 5. Japan; 6. USA). Again, proceeds through corporate bond issues are the highest, except for Africa/Middle East/Central Asia. Moreover, Figure 1-2 shows that corporate bonds play a key role in particular for Europe and the United States. Thus, the research focuses on these two regions.

Despite the growing importance of financing through bonds for non-financial firms, most investigations on the short-term effects of certain events on firm value are only conducted for stocks. For instance, a keyword search of "abnormal stock returns" with google scholar lead to approximately 10,900 hits, while the keyword "abnormal bond returns" only lead to approximately 282 hits.[4] Thus, it is the author's opinion that most research provides an incomplete view on the impact of events on listed firm values in the short run, as allegedly positive or negative events could have the opposite effect on a firm's debt capital. Moreover, the gap in empirical work devoted to (corporate) bond markets compared to equity markets is also criticized by prior research, which requests a stronger focus on bonds (e.g.

4 Conducted on March 20, 2015.

Biais, Declerck, Dow, Portes, & von Thadden, 2006). It is the main objective of this thesis to contribute to this request. Current research is utilized and enhanced with a new perspective, thereby contributing to the understanding of major corporate events on two different stakeholder classes: stockholders and bondholders.

Figure 1-2: Corporate Bond Issuance, Convertibles, SEO, and IPO Activity of Non-financial Firms by Region 1985–2014

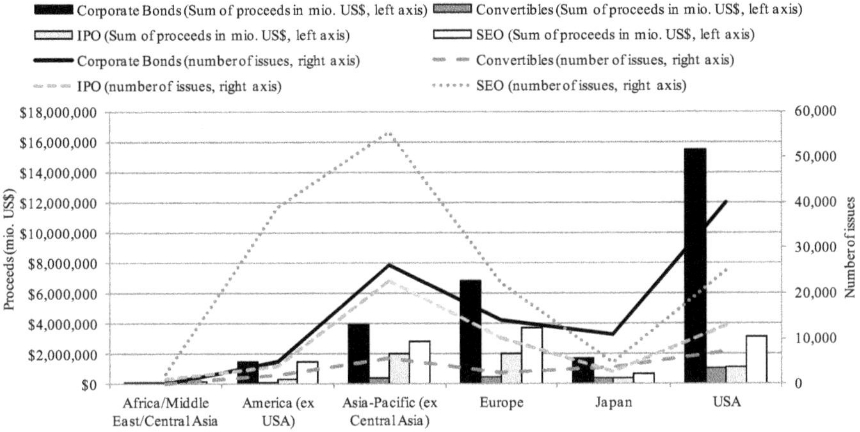

This graphic presents the number and proceeds of all straight corporate bond issues, convertible issues, SEO, and IPO of non-financial firms (indicated by Thomson Financial Macro Description) from Thomson One Banker database between 1985 and 2014 separated by region (Africa/Middle East/Central Asia; America (ex USA); Asia-Pacific (ex Central Asia); Europe; Japan; USA).

1.2 Thesis Structure

This thesis is divided into three main parts. For a start, chapter 2 provides a comprehensive overview of existing academic research on event studies concerning bondholder wealth effects. While reviewing more than 100 published and unpublished research papers, the innovative evolution of bond event study methodology since the mid-70s of the 20th century is discussed. Furthermore, past and present event study methods to calculate abnormal bond returns are illustrated and the applied parametric and non-parametric test statistics are evaluated. Besides, insight on how the availability of corporate bond data has evolved through the last four decades, as well as the impact on prevailing methodology is provided. Moreover, the relationship between abnormal bond returns and abnormal stock returns is reviewed. Altogether, a first extensive snapshot of the current bond event study methodology is conducted and guidance for future research offered.

Next, chapter 3 explores stockholder and bondholder wealth effects of synergy disclosing and non-disclosing mergers and acquisitions in the US energy sector. To the best knowledge of the author, this is the first study investigating the interdependence of synergy forecasts and bond price effects. In line with prior research, synergy estimates affect abnormal stock returns positively. Interestingly, bondholders of the respective companies experience a wealth loss, implying a wealth transfer from bondholders to stockholders. Regression analysis confirms a positive impact of synergy forecasts on stockholder wealth and a negative impact on bondholder wealth. Moreover, after controlling for multicollinearity and confounding events, evidence consistent with a wealth expropriation of bondholders is found. Overall, synergy forecasts no longer can be seen as purely firm value enhancing strategy, proving the necessity to regard both stakeholder classes to fully assess the impact.

Chapter 4 provides first evidence on the difference in wealth effects between new bond issues and reopenings. For a unique dataset of European companies, robust results are detected which indicate that equity investors react differently to both announcements. Excess stock returns turn out to be stronger for regular issues. Bondholders, on the other hand, experience similar negative wealth effects for both issue types. Furthermore, factors explaining bondholder and stockholder wealth effects diverge between issuing types. Thus, it is crucial for future research analyzing bond issues to distinguish between both offering types. Moreover, the results offer insights on how investors respond to different issue types thereby aiding management with the selection of the appropriate debt offering type.

Finally, chapter 5 summarizes the results of the empirical investigations. The main conclusions of this thesis are discussed and implications for financial markets drawn. In addition, the limitations of the empirical analyses are briefly described and possible future research outlined.

Overall, the results suggest that bond markets and their interaction with stocks play a key role in conclusively determining the wealth effects of major corporate events like mergers and acquisitions and debt offerings. Thus, future research ought to consider more than one stakeholder class to assess the impact of events and new information on firm value.

2. Review of Event Study Procedures to detect Wealth Effects in Bondholder Research

Lin, Liu, and Wu (2011), Bessembinder and Maxwell (2008) as well as Edwards, Harris, and Piwowar (2007) provide initial insights into the importance of the US corporate bond market.[5] At the end of 2006, the outstanding principal in US corporate bonds amounts to $5.37 trillion and is therefore larger than either US Treasury obligations or municipal bond obligations. Issuance of corporate bonds between 1997 and 2006 is more than three times the number of equity raised through IPO and SEO combined, with a total of $4.6 trillion. Obtaining trades reported to TRACE (Trade Reporting and Compliance Engine) between January 2003 and January 2005, Edwards et al. (2007) collect a sample of 12,320,016 trades, representing $9.3 trillion and almost 22,000 non-convertible bonds. Comparing the bond and stock data from Thomson One Banker presents the same pattern: between January 2000 and November 2014 non-financial US-Companies (European-Companies) issued non-convertible bonds with a total principal value of almost $13 trillion (over €6 trillion). Equity capital raised through initial and secondary offerings, on the other hand, only amounted to slightly more (less) than $3 trillion (€3 trillion). Despite the undeniable enormous importance of corporate bonds as a source of external financing, most researchers focus solely on stock price behavior to evaluate the impact of various corporate events. Conducting a census of event studies that focus on stock price effects in five top-tier journals[6] which are published between 1974 and 2000, Kothari and Warner (2005) find a total number of 565 articles. While the author is unaware of the exact number of event studies on stocks, it is safe to say that the actual figure is considerably higher, probably several thousands. Bond price effects, however, play a subordinate role in corporate finance research.

Nevertheless, over the last four decades several empirical papers applied event study methodology to investigate the impact of various events, such as mergers and acquisitions, rating changes, or earnings announcements on bondholder wealth effects. This development was partly driven by the improved data availability through new and superior databases. However, researchers faced a number of challenges related to bond data and the estimation of abnormal bond returns.

---

5 Primary market for bond event studies are the United States.

6 Journal of Business, Journal of Finance, Journal of Financial Economics, Journal of Financial and Quantitative Analysis, and Review of Financial Studies.

Consequently, numerous approaches and methodologies as well as theoretical refinements have been proposed until today aimed at improving the calculation of bond event study results. This chapter reviews solely the developments of methodology applied in event studies for bonds. The intention is to provide a thorough overview of research related to bond event studies, and to highlight the most prevailing and important methodologies based on the available research literature. Furthermore, the guidance that has been provided by researchers for the issues encountered in bond event studies is discussed and assessed. Thereby, this chapter provides valuable insight into the evolution of the event study methodology and some guidance for subsequent studies.

While many methodology reviews that deal with event study methodology for stocks are published (e.g., Binder, 1998; Corrado, 2011; Henderson, 1990; Peterson, 1989), to the best of the author's knowledge no paper provides an explicit overview for bond event studies. Overall, 108 research papers are found that deal with bond event studies. Table 2-1 below provides an overview, including the utilized event (Column 2), examined securities (Column 3), period (Column 4), sample size (Column 5), applied methodology (Column 6) and price data (Column 7) for calculating abnormal bond returns and testing for their statistical significance (Column 8), adjustment(s) for multiple bonds (Column 9), database (Column 10), and data frequency (Column 11). Column 12 specifies, whether the paper was published in one of 11 top finance and accounting journals including (in alphabetic order) the *Accounting Review* (AR), *Contemporary Accounting Research* (CAR), *Journal of Accounting and Economics* (JAE), *Journal of Accounting Research* (JAR), *Journal of Banking and Finance* (JBF), *Journal of Corporate Finance* (JCF), *Journal of Finance* (JF), *Journal of Financial and Quantitative Analysis* (JFQA), *Journal of Financial Economics* (JFE), *Journal of Money, Credit and Banking* (JMCB), and *Review of Financial Studies* (RFS), was published in a less prestigious journal (-), or is available as a working paper (WP).

Table 2-1: Prior Event Study Research with Corporate Bond Data

Author(s)	Area Under Investigation	Securities	Period	Number of Obs.	Event Study Model	Yields/Bond Returns	Test Statistics	Mutiple Bonds	Database	Frequency	Journal
Chen et al. (2014)	Ratings	Bonds	2005	57 upgraded bonds	Matching portfolio	Bond returns	–	Value weighted	TRACE FISD	Daily	WP
DeFond and Zhang (2014)	Earnings	Bonds Stocks	1996–2006	11,641 announcements 710 firms	FF factor model CDGM factor model	Bond spreads Yield spreads	t-statistic	Value weighted	Datastream FISD	Daily	CAR
Fortin et al. (2014)	Shareholder proposals	Bonds Stock	1996–2006	689 bonds of 86 PSP firms 219 bonds of 27 NPSP firms	Matched government bond	Bond returns	t-statistic z-statistic	Value weighted 1. level: Highest average daily trades 2. level: Highest number of trading days	TRACE	Daily	–
Kwan and León (2014)	Strategic alliances	Bonds Stocks	2003–2007	467 announcements	Market model with Matching portfolio	Bond returns	Sign Signed rank	Value weighted	TRACE FISD	Daily	WP
Lemmon et al. (2014)	Asset Securitization	Bonds Stocks	1996–2009	65 firms 185 bonds	Matching portfolio	Bond returns	t-statistic Signed rank	Equally weighted	Datastream	Daily	JF
Chen (2013)	Debt issue	Bonds Stocks	2005–2011	1,356 debt offerings 859 firm level offerings	Matching portfolio	Bond returns	t-statistic Signed rank	Equally weighted	TRACE FISD	Daily	WP
Li et al. (2013)	Collapse of Bear Stern and Lehman Brothers	Bonds	2007–2009	309 firms 689 bonds	Mean adjusted	Premium returns	t-statistic	All	TRACE FISD	Daily	–
Plunus et al. (2012)	Operational loss	Bonds	1994–2006	71 losses by 41 firms	Market model	Bond returns	t-statistic	Longest maturity	Datastream	Daily	–
Pu (2012)	Pension fund activism	Bonds Stocks	2002–2009	25 firms	Market adjusted	Bond returns	–	Value weighted	TRACE FISD	Daily	WP
Autore et al. (2011)	Short sale ban	Bonds Stocks	2008	59 firms	Matching portfolio	Bond returns	t-statistic Signed rank	Equally weighted	TRACE	Daily	JBF
Bhat et al. (2011)	MBS holdings	Bonds Stocks	2006–2010	28 banks 480 bonds	Market adjusted	Bond returns	t-statistic z-statistic	–	–	Daily	JAE
Billings et al. (2011)	Shareholder lawsuits	Bonds	1996–2008	579 firms	Paired comparison	Bond returns	t-statistic Signed rank	Representative	TRACE FISD	Daily	WP

Author(s)	Area Under Investigation	Securities	Period	Number of Obs.	Event Study Model	Yields/Bond Returns	Test Statistics	Mutiple Bonds	Database	Frequency	Journal
Blaylock et al. (2011)	Government intervention	Bonds Stocks	2009	265 firms 575 bonds	Market adjusted	Bond returns	–	Equally weighted	TRACE	Daily	WP
Cho et al. (2011)	Ratings	Bonds	2002–2006	759 upgrades 2,025 downgrades	Matching portfolio	Bond returns	t-statistic Signed rank	All	TRACE	Daily	WP
Clayton (2011)	IPO	Bonds	1983–2007	70 IPOs	Matching portfolio	Bond returns	–	Value weighted	LBBD NAIC TRACE FISD	Monthly	WP
DeFond et al. (2011)	SOX-related events	Bonds	2002	2,671 bonds	CDGM factor model Zhang factor model	Yield spreads	t-statistic	All	Datastream	Daily	–
Ellul et al. (2011)	Fire sales	Bonds	2001–2005	356 bonds 173 firms	Simple market model Matching portfolio Mean adjusted	Bond returns	t-statistic	All Random	NAIC FISD	Weekly	JFE
Gao et al. (2011)	Dodd Frank Act of 2010	Bonds Stocks	2009–2010	31 firms	Matching portfolio	Bond returns	t-statistic	Equally weighted Value weighted	TRACE FISD	Daily	WP
Klein and Zur (2011)	Hedge fund activism	Bonds Stocks	1994–2006	189 bonds short run 193 bonds long run	Matching portfolio	Bond returns	t-statistic Signed rank	Most recently issued Weighted	TRACE FISD	Daily	RFS
Marble III (2011)	Ratings	Bonds	2002–2005	49 downgrades 20 upgrades	Matching portfolio	Bond returns	t-statistic Signed rank	Value weighted	TRACE	Daily	–
Massa and Zhang (2011)	Natural catastrophe	Bonds	1998–2008	1,583 bonds 564 firms	Mean adjusted	Premium returns	t-statistic	–	BoA Merrill Lynch TRACE FISD	Daily Monthly	WP
Nishikawa et al. (2011)	Repurchases	Bonds Stocks	1994–2002	666 repurchases 359 firms	VPE for yield spreads	Yield spreads	t-statistic Signed rank	Largest combined trading volume	FISD	Daily	–
Okamoto et al. (2011)	LBO	Bonds Stocks	2007–2008	67 bonds 28 firms	Mean adjusted	Premium returns	t-statistic	Value weighted	Datastream FISD	Daily	–

Author(s)	Area Under Investigation	Securities	Period	Number of Obs.	Event Study Model	Yields/Bond Returns	Test Statistics	Mutiple Bonds	Database	Frequency	Journal
Wei and Yermack (2011)	Inside debt	Bonds Stocks CDS Exchange-traded options	2007	299 firms	Two index market model	Bond returns	t-statistic	Most heavily traded	Reuters TRACE FISD	Daily	RFS
Aslan et al. (2010)	Hedge fund activism	Bonds Stocks	1996–2008	558 firms 732 bonds	Matching portfolio	Bond returns	t-statistic	All Value weighted Median time to maturity	TRACE FISD Datastream	Daily	WP
Baran and King (2010)	LBO	Bonds Stocks	1981–2006	363 bonds 202 bids	Matching portfolio	Bond returns	t-statistic Signed rank	Standard error adjustment	FIDB Bond Record FISD Bloomberg	Monthly	JBF
Billett et al. (2010)	LBO	Bonds Stocks	1980–2006	49 bonds 18 firms	Matching portfolio	Bond returns	t-statistic	Weighted by bonds outstanding	Bond Record TRACE FISD	Monthly	JCF
Choi et al. (2010)	M&A	Bonds Stocks	1995–2002	147 mergers	EMW model	Yield spreads Bond spreads	z-statistic	Value weighted	Datastream LBBD Reuters	Weekly	JMCB
Francis et al. (2010)	Antitakeover laws	Bonds Stocks	1990–2000	489 firms 1,857 bonds	Mean adjusted	Premium returns	z-statistic Signed rank	All Value weigted	FISD SDC LBBD	Monthly	JFE
Kitsabunnarat-Chatjuthamard et al. (2010)	LREO	Bonds Stocks	1973–1997	66 exchange offer, 190 bonds 93 swap offer, 258 bonds	Mean adjusted	Premium returns	t-statistic Signed rank	Value weighted	LBBD	Monthly	–
May (2010)	Ratings	Bonds Stocks	2002–2009	1,769 rating changes	Matching portfolio	Bond returns	t-statistic Signed rank	Value weighted	TRACE	Daily Monthly	JBF
Michayluk and Zhao (2010)	Stock splits	Bonds	1999–2006	136 firms	Mean adjusted	Premium returns	t-statistic	Most frequently traded	Bridge Datastream Bloomberg	Daily	–

Author(s)	Area Under Investigation	Securities	Period	Number of Obs.	Event Study Model	Yields/Bond Returns	Test Statistics	Mutiple Bonds	Database	Frequency	Journal
Adams and Mansi (2009)	CEO turnover	Bonds Stocks	1973–2000	674 events 415 firms	Mean adjusted	Yield spreads	t-statistic	Value weighted	FIDB Bloomberg	Monthly	JBF
Bessembinder et al. (2009)	M&A	Bonds Stocks	2002–2006	50 firms	Mean adjusted Matching portfolio	Premium returns Bond returns	t-statistic Signed rank Sign	Value weighted	LBBD TRACE FISD	Daily Monthly	JFE
Cornil (2009)	Restatements	Bonds	2000–2002	49 firms 143 bonds	Mean adjusted	Yield spreads	t-statistic	–	–	Daily	–
Dbouk and Kryzanowski (2009)	Bond index revision	Bonds Stocks	1987–1997	25 additions 58 deletions	Market model with event month dummy Two index market model with event month dummy Unconditional three factor model with event month dummy	Bond returns	t-statistic Signed rank	All	FIDB	Monthly	–
Elliott et al. (2009)	SEO	Bonds Stocks	1990–2002	188 bonds 68 firms	Mean adjusted	Premium returns	t-statistic	All Value weighted	Tradeline WSJ Manual	Daily	JBF
Kedia and Zhou (2009)	M&A	Bonds Stocks	1994–2006	118 firms 299 bonds	Matching portfolio	Bond returns	t-statistic Signed rank	All Value weighted	FISD NAIC	Daily	WP
Ongena and Penas (2009)	M&A	Bonds Stocks	1998–2002	96 mergers 91 bidder, 781 bonds 18 targets, 117 bonds	Matching portfolio	Bond returns	t-statistic	Value weighted	Datastream	Daily	–
Shin et al. (2009)	Ratings	Bonds	1996–2003	131 rating changes	Mean adjusted	Premium returns	t-statistic z-statistic	Equally weighted	NEEDS	Daily	WP
Amromin et al. (2008)	Dividend tax cut	Bonds Stocks	2003	98 High dividend 109 Low dividend	Two index market model	Bond returns	-	–	–	Monthly	–
DeFond and Zhang (2008)	Earnings	Bonds Stocks	1994–2006	11,525 announcements 690 firms	DFHKZ factor model EGB factor model	Bond spreads	t-statistic	Value weighted	Datastream FISD	Daily	WP
Eberhart et al. (2008)	R&D intensity	Bonds Stocks	1990–1998	83 announcements 41 firms 218 bonds	EGB factor model	Bond spreads	–	Value weighted	SDC LBBD	Monthly	JAR

Author(s)	Area Under Investigation	Securities	Period	Number of Obs.	Event Study Model	Yields/Bond Returns	Test Statistics	Mutiple Bonds	Database	Frequency	Journal
Ongena et al. (2008)	Loan deals	Bond Stocks	1997–2003	896 deals 364 firms	CDGM factor model	Bond spreads	–	–	Datastream	Daily	–
Shi and Zhang (2008)	Restatements	Bonds	1997–2003	50 firms 137 bonds	Matched government bond	Bond returns	t-statistic Signed rank	All Firm level	NAIC TRACE	Daily	WP
Veld and Veld-Merkoulova (2008)	Spin-offs	Bonds Stocks	1995–2002	91 spin-offs 355 bonds	Mean adjusted	Premium returns	z-statistic Signed rank	All Median return	Datastream Bloomberg	Daily	–
Newberry and Parthasarathy (2007)	Restatements	Bonds	1997–2002	328 Debt issuances-Unique firms 640 Debt issuances-Non-unique firms	Pre- and Post-yield spread difference	Yield spreads	t-statistic	All	FISD	Yearly	WP
Renneboog and Szilagyi (2007)	M&A	Bonds Stocks	1995–2004	225 bidders 24 targets	Matching portfolio	Bond returns	Signed rank	Value weighted	Reuters	Monthly	WP
Dallocchio et al. (2006)	Ratings	Bonds	2000–2004	35 rating changes	Stationarity test GR methodology	Relative Spreads	t-statistic	–	Merrill Lynch	Daily	–
Minnick and Zhao (2006)	Repurchases	Bonds Stocks	1985–2005	1,510 repurchases	Mean adjusted	Premium returns	t-statistic	All Value weighted	LBBD	Monthly	WP
Billett et al. (2004)	M&A	Bonds Stocks	1979–1997	940 mergers 831 bidders, 3083 bonds 256 targets, 818 bonds	Matching portfolio	Bond returns	t-statistic Signed rank	Value weighted	FIDB	Monthly	JF
Devaney and Lizieri (2004)	Divestment	Bonds stocks	1999–2001	8 deals 6 firms	Market model Extended market model	Bond returns	–	–	Datastream GDMO	Weekly	–
Dittmar (2004)	Spin-offs	Bonds	1983–1995	16 spin-offs	Market model	Bond returns	–	–	FIDB	Monthly	–
Penas and Unal (2004)	M&A	Bonds Stocks	1991–1997	66 merger 282 bonds	Matching portfolio	Bond returns	t-statistic	Value weighted	FIDB	Monthly	JFE
Datta et al. (2003)	Divestment	Bonds Stocks	1982–1992	209 firms	Mean adjusted	Premium returns	Sign	Most frequently traded	WSJ Bond Record	Daily	JBF
Maxwell and Rao (2003)	Spin-offs	Bonds Stocks	1976–1997	80 spin-offs	Mean adjusted	Premium returns	t-statistic Signed rank	All Value weighted	LBBD	Monthly	JF

Author(s)	Area Under Investigation	Securities	Period	Number of Obs.	Event Study Model	Yields/Bond Returns	Test Statistics	Mutiple Bonds	Database	Frequency	Journal
Maxwell and Stephens (2003)	Repurchases	Bonds Stocks	1980–1997	945 repurchases 2,817 bonds	Mean adjusted	Premium returns	t-statistic Signed rank Sign	All Value weighted	LBBD	Monthly	JF
Eberhart and Siddique (2002)	SEO	Bonds Stocks	1980–1992	189 SEOs 140 firms	Matching portfolio EGB factor model	Bond returns	t-statistic Signed rank	–	FIDB	Monthly	RFS
Gropp and Richards (2001)	Ratings	Bonds Stocks	1989–2000	129 rating changes 30 banks	Market model	Bond returns	t-statistic	All	Bloomberg	Daily	–
Steiner and Heinke (2001)	Ratings	Bonds	1985–1996	546 rating changes 182 watchlistings 216 bonds 111 firms	Matched government bond	Bond returns	t-statistic Signed rank Corrado	One bond per issuer	DFDB Euromoney Bondware	Daily	–
Brewer III and Jackson III (2000)	Market maker withdrawal	Bonds Stocks	1990	3 junk bond porfolios	Market model with event day dummy	Porfolio returns	–	–	Merrill Lynch	Daily	–
Kliger and Sarig (2000)	Ratings	Bonds Stocks	1982	812 bonds	Return minus yield	Bond returns	–	Most recently issued	FIDB	Monthly	JF
Easterwood (1998)	Divestment	Bonds	1986–1990	134 divestments 110 bonds 41 firms	Return minus high yield index	Bond returns	t-statistic Signed rank	All Value weighted Equally weighted	Bond Guide	Monthly	JBF
Maquieira et al. (1998)	M&A	Bonds Preferred Convertibles	1963–1995	1,283 securities 520 firms 260 mergers	VPE	Yields	t-statistic Signed rank	–	Moody's Manual	Monthly	JFE
Akhigbe et al. (1997)	Debt issue	Bonds Stocks	1980–1992	574 issues 256 firms	Matching portfolio Mean adjusted	Bond returns Premium returns	t-statistic	–	CFC Dow-Jones Reuters	Weekly	–
Hite and Warga (1997)	Ratings	Bonds	1985–1995	>2,800 bonds >1,200 firms	Matching portfolio	Bond returns	t-statistic Signed rank	Equally weighted	Lehman	Monthly	–
Hotchkiss and Mooradian (1997)	Public debt/ equity purchase	Bonds Stocks	1991–1993	63 purchases 39 firms	Mean adjusted	Bond returns	z-statistic	Equally weighted	IDC Salomon Brothers	Daily	JFE

Author(s)	Area Under Investigation	Securities	Period	Number of Obs.	Event Study Model	Yields/Bond Returns	Test Statistics	Mutiple Bonds	Database	Frequency	Journal
Datta and Iskandar-Datta (1996)	Divestment	Bonds Stocks	1983–1990	73 sell-offs 54 firms	Mean adjusted	Premium returns	z-statistic	Most frequently traded	WSJ Bond Record	Daily	–
Datta and Iskandar-Datta (1995)	M&A	Bonds Stocks	1982–1990	63 mergers 43 firm	Mean adjusted	Premium returns	t-statistic Sign	Most frequently traded	WSJ Bond Record	Daily	JBF
Brown et al. (1994)	Asset sales	Bonds Stocks	1979–1988	22 asset sales	Mean adjusted	Bond returns	t-statistic	Value weighted	WSJ	Daily	JCF
Cook and Easterwood (1994)	Debt issue	Bonds Stocks	1988–1989	170 firms 877 bonds	Matching portfolio	Bond returns	t-statistic	Equally weighted	Bond Guide	Monthly	–
Dhillon and Johnson (1994)	Dividends	Bonds Stocks	1978–1987	131 firms	Mean adjusted	Premium returns	t-statistic Signed Rank	Most frequently traded	WSJ DRI	Daily	JF
Walker (1994)	M&A	Bonds	1980–1988	65 mergers 92 firms	Matched government bond	Bond returns	t-statistic	Value weighted	Bond Guide	Monthly	–
Datta and Dhillon (1993)	Earnings	Bonds Stocks	1984–1990	250 announcements 135 firms	Mean adjusted	Premium returns	Signed rank Sign	–	DRI WSJ Bond Record	Daily	JFQA
Kahan and Tuckman (1993)	Covenant changes	Bonds Stocks	–	42 changes	Matched government bond	Bond returns	t-statistic	–	Salomon Brothers Bear Stern IDC Bloomberg Moody's S&P's	Daily Monthly	–
Warga and Welch (1993)	LBO	Bonds Stocks	1985–1989	43 bonds 16 firms	Matching portfolio	Bond returns	t-statistic	–	Lehman	Monthly	RFS
Cook et al. (1992)	MBO	Bonds	1981–1989	29 MBOs 62 bonds	Matching portfolio Market adjusted	Bond returns Premium returns	t-statistic Sign	Equally weighted	CFC WSJ	Weekly	–
Hand et al. (1992)	Ratings	Bonds Stocks	1977–1983	1,301 bonds 624 firms	Matched government bond	Bond returns	t-statistic Binomial test	Equally weighted (max 5 bonds per firm)	IDC	Daily	JF

Author(s)	Area Under Investigation	Securities	Period	Number of Obs.	Event Study Model	Yields/Bond Returns	Test Statistics	Mutiple Bonds	Database	Frequency	Journal
Wansley et al. (1992)	Ratings	Bonds	1982–1984	351 rating changes 255 firms	Market adjusted	Bond returns	t-statistic	One bond selected	Merrill Lynch	Weekly	–
Crabbe (1991)	Ratings	Bonds	1983–1988	56 bonds	Matching portfolio	Bond returns Yields	t-statistic	Value weighted	Bond Guide	Monthly	JF
Gupta and Rosenthal (1991)	Leveraged recapitalization	Bonds Stocks	1984–1988	–	Market adjusted	Bond returns	t-statistic Binomial test	Equally weighted	WSJ DRI	Daily	–
Handa and Radhakrishnan (1991)	Leveraged recapitalization	Bonds Stocks	1984–1989	26 bonds 19 firms	Mean adjusted	Bond returns	t-statistic Signed rank	Max 2 bonds per firm	IDC	–	–
Rathinasamy et al. (1991)	M&A	Bonds	1970–1984	49 mergers 146 bonds	Mean adjusted	Premium returns	t-statistic	All	Bond Guide BQR	Monthly	–
Asquith and Wizman (1990)	LBO	Bonds Stocks	1980–1988	214 bonds 65 firms	Matching portfolio	Bond returns	t-statistic	Random Median time to maturity	Bond Guide IDD Bloomberg	Monthly	JFE
DeFusco et al. (1990)	Stock option plans	Bonds Stocks	1978–1982	36 announcements 34 firms	Matching portfolio	Bond returns	t-statistic Signed rank	One bond selected	WSJ	Daily	JF
Cornett and Travlos (1989)	Exchange offer	Bonds Stocks	1973–1983	11 firms debt-for-equity 56 firms equity-for-debt	Mean adjusted	Bond returns	z-statistic	–	WSJ Bond Guide	Daily	JF
Marais et al. (1989)	LBO	Bonds Stocks Preferred	1974–1985	290 LBOs 264 firms	Two index market model	Bond returns	z-statistic	Value weighted	Bond Record	Daily	JFE
Jayaraman and Shastri (1988)	Dividends	Bonds Stocks	1962–1982	154 bonds 63 firms	Mean adjusted	Premium returns	z-statistics	Most frequently traded	WSJ Manual Bond Record	Daily	JFQA
Kolodony and Suhler (1988)	Debt issue	Bonds Stocks	1973–1981	66 bonds	Paired comparison	Bond returns	t-statistic	One bond selected	Bond Record	Monthly	–
Kalay and Shimrat (1987)	SEO	Bonds Stocks	1970–1982	58 SEOs	Mean adjusted	Premium returns	z-statistic	Most frequently traded	IDC Bond Record	Daily	JFE
Strong and Meyer (1987)	Writedown	Bonds Stocks	1981–1985	32 bonds 32 firms	Matched government bond	Bond returns	t-statistic Sign	Equally weighted	WSJ	Daily	JF

Author(s)	Area Under Investigation	Securities	Period	Number of Obs.	Event Study Model	Yields/Bond Returns	Test Statistics	Mutiple Bonds	Database	Frequency	Journal
Dennis and McConnell (1986)	M&A	Bonds Stocks Preferred	1962–1980	132 mergers 81 targets 94 bidders	Mean adjusted Matching portfolio	Bond returns	t-statistic	Equally weighted	WSJ Bond Guide	Daily	JFE
Wansley and Clauretie (1985)	Ratings	Bonds Stocks	1981–1983	54 firms	Matching portfolio	Bond returns	t-statistic	–	Bond Guide	Monthly	–
Handjinicolaou and Kalay (1984)	Dividends	Bonds	1975–1976	1,967 announcements 255 bonds	Mean adjusted	Premium returns	t-statistic	Most frequently traded	WSJ	Daily	JFE
Settle et al. (1984)	M&A	Bonds	1961–1977	53 mergers 90 bonds 58 firms	Term adjustment procedure	Adjusted returns	t-statistic	–	Bond Record CFC	Monthly	–
Chow (1983)	1933 and 1934 Securities Act	Bonds Stocks	1933–1935	38 bonds	Matching portfolio	Bond returns	Rank sum	One bond selected	WSJ	Daily	AR
Eger (1983)	M&A	Bonds Stocks	1958–1980	38 mergers 39 firms 41 bonds	Matching portfolio	Jump returns Continuous returns	t-statistic	Largest trading volume	WSJ	Daily	JFQA
Hite and Owers (1983)	Spin-offs	Bonds Stocks Preferred	1963–1981	53 securities 31 firms	Mean adjusted	Bond returns	z-statistic	–	Compuserve WSJ	Daily	JFE
Woolridge (1983)	Dividends	Bonds Stocks Preferred	1970–1977	94 announcements 248 bonds 45 firms	Mean adjusted	Bond returns	t-statistic	Equally weighted	WSJ Bond Guide	Daily	JF
Asquith and Kim (1982)	M&A	Bonds Stocks	1960–1978	50 firms 62 bonds	Paired comparison	Bond returns	t-statistic	Equally weighted	BQR WSJ Bond Guide	Daily Monthly	JF
Dann (1981)	Repurchases	Bonds Stocks Preferred	1962–1976	51 repurchases 122 securities	Mean adjusted	Bond returns	t-statistic	–	WSJ Bond Guide	Daily	JFE
Mikkelson (1981)	Call options	Bonds Stocks Convertibles	1961–1978	27 bonds 19 convertibles	Announcement week return minus average	Bond returns	t-statistic	Equally weighted	Barrons	Weekly	JFE

Author(s)	Area Under Investigation	Securities	Period	Number of Obs.	Event Study Model	Yields/Bond Returns	Test Statistics	Mutiple Bonds	Database	Frequency	Journal
Masulis (1980)	Exchange offers	Bonds Stocks Preferred	1962–1976	17 offers 23 securities	Mean adjusted	Bond returns	t-statistic	Equally weighted	WSJ Bond Guide	Daily	JFE
Kim and McConnell (1977)	M&A	Bonds	1960–1973	39 firms 44 bonds	Paired comparison Two index market model	Bond returns	t-statistic	–	Bond Guide	Monthly	JF
Warner (1977)	Bankruptcy	Bonds	1930–1955	20 firms 73 bonds	Two parameter model Matching portfolio	Bond returns	t-statistic	–	BQR Manual	Monthly	JFE
Weinstein (1977)	Ratings	Bonds	1962–1974	123–315 bonds	Matching portfolio	Bond returns	t-statistic	All	BQR Bond Record Nat. Bond Summary Bond Guide	Monthly	JFE
Grier and Katz (1976)	Ratings	Bonds	1966–1972	66 firms 96 bonds	Matching portfolio	Bond returns	Sign test	–	BCC NYSE Library	Monthly	–
Katz (1974)	Ratings	Bonds	1966–1972	66 firms 115 bonds	Factor model	Yields	t-statistic	2 bonds per firm	Bond Guide	Monthly	JF

This table provides an overview of research studies that calculate event studies using bond data. Abbreviations in the event study model column are: CDGM = Collin-Dufresne, Goldstein, and Martin (2001); DFHKZ = DeFond, Hung, Karaoglu, and Zhang (2008); EGB = Elton, Gruber, and Blake (1995); EMW = Eckbo, Maksimovic, and Williams (1990); FF = Fama and French (1993); GR = Gropp and Richards (2001); VPE = Valuation prediction error. Sources of bond price data include: BCC = Baruch College Center for Financial Research Utility Data Base; BoA Merrill Lynch = Bank of America Merrill Lynch US Corporate and High Yield Master bond index database; Bond Guide = Standard and Poor's Bond Guide; Bond Record = Moody's Bond Record; BQR = Bank Quotation Record; CFC = Commercial and Financial Chronicle; DFDB = Deutsche Finanzdatenbank; Dow-Jones = Dow-Jones News Retrieval; DRI = Data Resources Inc.; IDC = Interactive Data Corporation; IDD = Investors Dealers Digest; LBBD = Lehman Brothers Bond Database; FIDB = Lehman Brothers Fixed Income Database; FISD = (Mergent) Fixed Income Security Database; GDMO = Government's Debt Management Office; Manual = Moody's Industrial Manual; NAIC = National Association of Insurance Commissioners; Nat. Bond Summary = The National Bond Summary; NEEDS = NEEDS-Financial Quest; NYSE Library = New York Stock Exchange Library; Salomon =Salomon Brothers; SDC = Securities Data Corporation; TRACE = Trade Reporting and Compliance Engine; WSJ = Wall Street Journal; Journals are: AR = Accounting Review CAR = Contemporary Accounting Research; JAE = Journal of Accounting and Economics; JAR = Journal of Accounting Research; JBF = Journal of Banking and Finance; JCF = Journal of Corporate Finance; JF = Journal of Finance; JFQA = Journal of Financial and Quantitative Analysis; JFE = Journal of Financial Economics; JMCB = Journal of Money, Credit and Banking; RFS = Review of Financial Studies; WP = Working Paper.

2.1 Bond Characteristics affecting Event Study Methodology

2.1.1 Illiquidity of Bond Price Data

Comparing the bond market with the stock market for liquidity yields two general results: On average, government bonds possess a higher liquidity than stocks (Chordia, Sarkar, & Subrahmanyam, 2005), yet corporate bonds are rather illiquid compared to stocks. Most US corporate bonds trade less than once a year, as compared with the equity market, where the median stock trades once every few minutes (Mahanti, Nashikkar, Subrahmanyam, Chacko, & Mallik, 2008). Examining the frequency of trade of US corporate bonds during the period 2000 to 2005, Mahanti et al. (2008) detect that over 40% from a sample of roughly 19,000 bonds do not trade once a year, while less than 0.032% trade approximately every day. Corroborating the illiquidity in corporate bond markets, although to a weaker extent, Bessembinder, Kahle, Maxwell, and Xu (2009) find an average trading of 52 days a year for TRACE data. The level of infrequent trading is confirmed by Bao, Pan, and Wang (2011), showing a statistically and economically significant illiquidity measure[7] for bond transaction data from 2003 to 2009, as well as by Chen, Fabozzi, and Sverdlove (2010).

This inherent illiquidity reflects the institutional nature of corporate bond markets where securities are held primarily by long-term buy-and-hold investors (i.e. pension funds, insurance companies, etc.) with extremely low portfolio turnovers (Mahanti et al., 2008). According to Schultz (2001), insurance companies hold almost 40% of outstanding investment-grade bonds, which illustrates the immense influence on bond liquidity.

Since illiquid data has implications for event study methods, causing poorly specified statistical tests (see Cowan and Sergeant (1996) for further details) most bond event studies impose trading restrictions to accommodate this infrequent trading. Usually researchers demand a certain number of trading days during an interval prior, during and/or after the event. For instance, May (2010) requires that a bond trades on at least ten of the twenty days starting thirty days after the event day and that it trades on the day before and after the event day. Another approach is provided by Maquieira, Megginson, and Nail (1998). They argue that the utilization of yield spreads would mitigate the infrequent trading problem that characterizes daily bond transactions. Thus, they state that calculating bond returns requires two fairly close consecutive prices, whereas one data

7 The amount of price reversal as captured by the negative of the autocovariance of price changes.

point is sufficient to calculate its yield making the first more vulnerable to infrequent data. While their reasoning is coherent, they do not provide any empirical evidence that bond event studies would significantly benefit from the utilization of yield spreads in place of returns.

2.1.2 Multiple Bonds Outstanding per Company

Obtaining trades reported to TRACE between 2003 and 2005, Edwards et al. (2007) observe an average number of over nine bonds outstanding per issuer, as well as a median number of two. This suggests a skewed distribution with a large number of companies having only a small number of bonds outstanding and a small number of firms with much more issues outstanding. In contrast to abnormal stock returns, researchers investigating bondholder wealth effects are presented with the question as to which bond to choose. So far, several methodologies have been utilized to overcome this discrepancy (see Table 1). Bessembinder et al. (2009) differentiate between these procedures: (i) the bond level approach, (ii) the representative bond approach, and (iii) the firm level approach.

With the bond level approach each bond is treated as a separate observation. This approach causes clustered data because the bond data can be classified into a number of different clusters (i.e. firms), each of which contains multiple observations (i.e. bonds). This clustering biases the standard errors downward because of the likely high correlation among bonds from the same firm, violating the assumption of independent observations and leading to an inflated t-statistic (Eberhart & Siddique, 2002). Non-parametric tests, like the Wilcoxon signed rank-test, provide no real alternative. The assumption for the applicability of non-parametric tests is that all observations are independent (Datta & Satten, 2005). However, investigating the effect of dependence among observations on the sign-, Wilcoxon signed rank-, and t-test, Gastwirth and Rubin (1971) note that the sign test is the least affected while the t-test is most affected. Researchers have developed several adjustments for existing parametric and non-parametric test statistics to account for the within-cluster correlation: Modifications of the Wilcoxon signed rank-test have been developed by Rosner, Glynn, and Lee (2006) as well as Datta and Satten (2008), and for the t-test by Subbaiah and Xia (2007). These tests could be used to mitigate the correlation issue without the need to reduce the sample. However, no bond event study has utilized these modifications so far. An exploration of that is left for future research.

Another drawback of the bond level approach is that firms with more than one bond tend to be overrepresented. Bessembinder et al. (2009) point out that these are typically larger firms with higher bond rating, causing another bias in the calculation.

Following the representative bond approach, researchers select a representative bond for each firm. The literature shows different procedures picking a single bond: a random issue (e.g., Asquith & Wizman, 1990), the most heavily (e.g., Wei & Yermack, 2011) or frequently (e.g., Handjinicolaou & Kalay, 1984) traded bond, the most recently issued (e.g., Klein & Zur, 2011), or the one with median time to maturity (e.g., Asquith & Wizman, 1990). Bessembinder et al. (2009) yet indicate that depending on how the representative bond is selected the results could be biased. Nonetheless, choosing the most heavily or frequently traded bond could be justified with the inherent illiquidity of the bond market. It is crucial to ensure certain liquidity for bond event studies. Therefore, this approach should not be excluded overhastily.

The firm level approach is equivalent to the approach B (reducing data to independent observations), presented by Galbraith, Daniel, and Vissel (2010) to treat clustered data. The multiple observations in a cluster are reduced to a single observation and the resulting data points are regarded as independent. The firm level approach can be subdivided into an equally weighted and a value weighted approach. With the equally weighted approach a firm's abnormal return is calculated as the sum of the abnormal returns, divided by the quantity of issued bonds. Following the value weighted approach, a firm's abnormal return is calculated as the sum of the market-value weighted abnormal returns of n bonds.

$$FBR_{j,t} = \sum_{i=1}^{n} ABR_{i,t} \cdot w_{i,t} \tag{1}$$

where

$FBR_{j,t}$ abnormal bond return of firm j

$ABR_{i,t}$ abnormal bond return of bond i issued by firm j

$w_{i,t}$ market value weight of bond i

Since a firm's bond returns are highly but not perfectly correlated, this procedure causes downward shifted t-statistics due to inflated standard errors (Eberhart & Siddique, 2002). Furthermore, only the value weighted approach represents the exact value change of the examined firm. Applying the equally weighted approach overestimates the price reaction of smaller bond issues and underestimates the price reaction of larger issues. On the other hand, Ederington, Guan, and Yang (2012) test four weighting schemes to combine standardized abnormal returns into a single firm return, among them the equally weighted average and the weighted approach from Bessembinder et al. (2009). Overall, results show only slight power differences between the four approaches. Hence, Ederington et al. (2012) recommend to disregard any complicated weighting scheme and use an equally weighted average of standardized bond returns.

2.2 Bond Event Study Methodology

2.2.1 Market Model

Traditionally, the market model is an example of a one-factor model which relates the return of any given security to the return of a market portfolio.[8] While the market model provides an elaborated procedure to measure abnormal returns for stockholders finding its way into many event studies, its application to bond event studies contains several empirical issues. One issue is the potential non-stationarity of the beta coefficient. Elton, Gruber, Brown, and Goetzmann (2011) discuss the application of the single-index model to bonds and argue that the bond beta equals the ratio of the duration of the bond and the duration of the index. On this basis, the beta decreases with time and the decrease becomes steeper as the bond approaches maturity. Elton et al. (2011) mention further influences affecting returns on bonds including liquidity premiums, tax effects, callability, and default risk. They argue that the single-index model only provides appropriate results if the impact of all these influences were constant over time. Alexander (1980) provides further support for this conclusion. Conducting an analysis of the use of the market model to long-term corporate bonds, he infers that the market model involves notable violations of regression assumptions and instances of parameter instability. Therefore, the interpretation of bond event studies that apply the market model has to be made with extreme caution.

Nevertheless, several published event studies apply a standard (e.g., Dittmar, 2004; Plunus, Gillet, & Hübner, 2012) or two index market model[9] (e.g., Kim & McConnell, 1977; Marais, Schipper, & Smith, 1989; Wei & Yermack, 2011). Two papers (e.i., Brewer & Jackson, 2000; Dbouk & Kryzanowski, 2009) follow the methodology recommended by Karafiath (1988) and add dummy variables for

8 See MacKinlay (1997) for calculation details.

9 Bessembinder et al. (2009) name this method also factor model while according to Eger (1983) it belongs to the market model approach. This thesis follows the understanding of Eger (1983) and defines them as two-index market models.

the event date to the right-hand side of the market model. For the two index market model the abnormal bond returns $ABR_{i,t}$ are calculated over the event period as follows.

$$ABR_{i,t} = BR_{i,t} - \hat{\alpha}_i - \hat{\beta}_{i1} \cdot S_t - \hat{\beta}_{i2} \cdot B_t \tag{2}$$

where

$BR_{i,t}$	return of corporate bond i
$\hat{\alpha}_i; \hat{\beta}_{i1}; \beta_{i2}$	coefficients calculated over the estimation period
S_t	return of a stock market index
B_t	return of a bond market index

After the single-index model, Elton et al. (2011) discuss the relevance of multi-index models and assert that using more than a single-market-factor seems to improve the explanatory power. For instance, to capture changes in the term structure researchers apply the changes in the long rate and changes in the spread between long and short rate as regression factors. To deepen this approach multi-factor models are discussed in the next section.

2.2.2 Multi-Factor Models

The first and probably most famous factor model used to estimate abnormal returns for bondholders is the five-factor model, provided by Fama and French (1993).

$$\begin{aligned} BR_{i,t} - R_{f,t} = \alpha + \beta_1 \cdot (R_{m,t} - R_{f,t}) + \beta_2 \cdot SMB_t + \beta_3 \cdot HML_t \\ + \beta_4 \cdot TERM_t + \beta_5 \cdot DEF_t + \varepsilon_{i,t} \end{aligned} \tag{3}$$

where

$BR_{i,t}$	return of corporate bond i
$R_{m,t}$	return of all the stocks in the created portfolios
$R_{f,t}$	one-month Treasury bill rate, observed at the beginning of the month
SMB_t	(Small Minus Big) difference between the returns of small- and big-size portfolios with about the same weighted-average book-to-market equity
HML_t	(High Minus Low) difference between the returns of high- and low-book-to-market portfolios with about the same weighted-average size

$TERM_t$ difference between the long-term government bond return and the one-month Treasury bill rate measured, observed at the beginning of the month

DEF_t difference between the return of a market portfolio of long-term corporate bonds and the long-term government bond return on day t

Altogether, Fama and French (1993) not only identify three stock-market-factors, but also two bond-market-factors explaining bond returns. This five-factor model is applied to several studies (e.g., Bessembinder et al., 2009; DeFond & Zhang, 2014). Bessembinder et al. (2009) test the Fama and French five-factor model to construct abnormal bond returns and find major problems. It consistently performs poorly, regardless of the used test statistics.

Better specified is the following factor model, at least with monthly data (Bessembinder et al., 2009). Utilizing fundamental economic variables as well as return indexes they develop different models successful in explaining expected bond returns. Based on the six-factor model by Elton, Gruber, and Blake (1995) the following model is applied in bond event studies (e.g., Eberhart & Siddique, 2002).

$$BR_{i,t} - R_{f,t} = \alpha + \beta_1 \cdot (UnxGDP_t) + \beta_2 (UnxCPI_t) + \beta_3 \cdot (DefaultRP_t) + \beta_4 .(BondMktRet_t) + \beta_5 \cdot (R_{m,t}) + \beta_6 \cdot (TERM_t) + \varepsilon_{i,t} \quad (4)$$

where

$BR_{i,t}$ return of corporate bond i

$R_{f,t}$ one-month Treasury bill return

$UnxGDP_t$ forecast of nominal GNP growth rates regressed on $Inflation_t$. Residuals with the sample mean added back as variable

$UnxCPI_t$ change in the consumer's forecast on inflation over the next year

$DefaultRP_t$ difference in return between the high-yield series and the intermediate government index

$BondMktRet_t$ return of the Lehman Brothers bond index

R_{mt} return of a market index (S&P 500)

$TERM_t$ difference in return between the long-term government bond index and the intermediate bond index (slope of the term structure)

Between this six-factor model and the one introduced by Elton et al. (1995) there is a noticeable difference. Considering seven explanatory variables, Elton et al. (1995) detect no influence by the variable measuring term spread. Therefore, they remove the $TERM_t$ variable from the regression. But an option index variable[10] is included into the analysis, omitted by subsequent bond event studies (Bessembinder et al., 2009; Eberhart & Siddique, 2002).

The third factor model is based on Collin-Dufresne, Goldstein, and Martin (2001).

$$\Delta CS_{i,t} = \alpha + \beta_1 \cdot R_{i,t} + \beta_2 \cdot \Delta r_t^{10} + \beta_3 \cdot (\Delta r_t^{10})^2 + \beta_4 \cdot \Delta slope_t + \beta_5 \cdot \Delta VIX_t + \beta_6 \cdot R_{m,t} + \beta_7 \cdot \Delta jump_t + \varepsilon_{i,t} \quad (5)$$

where

Δ	difference between two consecutive quotes
$CS_{i,t}$	difference between the yield of bond i and the associated yield of the Treasury curve at the same maturity
$R_{i,t}$	stock return for the issuer of bond i
r_t^{10}	10-year Benchmark Treasury rates
$slope_t$	difference between 10-year and 2-year Benchmark Treasury yields
VIX_t	VIX index for volatility of the S&P 500
$R_{m,t}$	return of a stock market index (S&P 500)
$jump_t$	probability and magnitude of a large negative jump in firm value as measured by changes in the slope of the "smirk" of implied volatilties of options on S&P 500 futures

The difference between the Collin-Dufresne et al. (2001) model and the two previous mentioned factor models is the analysis of spread changes instead of spreads. Therefore, not abnormal returns but unexpected changes in spreads are calculated. However, it is also used without calculating the difference between two consecutive quotes (e.g., Ongena, Roşcovan, Song, & Werker, 2008). To the best of the author's knowledge, no investigation of the empirical power or specification of the Collin-Dufresne et al. (2001) has been conducted.

10 $Option_t$: is the difference in return between the Lehman Brothers Government National Mortgage Association index and a government bond series with the same duration.

The latest factor model is provided by Ellul, Jotikasthira, and Lundblad (2011).[11] Following methodologies used by Bessembinder, Maxwell, and Venkataraman (2006) and Schultz (2001), they measure abnormal bond returns controlling for both market-wide and issuer-specific information by applying the following factor model.

$$ln\left(\frac{P_{i,t}}{P_{i,t-1}}\right) = \alpha + \beta_1 \cdot (\Delta YTM_t^{10} \cdot T_i) + \beta_2 \cdot (\Delta InvCS_t \cdot T_i) + \beta_3 \cdot (\Delta highCS_t \cdot T_i) + \beta_4 \cdot \Delta R_{m,t} + \beta_5 \cdot \Delta R_{i,t} + \gamma_0 \cdot \Delta Q_{i,t} + \gamma_1 \cdot \Delta(Q_{i,t} \cdot ln(S_{i,t})) + \varepsilon_{i,t} \quad (6)$$

where

Δ	difference between two consecutive quotes
$P_{i,t}$	trade price of bond *i*
YTM_t^{10}	10-year Treasury bond yield
T_i	years to maturity of bond *i*
$InvCS_t$	credit spread of investment-grade bonds
$highCS_t$	credit spread of high-yield bonds
$R_{m,t}$	return of a stock market index
$R_{i,t}$	stock return for the issuer of bond *i*
$Q_{i,t}$	indicator variable that equals one (minus one) if the transaction is a buy (sell)
$S_{i,t}$	size of the trade (par value)

Ellul et al. (2011) are the first to discuss an issue inherent in several factor models for bondholder wealth effects: equal coefficients for changes in stock market returns and/or changes in issuer returns for bonds of different rating categories, as well as no differentiation between bonds with varying maturities. They argue that bonds with lower ratings are more equity-like, and therefore load more on the change in the high-yield spread and stock market returns. Moreover, treating maturity adjustments the same way for all bonds would be inaccurate too, since the difference between modified duration and maturity grows with increasing maturity. Hence, they construct four different bond groups, classified by maturity at event-date (≤ 5 years or > 5 years) and pre-event rating (at BBB- or above BBB-),

11 Ellul et al. (2011) call it a "simple market model". However, since the regression contains more than just market returns, we list it under the section "factor models".

assuming that the parameters are the same for all bonds in one group. Subsequently, the estimation of abnormal bond returns is done separately for four groups.

2.2.3 Valuation Prediction Error

To determine the wealth effects of mergers on all of the publicly traded securities, including bonds, Maquieira et al. (1998) compute a valuation prediction error (VPE) for every security. Rather than the more common bond returns they assess excess changes in yield spreads. For each individual bond issue, a maturity and coupon rate matched outstanding government bond is allocated. Next, pre-event yield spreads are computed as the difference between the matched government bond's yield to maturity and the yield to maturity of the sample corporate bond.

$$YieldSpread_{i,t} = YTM_{i,t} - YTM_{Govt\ i,t} \tag{7}$$

where

$YTM_{i,t}$	Yield to maturity of the corporate bond i
$YTM_{Govt\ i,t}$	Yield to maturity of the matched government bond i

Next, it is assumed that the pre-event yield spread will remain unchanged over time. This assumption allows the computation of an expected yield to maturity for each bond, based on the observed value of its matching government bond during the post-event time. Knowing the expected yield to maturity, remaining maturity, and coupon rate, the expected post-event price of a bond can be computed using a standard internal rate of return bond price formula. The VPE for each bond is computed as the difference between the actual price and the expected price, after adjusting for bond redemptions, conversions, and sinking fund payments.

$$VPE_{i,t} = Price_{i,t} - Price_{expected,i} \tag{8}$$

where

$Price_{i,t}$	actual price of corporate bond i
$Price_{expected,i}$	expected price of corporate bond i

Nishikawa, Prevost, and Rao (2011) employ the above described methodology, yet compute abnormal changes in bond yield spreads instead of valuation prediction errors. They search for the closest trade within a pre-event ($-t_1$, -1) and post-event (0, t_2) window relative to the examined event, and calculate two corresponding yield spreads for each firm. The pre-event spread is assumed to be equal to the expected yield spread and the difference between the post-event and pre-event spread reflects the impact of the examined event on the credit risk component of the spread, equaling the abnormal change in bond yield spreads.

2.2.4 Mean Adjusted Model

Based on the mean adjusted returns model for stocks (Brown & Warner, 1980, 1985) Handjinicolaou and Kalay (1984) create a simple bond event study model that accounts for a specific challenge dealing with fixed income securities: bond returns are influenced by changes in the term structure. Few studies apply the unadjusted formula (e.g., Dann, 1981; Masulis, 1980). However, changes in the term structure of interest rates must be considered to ensure that abnormal bond returns are not the result of risk free rate changes. The concept is to disentangle the influence of bond specific information from information that affects interest rates market-wide.

The adjusted calculation is divided into three steps. First, they calculate premium bond returns $PR_{i,t}$ over a previously determined estimation and event period, calculated as follows.

$$PR_{i,t} = BR_{i,t} - TR_{i,t} \tag{9}$$

where

$BR_{i,t}$	return of corporate bond i
$TR_{i,t}$	return of matched Treasury security i

Conventionally, the Treasury security is the one with the most similar time to maturity and coupon. Another matching category used to identify the adequate Treasury security is duration (e.g., Elliott, Prevost, & Rao, 2009; Kitsabunnarat-Chatjuthamard, Lung, Nishikawa, & Rao, 2010). Duration is supposed to be a more precise measure of the bond's sensitivity to interest rate changes (Kraft & Munk, 2007).

Second, expected premium bond returns EPR_i are calculated as the average premium bond return over the estimation window.

$$EPR_i = \frac{1}{d} \cdot \left(\sum_{t=\tau_1}^{\tau_2} PR_{i,t} \right) \tag{10}$$

where

$\tau_{1(2)}$	first (last) day of the estimation period
d	number of days in the estimation period

Third, abnormal premium bond returns $APR_{i,t}$ are calculated for each bond by subtracting the expected premium bond returns EPR_i from the actual premium bond returns $PR_{i,t}$ on event day t.

$$EPR_i = \frac{1}{d} \cdot \left(\sum_{t=\tau_1}^{\tau_2} PR_{i,t} \right) \tag{11}$$

$$APR_{i,t} = PR_{i,t} - EPR_i \tag{12}$$

The assumption inherent in this methodology is that premium bond returns follow a stationary process, leading to a constant return over the matched Treasury bond. However, this comparison of estimation and event date premium returns is unable to disentangle the effects of bond-specific information from market-wide movements in credit spreads, making the mean adjusted model less convincing.[12] Testing the mean adjusted model, Bessembinder et al. (2009) observe that the model performs well with monthly data but always with less statistical power than the portfolio matching methods.

2.2.5 Matching Portfolio Model

A more sophisticated method uses bond portfolios to remove the influence of the overall market on bond returns. In the matching portfolio model, abnormal bond returns are measured using a procedure that compares portfolios. Early studies mentioning this approach are Kim and McConnell (1977), Asquith and Kim (1982), and Eger (1983). The first two papers apply the paired-comparison procedure, a special form of the matched portfolio model. With the paired-comparison procedure just one bond issued by a non-sample company is matched with the bond issued by a sample-company on four observable characteristics. These are (i) bond rating, (ii) term to maturity, (iii) coupon interest rate, and (iv) industry (Asquith & Kim, 1982; Kim & McConnell, 1977). Kim, McConnell, and Greenwood (1977) provide the theoretical and empirical justification for matching the bonds on these characteristics.

To calculate the abnormal returns to bondholders, the rate of return on each matching bond is subtracted from the return on its corollary sample bond over the event period. Few papers use matched government bonds instead of corporate bonds to construct a measure of market interest rate movements (e.g., Fortin, Subramaniam, Wang, & Zhang, 2014; Kahan & Tuckman, 1993; Steiner & Heinke, 2001; Strong & Meyer, 1987). However, this procedure conflicts with

12 Corrado (2011) provides the same explanation for stock returns.

the mean adjusted model, and therefore cannot be recommended for future research.[13]

Eger (1983) is the first to calculate abnormal bond returns by matching every sample bond with a portfolio of bonds. The control portfolio for each sample bond was selected from all publicly traded, non-convertible bonds in the same rating category and with the closest maturity. Thereby, the control samples vary in size from five to ten bonds. Subsequent papers apply this approach (e.g., Gao, Liao, & Wang, 2011; May, 2010) with equally- as well as value weighted portfolios. Bessembinder et al. (2009) use six rating and three time to maturity categories to create 17 portfolios[14] for monthly data, and six matching portfolios based on the rating categories for daily data, both equal- and value weighted. Their results show that the value weighted approach outperforms almost universally all other approaches.

Another alternative for a portfolio are bond indexes. An early study that utilized this approach is provided by Dennis and McConnell (1986). Although Dennis and McConnell (1986) mention the necessity of an appropriate risk adjusted market index, they do not explicate the appropriate measurements to ensure the risk adjustment. Their calculations seem to be similar to the simulations for stocks conducted by Brown and Warner (1985), neglecting the appropriate index matching. Later studies match their bond indexes by time to maturity alone (e.g., Asquith & Wizman, 1990; Cook, Easterwood, & Martin, 1992) or time to maturity and rating classification (e.g., Hite & Warga, 1997; Warga & Welch, 1993). Typically, the indexes are divided into different rating classes (e.g. Aaa, Aa, A, Baa, Ba, and B) and, within each ranking, into different term structures (e.g. long-term and intermediate term), providing several matching portfolios. While constructing abnormal bond returns and applying the Lehman Brothers indexes, Bessembinder et al. (2009) report that Lehman's inclusion of bankruptcies induces a significantly positive bias, and therefore should not be used as a benchmark portfolio. Furthermore, it remains unclear if the matched portfolio approach benefits from additional classification categories, e.g. firm size and industrial classification. Examining the impact of controlling for industry upon financial research, Kahle and Walkling (1996) find that size- and industry-matched comparison are more powerful than pure size matches. On the other hand, Chen et al. (2014) control in their bond event study for additional characteristics including index beta,

13 "Stationarity is the central assumption of the mean adjusted returns model" (Handjinicolaou & Kalay, 1984).

14 The Aaa sample was too small to split into three subsets. Instead, only two maturity categories were used.

liquidity, outstanding par size, coupon, and industry and obtain similar results. They conclude that any selection bias in the control sample is negligible when matching on just rating and maturity. Future research might explore more carefully the impact of further matching categories.

Regardless of the portfolio, the abnormal bond returns $ABR_{i,t}$ are calculated over the event period as follows.

$$ABR_{i,t} = BR_{i,t} - PBR_{i,t} \tag{13}$$

where

$BR_{i,t}$ return of corporate bond i

$PBR_{i,t}$ average return of matched bond portfolio i

2.3 Test Statistics

Previous research on bond event studies mostly utilizes the non-parametric sign (e.g., Cook et al., 1992; Datta & Dhillon, 1993; Maxwell & Stephens, 2003) and Wilcoxon signed rank (e.g., Billett, King, & Mauer, 2004; Klein & Zur, 2011; May, 2010) as well as the parametric t-test (e.g., Crabbe, 1991; Maquieira et al., 1998; Wei & Yermack, 2011); (see Table 2-1). The parametric t-test is, however, less powerful than non-parametric sign and signed rank-tests (Bessembinder et al., 2009; Ederington et al., 2012) while the sign appears to be more powerful than the signed rank-test (Ederington et al., 2012). The underlying source of the decreased explanatory power of the parametric test is the disregard of heteroskedasticity in bond returns (Ederington et al., 2012). This is caused by different abnormal return volatilities between bond groups: abnormal return variance rises as the time to maturity lengthens and ratings deteriorate (Bessembinder et al., 2009; Ederington et al., 2012). Moreover, prices of infrequently traded bonds appear to be even more volatile during the financial crisis. According to Ederington et al. (2012), an attempt to resolve this issue is a standardization of each bond's return by its estimated standard deviation s_i in the spirit of Jaffe (1974), Mandelker (1974), and Patell (1976) yielding the standardized abnormal return.

First, Ederington et al. (2012) compute s_i by calculating the standard deviation around event date t using observed 2-day returns from t–25 to t+25 but excluding event day returns.[15] Second, standardized abnormal bond returns

15 See Ederington et al. (2012) for further details.

$SABR_{i,t}$ are calculated by dividing the abnormal bond return by its standard deviation[16].

$$SABR_{i,t} = \frac{ABR_{i,t}}{s_i} \tag{14}$$

where

$ABR_{i,t}$	abnormal return of bond i
s_i	estimated standard deviation of abnormal returns of bond i

Another similar standardization procedure is applied by the construction of abnormal standardized bond returns $ASBR_{i,t}$. These are computed in a two step process: First, raw returns are divided by their standard deviation and then the standardized average returns are subtracted from the matched bond portfolio.

$$SBR_{i,t} = \frac{BR_{i,t}}{s_i} \tag{15}$$

$$ASBR_{i,t} = SBR_{i,t} - SPBR_{i,t} \tag{16}$$

where

$BR_{i,t}$	raw bond return of bond i
s_i	estimated standard deviation of raw returns of bond i
$SPBR_{i,t}$	standardized average return on matched bond portfolio i

Standardized returns are subsequently used to calculate parametric and non-parametric test statistics. According to Ederington et al. (2012), both parametric and non-parametric test-statistics benefit from the standardization, while the improvement of the t-test is the most impressive. Ederington et al. (2012) conclude, that the past poor performance of t-tests in bond event studies can be redirected to the violation of the homoskedasticity assumption. Nonetheless, instead of the t-test the Wilcoxon signed rank-test becomes the most powerful test for standardized returns. The sign test shows only minor improvements. Furthermore, Ederington et al. (2012) observe that the discrepancies between the

16 When calculated from market model residuals denominator is multiplied by $\sqrt{1+\frac{1}{T_i}+\frac{(R_{mE}-\bar{R}_m)^2}{\sum_{t=1}^{T_i}(R_{mt}-\bar{R}_m)^2}}$. See Patell (1976), Boehmer, Musumeci, and Poulsen (1991) and Corrado (2011) for further details.

$SABR_{i,t}$ and $ASBR_{i,t}$ results are negligible, therefore, presenting only the results for the second return measure.

As Brown and Warner (1985) show for stock returns, Bessembinder et al. (2009) verify the predominance of daily bond return data compared to monthly data in event studies. However, both fail to clarify whether the power and specification of the tests could be further increased by incorporating trades over longer event windows. Ederington et al. (2012) argue that a lengthened event window may produce more powerful tests, due to a higher number of event days with calculable returns, less undesirable noise in individual bond trade prices, and a higher number of bonds for constructing firm returns. On the other hand, longer event windows could cause greater non-event-induced fluctuations in bond returns reducing test power. To provide an answer, Ederington et al. (2012) construct a composite standardized abnormal return while allocating increased weights to returns calculated from transactions closest to the examined event. It is constructed as the average return of all possible return calculations for a predetermined event window, starting at least one day before and ending at least one day after event day [0;0].[17] The weighing is completed automatically because volatility for shorter windows is normally lower than for longer windows. Overall, Ederington et al. (2012) find that tests based on composite returns are more powerful, and this power even increases with the window length[18], albeit at a decreasing rate.

2.4 Data and Data Sources

To examine the impact of various events on bondholder returns, researchers screened different databases for availability of bond return data and issuer characteristic data. The quality and availability of the data to a great degree increased over time. Early empirical bond studies utilize daily exchange-based data provided by the Wall Street Journal (WSJ) or monthly data provided by the Moody's Bond Record, the S&P's Bond Guide, and the Bank and Quotation Record (BQR) (see Table 2-1). Exchange quotes are defined as prices that represent the trading conditions on organized exchanges (Nunn, Hill, & Schneeweis, 1986). However, the application of exchange prices is connected with major drawbacks. First, exchange trades reflect primarily the odd-lot activities of individual investors accounting only for a negligible portion of the total trading

17 See Ederington et al. (2012) for examples.

18 Ederington et al. (2012) calculate abnormal standardized returns over the (t−2, t+2), (t−3, t+3), (t−4, t+4), and (t−5, t+5) window.

in listed corporate issues, as the vast majority of listed bond trading occurs over the counter (OTC) between institutional investors (Nunn et al., 1986). Second, exchange based data relies heavily on prices determined by using an algorithm on bond characteristics, known as matrix prices[19] (Warga & Welch, 1993). Hence, exchange prices may not accurately represent bond values. Third, exchange based data leads to lagged response and to weaker statistically and economically significance, as shown by Warga and Welch (1993). Furthermore, the data has to be hand-collected what frequently leads to rather small sample sizes. Thus overall, bond event study results obtained from exchange prices may be suboptimal and could be misleading. Therefore, the need for databases that provide institutional prices from major OTC bond dealers is predominant.

Since the 1990s, yet before the implementation of TRACE, many studies relied on the Lehman Brothers Bond Database (LBBD), also known as the Lehman Brothers Fixed Income Database (FIDB)[20], to calculate abnormal bond returns (see Table 2-1). LBBD provides month-end price information over the period from January 1973 to March 1998 based on bid quotes from its dealers for publicly traded corporate bonds, as well as bond-specific diagnostics and descriptive information, such as S&P's and Moody's credit ratings, bond yields, coupons, accrued interests, and callability (Elton et al., 2001; Hong & Warga, 2000; Kitsabunnarat-Chatjuthamard et al., 2010). According to Hite and Warga (1997) only bonds with a principal value of at least $1 million, an investment grade at some point in their life, or an non-investment grade but traded by Lehman Brothers are included. The advantage of the Lehman bond data is the data-availability which enables increased sample sizes, and provides trader quoted prices which are found to offer more robust results than exchange based data (Warga & Welch, 1993). A disadvantage of this database, however, is that solely monthly data is provided which is found to cause decreased power and specification of the test statistics (Bessembinder et al., 2009). Besides, this database incorporates a bias towards large companies (Hite & Warga, 1997) and contains matrix prices (Hong & Warga, 2000). Matrix prices are not actual trader quotes but algorithmically determined prices. Whenever dealers do not supply a bond price, prices are determined by rules of thumb that specify the addition of a fixed spread over either an actively traded benchmark issue of the same company, another company's issue with similar rating, maturity, and coupon, or a Treasury bond

---

19 Matrix prices are discussed later in greater detail with the Lehman Brother Bond Database.

20 Data from the Lehman Brothers Fixed Income Database was distributed by Warga (1998) (e.g., Elton, Gruber, Agrawal, & Mann, 2001).

(Warga & Welch, 1993). Thus, matrix prices do not always incorporate all publicly available information.

Warga and Welch (1993) discuss the use of matrix pricing in event studies and find significant differences between trader-quoted and matrix-based prices, showing an undeniable weakness inherent in matrix prices. Quotes generated by matrix pricing may bias event month abnormal returns towards zero and cause event month and non-event month abnormal return to be equal (Easterwood, 1998). Therefore, most studies that rely on Lehman data eliminate matrix priced bonds from their sample (e.g., Bessembinder et al., 2009; Elton et al., 2001; Penas & Unal, 2004). Despite these drawbacks, many researchers nonetheless obtain bond data from the Lehman database because it provides information for a diverse variety of bonds without the need to hand collect them.

Insurance companies are required to provide a record of all bond transactions via a Schedule D to the National Association of Insurance Commissioners (NAIC) every quarter (Hong & Warga, 2000). This schedule provides detailed transaction information, including trade date, total market value, par value of the bonds, as well as buyers' and sellers' identity and are available electronically since 1995 (Hong & Warga, 2000; Schultz, 2001). The major disadvantage of this database is the limitation to insurance companies, which might not trade as actively as other market participants (Bessembinder et al., 2006). However, Schultz (2001) along with Campbell and Taksler (2003) estimate that insurance companies hold between 33% and 40% of all outstanding corporate bonds, thus represent a considerable portion of the corporate bond market. Therefore, it was also applied in bond event studies (e.g. Ellul et al., 2011).

In July 2002, the National Association of Security Dealers (NASD predecessor of FINRA) introduced the Trade Reporting and Compliance Engine (TRACE) in an effort to increase the transparency of the US corporate debt market, which facilitates the mandatory reporting of OTC secondary market transactions in publicly traded eligible securities (investment grade, high yield, and convertible corporate debt) (FINRA, 2012). All members are required to report bond identification (CUSIP or NASD/FINRA symbol), time and date of execution, price, yield, size and a sell or buy indication for each trade. However, only the first five are disseminated to the public (Bessembinder et al., 2006). Trade size is provided for investment-grade bonds with a face value of at least $5 million, and for speculative-grade bonds with a face value of at least $1 million. Otherwise, an indicator variable denotes a trade exceeding the aforementioned size (Bessembinder & Maxwell, 2008).

Due to intraday data, prices can be used to construct return data at a daily or even finer frequency what allows the construction of trade-weighted prices. This is accomplished by weighting each trade on a given day by its size and computing volume-weighted average prices. Bessembinder et al. (2009) argue that this approach emphasizes the institutional trades that incur lower execution costs and find that statistical tests estimated with this method are better specified and more powerful than those computed with end-of-day prices. Constructing daily returns by relying on the last trade of the day could introduce noise because prices reported in TRACE include bid-ask fees, which are negatively related to trade size and considerably large for small trades (May, 2010). The trade-weighted price approach mitigates this issue by allocating more weight to large trades that are assumed to have lower trading costs. Utilization of the square root of trade size produces only slightly more powerful test statistics (Ederington et al., 2012).

Moreover, eliminating non-institutional trades by using only trades of $100,000 or more lowers the standard deviation of abnormal returns even further, increasing the power of the test statistic (Bessembinder et al., 2009). However, this approach has the disadvantage of losing daily observations for bonds that only trade of less than $100,000. Therefore, Ederington et al. (2012) investigate whether the positive effect of restricting the sample to trades of 100 or more bonds[21] or the negative effect of the sample size reduction is the predominating effect. Restricting the sample to trades of at least 100 bonds produces small differences when compared to all trades (Ederington et al., 2012). The t-test is slightly more powerful, the sign test slightly less powerful, and the Wilcoxon signed rank-test shows mixed results. Thus, altogether there is no conclusive evidence of an improvement. Furthermore, restricting the sample to interdealer dates causes less noisy returns due to smaller bid-ask spreads and better informed market participants, hence, reduces the power of all test statistics.

Access to the information is either provided by the NASD website or investors rely on third-party vendors. Since its initiation in 2002, TRACE was expanded successively and by January 9, 2006, trades for nearly all publicly issued bonds were disseminated to the public (Bessembinder & Maxwell, 2008). Omitted, however, are only those trades that occurred on exchanges, like the NYSE's Automated Bond System. But these represent only a minor part of all trades (Edwards et al., 2007). Disadvantages of TRACE are data availability (only since 2002, and full coverage since mid-2005) and that price information reflected in TRACE are prices without accrued interest ("clean prices"). While the first disadvantage will resolve over time, most papers rely on the Mergent Fixed Income Security Database (FISD) to

21 Trades of $100,000 par value equal 100 bonds with $1,000 par value.

supplement the TRACE data with accrued interests.[22] Mergent FISD provides issue details on US debt securities, including credit rating, time to maturity, callability, coupon rates, and coupon frequency (Massa & Zhang, 2011).

According to Ederington et al. (2012), most researchers choose to calculate returns in terms of the "dirty price". Ederington et al. (2012) discuss the problem that "dirty prices", but not "clean prices", tend to fall by the amount of the coupon payment on the coupon payment date, leading to large negative returns on the payment date. Therefore, they recommend utilizing "clean prices" to compute bond returns. On the other hand, Bessembinder et al. (2009) point out that using "clean prices" could bias the results for bonds with significantly different accrued interests, but their results only show small difference in power if accrued interest is included or not. Therefore, accrued interest does not seem to be a requirement to conduct a bond event study.

Studies validating the implementation of TRACE conclude that investors benefit from the increased transparency through reduced transaction costs (Bessembinder & Maxwell, 2008; Bessembinder et al., 2006; Edwards et al., 2007).

Further sources for daily pricing quotes are the Reuters Fixed Income Database and Thomson Financials Datastream. Reuters provides end-of-day pricing quotes based upon market quotes. According to Wei and Yermack (2011), Reuters gathers daily closing price quotes for corporate bonds throughout each trading day, even if no trading took place. Then, Reuters releases provisional prices and allows clients to submit evidence to dispute Reuters' pricing. Whenever the dispute is justified, the data vendor initiates corresponding adjustments. Validating the accuracy of the Reuters bond data, Wei and Yermack (2011) obtain R^2 statistics from several regressions of close to 100% and therefore conclude that TRACE and Reuters contain similar information. Since all Reuters prices are dealer quotes, they can contain matrix prices (Renneboog & Szilagyi, 2007) causing the same shortcoming as with the Lehman data.

Datastream also uses quotes from dealers, but in contrast to Reuters does not calculate matrix prices if no new quotes are available. In the absence of dealer quotes, ex-coupon bond prices remain unchanged in Datastream (DeFond & Zhang, 2008; DeFond, Hung, Carr, & Zhang, 2011). To calculate bond prices the price across all market makers for the bond is averaged (Chen, Lesmond, & Wei, 2007). A potential advantage of Datastream relative to TRACE is that Datastream's

22 For instance, May (2010) calculates accrued interests relying on the raw return for a day on which the bond did not trade.

full coverage begins in 1994[23] while TRACE has only limited coverage prior to 2006 (DeFond & Zhang, 2008). According to Chen et al. (2007), Merrill Lynch[24] is Datastream's source for price data, which covers most rated US publicly issued corporate bonds (Acharya, Amihud, & Bharath, 2013).

2.5 The Link between Bondholder and Stockholder Returns

The two dominating hypotheses which deal with the relation between bondholders and stockholders abnormal returns are the wealth-transfer or -redistribution hypothesis and the signaling or information content hypothesis (e.g., Datta & Iskandar-Datta, 1995; Handjinicolaou & Kalay, 1984; Kitsabunnarat-Chatjuthamard et al., 2010; Maxwell & Rao, 2003; Maxwell & Stephens, 2003; Nishikawa et al., 2011). Past event studies frequently focused exclusively on stock price behavior without investigating corresponding bond price behavior and its interaction with stock prices. Therefore, the fundamental question of the overall firm value change could not be answered conclusively. The wealth transfer hypothesis stems from the agency conflict between different classes of security holders (Handjinicolaou & Kalay, 1984) and predicts that price of one class of security (i.e. stocks or bonds) should rise at the expense of another class of security (Vermaelen, 1981). The actual relationship depends on the examined event. According to Maxwell and Stephens (2003), disregarding transaction costs, a wealth-transfer is a zero-sum game. Gains to one class of security holder emerge at the expense of another class. Alternatively, the signaling hypothesis suggests that an information signal is given to investors concerning firm value and, consequently, bond and stock prices will move in the same direction (Maxwell & Stephens, 2003; Woolridge, 1983). This "informational content" hypothesis was first mentioned by Miller and Modigliani (1961) citing that dividend announcements are often followed by a change in the market price. Due to the riskiness of direct communication between managers and investors concerning a company's prospect, managers use financial signals[25] to convey their expectations to the market (Woolridge, 1983). The direction of this signal is ambiguous and depends on the signal itself. Comparing both hypotheses lead to the following empirical

---

23 Chen et al. (2007) argue that daily prices are more regularly available through Datastream after 1995.

24 Since 2009 Bank of America Merrill Lynch.

25 Possible signals are dividend announcements (Handjinicolaou & Kalay, 1984), stock repurchases (Vermaelen, 1981), and seasoned issue of new equity (Kalay & Shimrat, 1987), among others.

implication: The signaling hypothesis predicts that, on average, both bond and stock prices respond in the same way to the new information since it is relevant for all participants in capital markets. Conversely, the wealth-transfer hypothesis predicts that changes in both security classes will be negatively correlated. However, both alternative hypotheses are not mutually exclusive. Thus, both effects can be reflected in security prices but one can be the predominant effect. Moreover, if the signaling and the wealth-transfer hypotheses are both valid, their conflicting effects could result in no bond price reaction (Kalay & Shimrat, 1987).

To examine the predominant effect different approaches are applied. First, the possible gains or losses to stockholders and bondholders are observed and compared. Uniform signs of abnormal stock and bond returns suggest that the signal dominates the wealth-transfer while different signs are considered to be consistent with a wealth transfer among claimants. However, it is conceivable that the observed loss to one claimholder could be merely a wealth loss that is not necessarily associated with a transfer of wealth to another claimholder (Maxwell & Rao, 2003). The wealth-transfer hypothesis proposes that wealth is transferred from one class of securityholder to another. Therefore, researchers tend to also analyze the effect of their examined event on the value of the entire firm[26] (e.g., Kitsabunnarat-Chatjuthamard et al., 2010; Maxwell & Rao, 2003; Maxwell & Stephens, 2003). Should wealth effects to stockholders roughly offset the wealth effects to bondholders, then, the event is arguably a pure wealth-transferring one with no firm value change whatsoever (Maxwell & Stephens, 2003). On the other hand, if wealth gains (losses) to stockholders exceed the corresponding loss (gain) to creditors causing an overall increase (decrease) in firm value, the wealth-redistribution hypothesis provides only a partial explanation for the abnormal returns on stockholders, and possibly leaves additional value change associated with the information signal.

To better quantify the relation between the abnormal change in stock value and bond value and differentiate the hypotheses usually two methodologies are applied: correlation coefficient (e.g., Billett et al., 2004; Maxwell & Rao, 2003; Maxwell & Stephens, 2003; Nishikawa et al., 2011) and cross sectional regression analysis between stock and bond abnormal returns (e.g., Brown, James, & Mooradian, 1994; Datta & Dhillon, 1993; Datta & Iskandar-Datta, 1995) and/or between abnormal changes in the stock value and bond value[27] (e.g., Baran & King, 2010;

26 Abnormal firm returns are calculated as the weighted sum of the abnormal monthly changes in the value of stocks and bonds.

27 The abnormal change in the stock (bond) value is the abnormal return multiplied by the market value of securities (Maxwell & Rao, 2003).

Kitsabunnarat-Chatjuthamard et al., 2010; Maxwell & Stephens, 2003). According to Kitsabunnarat-Chatjuthamard et al. (2010), the usage of abnormal value changes is more revealing when the redistribution of actual dollar gains from one security class to another are analyzed.

If there is a wealth-transfer, a significant negative relation should exist, that is, larger gains to one group are associated with larger losses to the other group. On the other hand, if signaling is the dominating effect, the relation should be positive. The advantage of a multivariate regression framework over a simple correlation coefficient is that controlling for the influence by other factors is possible. Maxwell and Rao (2003) also apply cross sectional regression in a second way to test the hypotheses in a more indirect way: Given a redistribution of wealth, coefficients that significantly affect stockholders wealth should also be significant but opposite for bondholders. Nishikawa et al. (2011) combine both approaches and relate announcement period excess bond returns[28] not only on excess stock returns, but also on several wealth transfer indicators while controlling for non-wealth transfer motivations (e.g, signaling).

2.6 Summary and Conclusion

The purpose of this review is to fill a gap in the existing literature and provide a comprehensive overview of the applied methodology in bond event studies. First, those bond characteristics that affect event study results are summarized and the adjustments developed by researchers discussed. The low liquidity of bonds as well as the fact that several firms issue more than one bond are characteristics that differentiate bonds from stocks. Second, the favored models to calculate abnormal bond returns are illustrated and the applied parametric and non-parametric test statistics are discussed. One conclusion of past studies is that the matched portfolio approach using value weighted portfolios works well in event studies utilizing bond returns. With raw returns, non-parametric tests are more powerful than parametric t-tests. However, standardization of bond returns leads to a considerable increase in the power of the t-test. Third, the change in the availability of corporate bond data in the last four decades as well as the impact of improved databases on event study methodology are discussed. The introduction of the Lehman Brothers Bond Database in the 1990s providing monthly data, as well as the TRACE data set in 2002 providing daily data had a great influence on the occurrence of event studies concerning bondholder

28 Nishikawa et al. (2011) use excess changes in bond yield spreads.

wealth effects. Finally, insight into the major hypotheses explaining the relationship between bondholders and stockholders abnormal return is provided, implying different bond price behavior around corporate events. A wealth transfer between bondholders and stockholders implies that gains to one class should emerge at the expense of another, while the signal hypothesis suggests that bond and stock prices will move in the same direction. However, both alternative hypotheses are not mutually exclusive.

While a variety of important issues concerning event studies examining the impact of corporate events on bondholder wealth have been pointed out by previous studies, researchers have developed a number of simple adjustments to ultimately obtain robust results. This challenge and the introduction of new databases lead to a noticeable evolution of bond event study methodology over time. Today, researchers can utilize assessed methods and test statistics with strong empirical power to detect abnormal bond returns.

This methodology review offers some guidance for researchers in choice of event study method. However, the methodology will continue to be a popular area of investigation and innovation with the attempt to enhance the validity of bond event studies. In chapter 3 and 4 the author will use various insights from this review to present two bond event studies in broader research frameworks.

3. Wealth Effects of Synergy disclosing M&A Announcements in the US Energy Sector

Prior research on wealth effects for share- and bondholders during M&A lead to diverging value implications for not only the respective party (i.e. target and acquirers), but also for the holding entity (i.e. share- or bondholder). On a theoretical level, bondholders, regardless of whether they are target or bidder bondholders, should experience a value creation due to the so-called co-insurance effect: as the cash flows of the merging entities are imperfectly correlated, the debt default risk is reduced, which leads to a value appreciation for bonds (Kim & McConnell, 1977). Along this reasoning, Galai and Masulis (1976) propose that during non-synergetic mergers this value creation is directly offset by the wealth loss of the shareholders. On the contrary, other researchers like Settle, Petry, and Hsia (1984) or Dennis and McConnell (1986) indicate that there may also exist a so-called synergy effect during which bondholders share emerging synergies with shareholders, thus both parties experience a value creation. This, however, requires M&A to result in synergies, which is yet not the case for all transactions. Occasionally, firms voluntarily communicate along with the M&A announcement a quantitative synergy forecast which is expected to result in diverging value consequences for bondholders.

Voluntary disclosure in general, according to Lang and Lundholm (1996), has proved to have important capital market consequences, thus it is expectable that these also affect bonds and have in particular value consequences if synergies are projected. According to the author's best knowledge no prior study on wealth effects for shareholders and bondholders, however, has distinguished between synergy expecting and not disclosing M&A. By considering all M&A to be equal, the value effects of emerging synergies for shares and bonds cannot be extracted and hence their value influence not be investigated. This chapter intends to respond to this gap in research by distinguishing between those transactions which voluntarily disclose a synergy forecast at announcement and those which chose not to do so.[29]

This research focus is especially relevant as synergy forecasts during M&A have proven to lead to substantial value consequences for in particular the acquiring shareholders (Bernile & Bauguess, 2011; Bernile & Lyandres, 2013; Dutordoir, Roosenboom, & Vasconcelos, 2014; Fraunhoffer & Schiereck, 2012a). Preceding

29 Acknowledgement: I am thankful to Robert Fraunhoffer for helpful comments and support, which lead to a prior version of this chapter (see Fraunhoffer, Maul, & Schiereck, 2011).

research finds that bidding shareholders frequently lose value at announcement (Moeller, Schlingemann, & Stulz, 2005; Morck, Shleifer, & Vishny, 1990) owing to existing information between the market and the firm (Moeller, Schlingemann, & Stulz, 2007; Officer, Poulsen, & Stegemoller, 2009). Yet, if a quantitative synergy forecast is disclosed along with the announcement, investors are informed about the existence of synergies as well as implied wealth gains which subsequently serve as a value creation signal for rational market participants. Therefore, the reduction of existing information asymmetries as well as the implied value generation translates into an appreciation of the share prices. However, present research lacks results on how synergy forecasts affect bidder bondholders. On the one hand, bondholders might share the benefits of management forecasts of merger-related gains with shareholders, leading to positive impact on bondholder's wealth. On the other hand, gains for shareholders might be expropriated from the firm's bondholders, causing negative bond returns. Thus, a more detailed investigation on this aspect will eventually shed light on the potential interdependent wealth transfer.

Prior research by Bernile and Bauguess (2011) shows that synergy disclosure substantially differs across industries, thus the need for a detailed industry analysis arises, in particular, as idiosyncratic industry features may also lead to misleading industry specific conclusions. With respect to bondholder wealth effects, industry studies have also proved to diverge from general market implications (e.g. Penas & Unal, 2004), again highlighting the necessity of industry specific research. Therefore an industry with one of the highest synergy disclosure ratios, homogenous business models between its sectors, as well as high bond issuing rates is used. To further increase sample homogeneity with respect to general market conditions a geographic focus on the US energy sector is taken.

In accordance with preceding research, voluntary synergy disclosure is expected to also reduce information asymmetries in the sample leading to an increased share price reaction for disclosing acquiring firms. With respect to bondholders, the impact of synergy forecasts is an empirical question. A redistribution of wealth from bondholders to stockholders is possible, indicating that synergy disclosing is not a purely firm value enhancing strategy, as well as positive bondholder returns, suggesting that disclosing deals are considered as less risky investments.

3.1 Literature Review

3.1.1 Voluntary Synergy Disclosure and Shareholder Wealth Effects

The majority of the voluntary disclosure literature has focused on the effects of accounting related releases (e.g. Baginski, Hassell, & Waymire, 1994; Baginski &

Hassell, 1997; Healy, Hutton, & Palepu, 1999; Hutton, Miller, & Skinner, 2003; Lev & Penman, 1990). Unanimously these studies show that voluntary information disclosure has the potential to influence shareholder value. As such, Healy et al. (1999) for instance demonstrate that a more detailed information disclosure is accompanied by an improved stock performance. Other voluntary disclosure aspects are concerned with extended press releases or conference calls, providing the respective target group with an increased amount of information (e.g. Bowen, Davis, & Matsumoto, 2002; Bushee, Matsumoto, & Miller, 2004; Francis, Schipper, & Vincent, 2002; Kimbrough, 2005; Kimbrough & Louis, 2011). Again, these studies also show a capital market influence on disclosure. For instance, Bowen et al. (2002) find that conference calls that expand on earnings forecasts lead to increased analyst earnings forecast accuracy which indicates that voluntary disclosure reduces existing information asymmetries.

Disclosure at M&A, however, greatly differs from routine situation such as earnings estimates, as the communication strategy has proven to be one of the decisive success factors, and hence a value creation factor for shareholders or respective bondholders (Sirower & Lipin, 2003). Thus, if the market is aware of private information which is, however, not communicated, a negative content is implied. Therefore, disclosure decisions greatly impact post-announcement share price performance (Dye, 1985). Merger research in general finds that acquiring firms' shareholders experience no significant wealth effect or a value loss at the announcement (Moeller et al., 2005; Morck et al., 1990), while targets are associated with an value appreciation (Andrade, Mitchell, & Stafford, 2001; Bruner, 2004). For a review of M&A research see Haleblian, Devers, McNamara, Carpenter, and Davison (2009). In the light of voluntary disclosure at M&A and their effects for bidding and target shareholders, Kimbrough and Louis (2011) investigate the effects of conference calls at announcement. They find that bidders in general released a greater amount of information relative to mergers without conference calls (hence solely convey the M&A through press releases) and that the complexity as well as size of the transaction motivates managers to hold calls. With respect to shareholder value influences, the study shows that bidders with an associated call experience an increased capital market valuation which does not reverse on the long-term.

With respect to the focus of the conducted research, voluntary synergy disclosure, comparable results are retrieved yet again solely for the stock market. Both Bernile and Bauguess (2011) as well as Dutordoir et al. (2014) collect synergy estimates for the US M&A market from 1990–2005 and 1995–2008, respectively. Bernile and Bauguess (2011) find that the combined excess returns of the bidding and target firms are significantly higher for deals with an associated synergy disclosure. They argue that either disclosing deals generate larger synergies or management projections have a positive impact on investors' reaction to merger announcements. Utilizing the same sample, Bernile and Lyandres (2013) examine the impact of synergy disclosures on the merging firms' competitors, suppliers, and customers. They find that, consistent with their predictions, announcement returns increase with the synergy estimate for horizontal merger, decrease for competitors, and increase for merging firms' customers. Regarding the effects of forecasted synergies on merging firms' suppliers, Bernile and Lyandres (2013) find that firms with low tangibility within the subsample of horizontal mergers experience lower abnormal returns. Overall, they conclude that projected synergies not only affect bidders' and targets' returns, but also merging firms' competitors, customers, and suppliers. Dutordoir et al. (2014) confirm higher announcement returns for disclosing bidding firms specifically. They find that synergy forecasts reduce the negativity of acquirer abnormal returns by approximately 5%. Thus, synergies appear to be an effective instrument to decrease information asymmetries and convey rational investors of the value creation.

However, Bernile and Bauguess (2011) also show that synergy disclosure behavior substantially differs across industries; the durable goods industry has for instance a synergy disclosure ratio of 10.7%, while the energy sector has a ratio of 30.7%. These discrepancies therefore also suggest different capital market responses for various sectors, proposing the need for detailed industry level analysis. Houston, James, and Ryngaert (2001) complete a sector specific synergy disclosure study for 64 large US banking mergers between 1985 and 1996. Generally, they confirm the finding that disclosing deals experience increased returns, however, with the following limitations, which again underline the necessity of sector specific research. Not only is the synergy disclosure ratio substantially larger (64%), but the market also values management estimates differently, as synergies are discounted by a lower magnitude.

The industry of reference in this chapter, the US energy sector, has been subjected to an increased rate of M&A. This wave was primarily fostered by government enforced market liberalization and deregulation in the 1990s, in particular by the Energy Policy Act in 1992 (Becher, Mulherin, & Walkling, 2008). Moreover, this sector is attributed with one of the highest synergy disclosure ratios (Dutordoir et al., 2014) and, as Fraunhoffer and Schiereck (2012b) show, has great synergy potential throughout the value chain. Thus, the investigation of this particular sector is predominantly relevant.

3.1.2 Bondholder Wealth Effects associated with M&A

In contrast to shareholder wealth research upon M&A, the effects for bondholders are less clear. Bondholders, from a theoretical point of view, should experience a wealth increase if the merger leads to a reduction of the default risk, thus if the merging entities induce sufficient co-insurance, which in turn requires uncorrelated cash flows (co-insurance hypothesis) (e.g. Galai & Masulis, 1976; Kim & McConnell, 1977; Lewellen, 1971). The value increase primarily results from a value decrease of the shareholders, which is redirected to the low economic relationship between the merging firms. Thus, a wealth transfer from stockholders to bondholders would be the result. Contrary to this hypothesis but following the reasoning of Jensen and Meckling (1976), Asquith and Kim (1982) argue that stockholders have the incentive to increase a firm's default risk and earn positive returns at the expense of bondholders (incentive hypothesis). Consequently, if a merger is perceived as a risk increasing event, wealth is transferred from bondholders to stockholders. Additionally, Settle et al. (1984) as well as Dennis and McConnell (1986) argue that shareholders may induce such wealth transfers by either increasing the operational risk or the leverage. Finally, the M&A may lead to a synergy effect (synergy hypothesis). Here, share- and bondholder divide the value appreciation among each other and both parties experience a wealth increase (e.g. Dennis & McConnell, 1986; Eger, 1983; Settle et al., 1984).

Empirically, the evidence for the US market is inconclusive and thus by far no clear evidence for one of the theoretical foundations has evolved. Billett et al. (2004) show that acquiring bondholders do not experience a value increase upon the M&A, regardless of the bond rating, payment method, or whether the deal is a conglomerate one. Acquirer bonds result in significantly negative excess returns of –0.17%. In contrast, Kim and McConnell (1977), Asquith and Kim (1982), Dennis and McConnell (1986), as well as Walker (1994) find neither positive nor negative bidder wealth consequences. Eger (1983) along with Maquieira et al. (1998) furthermore analyze pure stock-for-stock mergers and thus the influence of the payment method, however, with again inconclusive results. Eger (1983) shows significantly positive excess returns while Maquieira et al. (1998) demonstrate these solely for non-conglomerate mergers, thereby directly contradicting the findings from Billett et al. (2004). Thus overall, there is so far no consensus upon acquiring bondholder wealth effects. As for the target bondholders, all studies show insignificant abnormal returns. Only Billett et al. (2004) retrieve significantly positive effects (even though not for all subsamples) and provide some evidence for the conglomerate hypothesis. They find that junk-graded targets (with a rating below BBB-) benefit from relatively higher rated bidders as their rating should improve upon M&A completion. For this subsample a positive return of 4.3% is reported. A different impact of M&A announcements on the wealth transfer between shareholders and creditors is detected by Imbierowicz and Wahrenburg (2013). Examining negative rating announcements as a signal for reduced credit quality, they find that effects for stockholders and bondholders are mitigated when the changes in the firm's credit quality are related to a contemporaneous M&A event.

Interestingly, other market places appear to exhibit diverging bond related value reactions following M&A announcements. In this light, Renneboog and Szilagyi (2007) show that for European bonds both the bidder and target receive positive excess returns with the latter yet being insignificant. In addition, the geographic proximity reveals to influence bondholder returns as cross-border mergers decrease acquiring bondholder returns relative to domestic transactions.

So far, industry sector bond research has solely been conducted for the US banking industry. Penas and Unal (2004) show that both bidder and target bondholders experience significantly positive excess returns, hence bank mergers are perceived as default-risk reducing events. Thereby, Penas and Unal (2004) directly contradict prior cross-industrial findings which are not able to show significant returns for target shareholders at all, and provide evidence for the "Too-Big-to-Fail" argument in banking. They argue that banks benefit from becoming or getting closer to become systematically important institutions (see Brewer and Jagtiani (2013) for further information on this topic). Additionally, Choi, Francis, and Hasan (2010) document that cross-border banking M&A lead to significantly positive abnormal returns for acquiring bondholders which implies that bondholders require a higher yield for the perceived increase in risk. Overall, it can be concluded that on an industry level, general market implications may vary significantly proposing the need for industry specific research, in particular as prior studies were not able to provide consisting results. To the author's knowledge, no other industry specific studies have so far been conducted. Thus, the intention is to further advance the discussion upon bondholder wealth returns with respect to the US energy sector.

Moreover, the effects of voluntary disclosure are introduced to the framework, which have proven to significantly influence shareholder returns to the field of bondholder wealth effects. Obviously, one could expect voluntary synergy forecasts to signal corresponding synergies and cause positive abnormal returns to stockholders and bondholders of the acquiring firm, thereby confirming the synergy hypothesis. On the other hand, management's synergy estimates do not state whether the transaction increases the firm's riskiness, causing a wealth transfer from bondholders to stockholders. Investors might interpret synergies in a way having the effect that management put itself in a tight spot by predicting exact figures and plans to increase operational risk or leverage to achieve them, leading to higher default risk for outstanding bonds. A reduced risk of default due to imperfectly correlated cash flow streams (co-insurance hypothesis) is rather unlikely, since only M&A in the energy sector are analyzed. To detect which effect dominates stockholder and bondholder returns, it is necessary to investigate both.

3.2 Data and Methodology

3.2.1 Data

Thomson One Banker Deals Analysis module for M&A is used to construct a sample with all completed, energy-related M&A occurred between January 1, 1998 and October, 31 2012 in the United States; to identify the respective M&A two-digit Standard Industrial Classification (SIC) codes 13, 49 (except Sanitary Services[30]) as well as 46 and 29[31] are utilized.[32] Moreover, the sample is limited by (i) a minimum transaction value of $1 million, (ii) majority transactions with a voting rights transfer of at least 50%, and (iii) the bidder has to be publicly listed to identify diverging wealth implication. Further, minority stake purchases, leverage buyouts, spin-offs, exchange offers, self-tenders, recapitalizations, and repurchases are eliminated which leads to a sample size of 1,309 M&A. Next, the bidding companies are checked for outstanding bonds, using the Thomson One Banker Bonds module. As not all firms issue bonds during the applied timeframe, those M&A without an associated bond outstanding at the announcement are eliminated. To deal with the illiquidity of the corporate bond market, bonds having only zero returns during the main event window [−10;10] are excluded. Since a bond credit rating is required to calculate abnormal returns, all bonds without a rating classification from Standard & Poor's (S&P) are eliminated.[33] These requirements and the availability of stock market data leads to a final sample size of 205 M&A, announced between 2000 and 2012, and associated with 689 bonds. Thereby, zero-coupon bonds, convertibles, as well as perpetual

30 4952 (Sewerage systems), 4953 (Refuse systems), 4959 (Sanitary services, nec).

31 Except 2951 (Asphalt paving mixtures and blocks) and 2952 (Asphalt felts and coatings).

32 The considered SIC codes belong to the two main groups "Electric, Gas, and Water Distribution" and "Oil and Gas; Petroleum Refining".

33 Ratings from Moody's cannot be used as Datastream only provides historical ratings from S&P.

bonds are not considered as these tend to behave more like stocks (Bessembinder et al., 2009). Stock and bond price information is retrieved from Thomson Reuters Datastream. For stocks returns based on the Total Return Index (RI) are utilized. Following Ederington et al. (2012) clean prices are utilized to compute bond returns.

Table 3-1: Number of M&A deals by year of announcement

Year	No. of Deals	No. of Deals with Synergy Dislosure	Percentage of Deals with Synergy Disclosure
2000	2	0	0.00%
2001	7	2	28.57%
2002	5	0	0.00%
2003	15	4	26.67%
2004	21	3	14.29%
2005	20	3	15.00%
2006	13	2	15.38%
2007	15	0	0.00%
2008	15	3	20.00%
2009	14	3	21.43%
2010	32	3	9.38%
2011	31	5	16.13%
2012	15	5	33.33%
Total	205	33	16.10%

This table presents the number of deals and the relative number of disclosing deals per year. Disclosing deals are deals in which bidding-firm managers publicly disclose a forecast of the value of synergies they expect to achieve. The sample consists of M&A announced between January 1, 2000 and October 31, 2012 within the US energy sector.

In a following process, press releases and news reports for all transactions are researched to identify those deals with an associated synergy disclosure at announcement utilizing corporate press releases as well as Nexis database. Thereby, only management indicated estimates are considered to ensure their credibility and accuracy; investors, analysts, or press estimates are not considered. Moreover, only quantitative forecasts are captured which signal a value creation to rational market participants. Table 3-1 documents the use of synergy forecasts during the research time window. The percentage of deals with synergy disclosure ranges from 0% in 2000, 2002, and 2007 up to 33.33% in 2012. Overall, disclosed synergy estimates account for 16.1% of the total sample.

The following Table 3-2 below provides descriptive statistics for the final sample of bidding firms. All information is presented for the whole sample, as well as for disclosing and non-disclosing deals separately. Panel A contains general financial information regarding the sample. The typical sample firm shows mean net sales of $10 billion, total debt of $4.8 billion, and a mean market capitalization of $10 billion. Utilizing a univariate comparison of non-disclosing and disclosing deals reveals no evidence that any of the four figures are significantly different between these two groups.

Panel B provides data on various financial ratios for liquidity, profitability, leverage, and growth opportunity. Non-disclosing deals have a significantly smaller current ratio and a significantly smaller leverage. This provides some evidence that more liquid and higher leveraged firms more frequently disclose synergy estimates. In line with Dutordoir et al. (2014) evidence is found, albeit weak, for lower proprietary costs for disclosing deals, as the t-statistic confirms smaller market to book ratios for disclosing deals at the 10% level.

Panel C contains information about the amount paid for the target firm, i.e. the deal value. Comparing non-disclosing with disclosing deals uncovers statistically highly significant differences regarding deal size. Disclosing deals are significantly larger, which is in line with the information quality rationale of Verrecchia (1990) but contradicts the signaling hypothesis. Panel D shows the number of bonds per firm in the sample and the average market value per bond. The mean (median) number of bonds per firm is 3.3 (2.0) and the mean (median) market value per bond is $478 million ($403 million). Finally, Panel E provides data on the different industry categories among the energy sector. 80% of all deals belong to the two-digit SIC code family starting with 49 or 13 and 77% of all bidding firms have the same two-digit SIC code as the target.

Table 3-2: Descriptive Statistic for Sample Bidding Firms

	All Deals		Non-disclosing Deals		Disclosing Deals			
Panel A: General Financial Information	**Mean**	**Median**	**Mean**	**Median**	**Mean**	**Median**	**t-test**	**rank sum-test**
	N = 204		N = 171		N = 33			
Net Sales [Mio $]	10,169	4,529	10,133	3,928	10,355	6,963	-0.057	1.536
Total Debt [Mio $]	4,761	2,746	4,506	2,469	6,078	4,313	-1.627	1.063
Market Cap [Mio $]	10,120	4,914	10,355	5,215	8,901	4,238	0.473	-0.142
Panel B: Ratios								
Current Ratio	1.12	1.05	1.09	1.00	1.29	1.19	-2.379**	2.606***
ROA	6.72	5.61	6.72	5.61	6.75	5.62	-0.034	0.174
Bidder Leverage	0.70	0.54	0.66	0.53	0.94	0.68	-2.407**	1.974**
Market to book	3.67	2.15	3.07	2.14	6.75	2.18	-1.864*	-0.329
Panel C: M&A Data								
Deal Size [Mio $]	1,116	325	764	292	2,937	920	-5.006***	3.342***
Panel D: Bond Data								
No. of bond issues per firm	3.338	2	3.216	2	3.970	2	-1.196	0.578
	N = 689		N = 557		N = 132			
Market Value [Mio $]	478	403	472	405	502	375	-0.858	0.172
Panel E: Other Information								
No. of bidder with two-digit SIC 49	76		60		16			
No. of bidder with two-digit SIC 46	17		14		3			
No. of bidder with two-digit SIC 29	23		19		4			
No. of bidder with two-digit SIC 13	88		78		10			
No. of bidder with the same industry as the target's	157		129		28			

This table presents descriptive statistics about the sample bidding firms. Shown are the mean and median values for various variables, as well as the number of bidders with specific attributes. Net Sales presents the net sales or revenues measured at fiscal year-end prior to the announcement (Source: Worldscope). Total Debt presents the total debt measured at fiscal year-end prior to the announcement (Source: Worldscope). Market Cap is the market capitalization at fiscal year-end prior to the announcement (Source: Datastream). Current Ratio presents the ratio of current assets and current liabilities measured at fiscal year-end prior to the announcement (Source: Worldscope). ROA is the return on assets measured at fiscal year-end prior to the announcement (Source: Worldscope). Bidder leverage presents the ratio of total debt and the market value of equity measured at fiscal year-end prior to the announcement (Source: Own calculation). Market to Book presents the ratio of the market value and the book value per share (Source: Worldscope) measured at fiscal year-end prior to the announcement. Deal Size presents the amount paid for the target firm in the merger transaction (Source: Thomson One Banker). The number of bond issues pertains to the event day [−0;0]. Market Value presents the average market value of bonds at the M&A announcement date (Source: Datastream). Due to missing financial data, one observation had to be removed from the sample for this analysis.

3.2.2 Calculation of Abnormal Bond Returns

The matching portfolio approach (Bessembinder et al., 2009) is applied to estimate bond excess returns.[34] 12 matching reference portfolios are built according to the respective bond's maturity and rating. For that reason, one portfolio according to six risk categories (AAA plus AA, A, BBB, BB, B, CCC and lower) is utilized and two different maturities (long- and short-term) considered. To split the portfolios by maturity, the maturity median calculated for every single trading day in the event window is used. S&P's rating classification is used for the risk category as Datastream only provides historical ratings from this rating agency. To exclude any possible industry effect just bonds belonging to US energy and power[35] industry are considered. To gain an impression about the portfolio size, Table 3-3 displays the number of bonds included in the portfolios for all M&A announcements on the event date [0;0]. As can be seen, over half of all portfolios contain more than 100 bonds, revealing that the utilized number of bonds can be considered as sufficient.

Table 3-3: Distribution of the number of portfolio bonds for the event day [0;0]

Mean	1st Quartile	Median	3rd Quartile	Maximum	Minimum
189.57	78	172	331	368	2

In a last step, the value weighted average of all bond returns in a portfolio is calculated.[36] These matching portfolios serve as the bond's expected return (*EBR*) which is deducted from the observed bond return (*OBR*) to retrieve the abnormal bond return (*ABR*) of firm *k*

$$ABR_k = OBR_k - EBR_k \qquad (17)$$

If *a* firm *k* has multiple bonds outstanding two different approaches are utilized: the bond level and the firm level approach. With the firm level approach a

34 See chapter 2.2.5 for a detailed description and critical assessment of the matching portfolio model.

35 As indicated by the Thomson Financial Macro Description.

36 Equally weighted portfolios are also calculated, but this method is not further pursued as the results remain qualitatively the same.

firm's individual abnormal bond returns are averaged into a single firm return. Bessembinder et al. (2009) apply a value weighted approach. Thereby, the abnormal bond return (*ABR*) is value weighted according to the market value of the bond *i* outstanding with *J* as the number of bonds outstanding for firm *k* and w_i as the ratio of bond *i*'s market value to the total market value of firm *k*'s sample bonds.

$$FBR_k = \sum_{i=1}^{J} ABR_t \cdot w_i \tag{18}$$

On the other hand, Ederington et al. (2012) compare the advantages of weighted averages to unweighted firm returns and conclude that only little can be gained by using the more complex approach. Therefore, following the recommendation by Ederington et al. (2012) equally weighted firm returns are used. Overall, the sampling procedures have significant advantages over other procedures used in literature as Bessembinder et al. (2009) show. Utilizing each bond as an event violates the assumption that each observation is independent, hence the correlation across the sample increases leading to a downward biased standard deviation. Moreover, firms with multiple bonds experience an unjustifiable excess weighting again biasing the results. Following a representative approach, thus choosing a single bond which represents a firm's bond portfolio, will not accurately capture the value change, if the event only affects certain bond segments or risk classes. However, the firm level approach can also lead to misinterpretations. According to Eberhart and Siddique (2002), using a value weighted average of each of the firm's bond returns biases the standard error estimate upward because bonds from the same firm are not correlated perfectly. Therefore, abnormal returns are also calculated with a bond level approach to test whether this procedure validates the results from the firm level approach.

To test for the statistical significance of the abnormal bond returns, a parametric (one-sample t-test) and a non-parametric (Wilcoxon signed rank-test) test statistic are employed. Additionally, the advice by Ederington et al. (2012) that bond returns suffer from substantial heteroskedasticity leading to weaker statistical tests is considered and bond returns are standardized by their estimated volatility before applying the test statistics once more. Standardized abnormal bond returns ($SABR_{i,t}$) are calculated as the quotient of the abnormal return to the standard deviation of abnormal returns (STD_i) over the main event period [−10;10], excluding returns on the event day [0;0]:

$$SABR_{i,t} = \frac{ABR_{i,t}}{STD_i} \tag{19}$$

According to Ederington et al. (2012) this procedure leads to more powerful parametric and non-parametric test statistics.

3.2.3 Calculation of Abnormal Stock Returns

Stock market excess returns are computed following standard event study methodology (Brown & Warner, 1980, 1985; Fama, Fisher, Jensen, & Roll, 1969; MacKinlay, 1997) utilizing the market model and the announcement of the M&A as the event in [0;0]. The expected return (*ER*) is deduced from the actual return (*R*) to calculate abnormal stock returns (*ASR*) for firm *k* on day *t*. First, the following market model ordinary least square (OLS) regression is estimated over a period of –11 to –262 days prior to the announcement (i.e. the estimation window) utilizing the S&P 500 subsector energy as the reference market $R_{m,t}$ to get the expected return:

$$R_{k,t} = \alpha_k + \beta_k \cdot R_{m,t} + \varepsilon_{k,t} \tag{20}$$

From this regression the coefficients $\hat{\alpha}_k$ and $\hat{\beta}_k$ are obtained which then are used to calculate the expected return over the event window, starting –10 days before and ending 10 days after the M&A announcement:

$$ER_{k,t} = \hat{\alpha}_k + \hat{\beta}_k \cdot R_{m,t} + \varepsilon_{k,t} \tag{21}$$

Finally, deducting the expected return ($ER_{k,t}$) from the actual return ($R_{k,t}$) over the event window [–10;10] leads to the abnormal stock return ($ASR_{k,t}$):

$$ASR_{k,t} = R_{k,t} - ER_{k,t} = R_{k,t} - (\hat{\alpha}_k + \hat{\beta}_k \cdot R_{m,t}) \tag{22}$$

Subsequently, abnormal stock returns are calculated once more to check the robustness of the results adding further explanatory variables regularly used to calculate abnormal stock returns to the OLS regression in (19). Factors from the Fama-French-three-factor model (Fama & French, 1993) are included i.e. the difference in returns of small and big firms (Small Minus Big, SMB_t) and the difference in returns of high and low market-to-book values (High Minus Low, HML_t), as well as the momentum variable from the Carhart (1997) four-factor model (Up Minus Down, UMD_t). This leads to a four-factor model as follows:

$$R_{k,t} = \alpha_k + \beta_k \cdot R_{m,t} + s_{k,t} \cdot SMB_t + h_{k,t} \cdot HML_t + p_{k,t} \cdot UMD_t + \varepsilon_{k,t} \tag{23}$$

All necessary data has daily frequency and is kindly provided by Andrea Frazzini's data library (Frazzini, 2014). To calculate excess returns, the steps above are repeated as with the market model.

Cumulative abnormal returns (CAR_k) and cumulative average abnormal returns ($CAAR$) for both stock or bond abnormal returns (below as AR) for different event periods $[t_1;t_2]$ are calculated as:

$$CAR_k = \sum_{t=t_1}^{t_2} AR_{k,t} \tag{24}$$

$$CAAR_k = \frac{1}{N}\sum_{k=1}^{N} CAR_k \tag{25}$$

with N being the number of transactions.

With the abnormal stock returns two parametric and two non-parametric test statistics are utilized. Again, as with the bond returns, the standard one-sample t-test and Wilcoxon signed rank-test are applied. Additionally, another parametric test (Boehmer-test) is applied, as proposed by Boehmer et al. (1991), which was specifically developed for detecting abnormal stock returns. The advantage of this test is, that it controls for increases in variance at the event that cause the rejection of the null hypothesis too often, when it is actually true. This is achieved through a simple adjustment to the cross sectional t-test which includes the standard deviation of abnormal returns during the estimation window. The subsequent section presents a detailed description of the computation of the Boehmer-test.

First, the abnormal returns $ASR_{k,t}$ of security k on event day t are standardized utilizing security k's standard deviation of market model regression residual $\varepsilon_{k,t}$ during the estimation period [–262;–11] ($\widehat{s_k}$), the number of trading days in the estimation period (T_k), the benchmark returns on event day t ($R_{m,t}$), and benchmark returns day e in the estimation period ($R_{m,e}$), as follows:

$$SR_{k,t} = \frac{ASR_{k,t}}{\widehat{s_k}\cdot\sqrt{1+\frac{1}{T_k}+\frac{\left(R_{m,t}-\frac{1}{T_k}\cdot\Sigma_{e=1}^{T_k}R_{m,e}\right)^2}{\Sigma_{e=1}^{T_k}\left(R_{m,e}-\frac{1}{T_k}\cdot\Sigma_{e=1}^{T_k}R_{m,e}\right)^2}}} \tag{26}$$

Second, the following *z-statistic* for event day t is computed as:

$$Z_t = \frac{\frac{1}{N}\Sigma_{k=1}^{N}SR_{k,t}}{\sqrt{\frac{1}{N\cdot(N-1)}\cdot\Sigma_{k=1}^{N}\left(SR_{k,t}-\Sigma_{k=1}^{N}\frac{SR_{k,t}}{N}\right)^2}} \tag{27}$$

The second non-parametric test was created by Corrado (1989) and enhanced for missing returns by Corrado and Zivney (1992). Its benefit compared to the signed rank-test is that it does not require a symmetrical distribution of abnormal returns. To compute this test statistic, first security k's abnormal returns $ASR_{k,t}$ needs to be transformed over the estimation[37] and event window [−262;+10] into their ranks $K_{k,t}$.[38] After that, ranks are divided by the number of non-missing returns M_k plus one, yielding the adjusted ranks $U_{k,t}$:

$$U_{k,t} = \frac{K_{k,t}}{(M_k + 1)} \tag{28}$$

Third, the necessary standard deviation $S(U)$ of adjusted ranks is calculated for the entire period starting −262 trading days before and ending 10 trading days after the announcement with d yielding the number of days and N_t the number of securities with non-missing returns on day t as:

$$S(U) = \sqrt{\frac{1}{d} \cdot \sum_{t=1}^{d} \left(\frac{1}{\sqrt{N_t}} \sum_{k=1}^{N_t} (U_{k,t} - 0.5) \right)^2} \tag{29}$$

Finally, the non-parametric test statistic for event day t is computed as follows, with N representing the number of securities:

$$Z_t = \frac{\frac{1}{\sqrt{N}} \Sigma_{k=1}^{N} (U_{k,t} - 0.5)}{S(U)} \tag{30}$$

3.3 Empirical Results

3.3.1 Bond Event Study

To infer the capital market's valuation of debt securities at the merger announcement, two research methodologies are conducted to present a diversified perspective and to moreover check the retrieved results for robustness. Initially, a bond level approach is used, i.e. each bond is treated as an individual observation.

37 The abnormal stock returns on estimation day t are equivalent to the residual $\varepsilon_{k,t}$ of the market model regression to estimate $\hat{\alpha}_k$ and $\hat{\beta}_k$.

38 More specifically, tied ranks are computed i.e. identical numbers receive their average rank.

The second research method is the firm level approach, i.e. if a firm has multiple bonds outstanding these are equally weighted to a single firm observation.

Every table in this section has the same shape. Panel A presents the results for the whole sample, Panel B for non-disclosing deals, and Panel C for disclosing M&A. The remaining Panel D provides the results of a univariate comparison between firms in Panel B and Panel C. Confounding events are accounted for, to ensure the validity of the results by computing abnormal returns for two different samples: the "Complete Sample" and the "Control Sample". Confounding events are major firm events such as the announcement of stock offerings, reporting of financial results, or the declaration of dividends. The sources for confounding events are the news and events section or press releases on the respective company's homepage and Nexis Academic press releases for the US. Failing to control for such events can lead to misinterpretations and false conclusions about the impact of the examined event (Broughton & Smith, 1997; McWilliams & Siegel, 1997).

With the "Complete Sample" no adjustments for confounding events are performed. Hence, it provides the largest sample size. Nevertheless, results could be affected by undesired events that coincide with the M&A announcement and are not the objective of the analysis. Deals with confounding events at the three-day-window surrounding the announcement [–1;1] are excluded with the "Control Sample". Hence, this sample provides the more robust results with regard to confounding events. However, it presents a smaller sample size, demonstrating a clear trade-off between sample size and controlling for confounding events.

Table 3-4: Bidder's Abnormal Bond Returns and Univariate Comparison for the "Complete Sample" (Bond Level Approach)

Event Window	(C)AAR		t-test	signed rank-test	N	t-test	signed rank-test	N
Panel A: All Issues	**Mean**	**Median**	**Unstandardized AR**			**Standardized AR**		
[-1;0]	-0.046%	-0.043%	-1.885*	-3.316***	686	-3.523***	-4.007***	681
[0;0]	-0.058%	-0.023%	-3.516***	-3.449***	689	-3.485***	-3.885***	681
[0;1]	-0.055%	-0.037%	-1.915*	-3.231***	689	-3.762***	-3.978***	681
[-1;1]	-0.044%	-0.039%	-1.284	-3.056***	686	-3.863***	-3.888***	681
[-2;2]	-0.055%	-0.068%	-1.408	-3.299***	685	-3.339***	-3.542***	681
[-5;5]	-0.048%	-0.073%	-1.003	-1.773*	685	-1.802*	-1.824*	681
[-10;10]	-0.025%	-0.057%	-0.382	-2.036**	681	-2.018**	-2.008**	681
Panel B: Non-disclosing M&A								
[-1;0]	-0.006%	-0.030%	-0.213	-1.866*	555	-1.811*	-2.720***	550
[0;0]	-0.023%	-0.014%	-1.419	-1.899*	557	-1.712*	-2.390**	550
[0;1]	-0.017%	-0.035%	-0.528	-1.940*	557	-2.194**	-2.631***	550
[-1;1]	-0.001%	-0.027%	-0.029	-1.514	555	-2.282**	-2.452**	550
[-2;2]	0.008%	-0.034%	0.171	-1.647*	554	-1.561	-2.044**	550
[-5;5]	-0.003%	-0.048%	-0.063	-0.597	554	-0.445	-0.593	550
[-10;10]	0.019%	-0.047%	0.249	-1.236	550	-0.767	-0.724	550
Panel C: Disclosing M&A								
[-1;0]	-0.216%	-0.100%	-4.074***	-3.733***	131	-3.335***	-3.285***	131
[0;0]	-0.206%	-0.045%	-4.028***	-3.782***	132	-3.264***	-3.648***	131
[0;1]	-0.214%	-0.038%	-3.955***	-3.346***	132	-3.363***	-3.547***	131
[-1;1]	-0.228%	-0.120%	-4.204***	-3.852***	131	-3.513***	-3.673***	131
[-2;2]	-0.319%	-0.188%	-4.645***	-4.117***	131	-3.794***	-3.715***	131
[-5;5]	-0.238%	-0.153%	-2.574**	-2.853***	131	-2.970***	-2.764***	131
[-10;10]	-0.208%	-0.271%	-1.964*	-2.159**	131	-3.043***	-3.136***	131
			t-test	**ranksum-test**		**t-test**	**ranksum-test**	
Panel D: Difference between Panel B and C			**Unstandardized AR**			**Standardized AR**		
[-1;0]	0.210%	0.070%	3.418***	-2.932***		3.821***	-2.749***	
[0;0]	0.183%	0.031%	4.445***	-2.957***		4.166***	-3.033***	
[0;1]	0.196%	0.003%	2.701***	-1.978**		3.351***	-2.207**	
[-1;1]	0.227%	0.094%	2.585***	-2.842***		3.234***	-2.607***	
[-2;2]	0.327%	0.153%	3.327***	-3.259***		3.571***	-2.930***	
[-5;5]	0.234%	0.105%	2.553***	-2.233**		2.643***	-1.988**	
[-10;10]	0.227%	0.224%	2.281**	-2.643***		3.240***	-2.894***	

This table presents (cumulative) abnormal bond returns of bidding firms over the windows [-1;0], [0;0], [0;1], [-1;1], [-2;2], [-5;5], and [-10;10] surrounding the M&A announcement date for the "Complete Sample", i.e. no adjustments for confounding events are performed. Abnormal bond returns are computed as the bond's return minus the return on a risk and maturity matched portfolio. Each bond is treated as a separate observation (Bond Level Approach). To check for statistical significance, one parametric and one non-parametric test is used: the one-sample standard t-test and the Wilcoxon sign rank-test. Following Ederington et al. (2012) both test statistics are calculated utilizing standardized bond returns. Standardized abnormal bond returns are computed by dividing the abnormal return by the standard deviation of abnormal returns over the [-10;10] period, excluding returns across event day [0;0]. Panel A reports (cumulative) abnormal bond returns for the complete sample. Panel B reports (cumulative) abnormal bond returns for non-disclosing deals. Panel C reports (cumulative) abnormal bond returns for disclosing deals. Panel D reports the difference in means and difference in medians between Panel B and Panel C. To check for statistical significance, the parametric two-sample standard t-test and the non-parametric Wilcoxon ranksum-test are used. The symbols ***, **, and * denote statistical significance at 1%, 5%, and 10% level, respectively.

Table 3-5: Bidder's Abnormal Bond Returns and Univariate Comparison for the "Control Sample" (Bond Level Approach)

Event Window	(C)AAR		t-test	signed rank-test	N	t-test	signed rank-test	N
Panel A: All Issues	**Mean**	**Median**	**Unstandardized AR**			**Standardized AR**		
[-1;0]	-0.034%	-0.037%	-1.204	-2.518**	549	-3.197***	-3.126***	544
[0;0]	-0.061%	-0.028%	-3.311***	-3.475***	552	-4.014***	-4.151***	544
[0;1]	-0.031%	-0.034%	-0.927	-2.144**	552	-3.574***	-3.319***	544
[-1;1]	-0.005%	-0.031%	-0.120	-1.761*	549	-3.037***	-2.628***	544
[-2;2]	0.009%	-0.022%	0.204	-1.408	548	-1.898*	-1.834*	544
[-5;5]	0.012%	-0.044%	0.230	-0.527	548	-0.765	-0.795	544
[-10;10]	-0.044%	-0.056%	-0.624	-2.123**	544	-1.445	-1.655*	544
Panel B: Non-disclosing M&A								
[-1;0]	0.017%	-0.024%	0.522	-0.851	433	-1.174	-1.606	428
[0;0]	-0.024%	-0.020%	-1.348	-1.842*	435	-2.266**	-2.569**	428
[0;1]	0.013%	-0.030%	0.331	-0.741	435	-1.850*	-1.779*	428
[-1;1]	0.053%	-0.016%	1.108	-0.049	433	-1.143	-0.942	428
[-2;2]	0.078%	0.011%	1.466	-0.255	432	-0.018	-0.222	428
[-5;5]	0.072%	0.021%	1.136	-0.811	432	0.705	-0.536	428
[-10;10]	-0.009%	-0.047%	-0.101	-1.334	428	-0.249	-0.477	428
Panel C: Disclosing M&A								
[-1;0]	-0.222%	-0.095%	-3.943***	-3.766***	116	-3.468***	-3.320***	116
[0;0]	-0.198%	-0.046%	-3.690***	-3.806***	117	-3.428***	-3.747***	116
[0;1]	-0.194%	-0.038%	-3.589***	-3.271***	117	-3.414***	-3.681***	116
[-1;1]	-0.222%	-0.118%	-3.981***	-3.793***	116	-3.534***	-3.659***	116
[-2;2]	-0.247%	-0.184%	-3.935***	-3.554***	116	-3.335***	-3.303***	116
[-5;5]	-0.210%	-0.168%	-2.407**	-2.829***	116	-2.706***	-2.526**	116
[-10;10]	-0.173%	-0.214%	-1.766*	-2.083**	116	-2.626***	-2.722***	116
			t-test	**ranksum-test**		**t-test**	**ranksum-test**	
Panel D: Difference between Panel B and C			**Unstandardized AR**			**Standardized AR**		
[-1;0]	0.239%	0.071%	3.504***	-3.250***		4.153***	-3.060***	
[0;0]	0.173%	0.026%	3.880***	-2.912***		4.159***	-2.988***	
[0;1]	0.207%	0.008%	2.557**	-2.231**		3.466***	-2.536**	
[-1;1]	0.276%	0.103%	2.826***	-3.284***		3.696***	-3.118***	
[-2;2]	0.325%	0.194%	3.022***	-3.393***		3.651***	-3.137***	
[-5;5]	0.282%	0.189%	2.384**	-2.429**		2.832***	-2.183**	
[-10;10]	0.164%	0.167%	2.559**	-3.179***		3.654***	-3.341***	

This table presents (cumulative) abnormal bond returns of bidding firms over the windows [-1;0], [0;0], [0;1], [-1;1], [-2;2], [-5;5], and [-10;10] surrounding the M&A announcement date for the "Control Sample", i.e. deals with confounding events at the three days surrounding the announcement day are excluded from the sample. Abnormal bond returns are computed as the bond's return minus the return on a risk and maturity matched portfolio. Each bond is treated as a separate observation (Bond Level Approach). To check for statistical significance, one parametric and one non-parametric test is used: the one-sample standard t-test and the Wilcoxon sign rank-test. Following Ederington et al. (2012) both test statistics are calculated utilizing standardized bond returns. Standardized abnormal bond returns are computed by dividing the abnormal return by the standard deviation of abnormal returns over the [–10;10] period, excluding returns across event day [0;0]. Panel A reports (cumulative) abnormal bond returns for the complete sample. Panel B reports (cumulative) abnormal bond returns for non-disclosing deals. Panel C reports (cumulative) abnormal bond returns for disclosing deals. Panel D reports the difference in means and difference in medians between Panel B and Panel C. To check for statistical significance, the parametric two-sample standard t-test and the non-parametric Wilcoxon ranksum-test are used. The symbols ***, **, and * denote statistical significance at 1%, 5%, and 10% level, respectively.

Table 3-4 and Table 3-5 cover the daily abnormal bond returns utilizing the bond level approach. Panel A of both tables presents bondholder wealth effects for all bidder bonds. Bondholders experience a mean (median) abnormal return of approximately –0.06% (–0.02%) on the announcement date [0;0], significant at the 1% level, regardless of the test-statistic or standardization procedure. Moreover, the three windows [–1;0], [0;1], and [–1;1] show highly significant returns for the standardized ARs. Examining Panel B of Table 3-4 and Table 3-5, which shows abnormal bond returns for bidding firms that do not disclose synergy estimates, weaker evidence for significant effects is found, particularly after controlling for confounding events. Only the announcement day [0;0] displays returns significant at the 5% level and that only holds after standardization. Bearing in mind the shortcomings of the bond level approach, i.e. upward biased standard deviations, this result implies that bonds issued by non-disclosing bidding firms are potentially unaffected by the announcement of a merger.

In contrast, bonds of bidding energy firms that do communicate synergy estimates (Panel C of Table 3-4 and Table 3-5) show statistically significant negative mean abnormal returns, regardless of the applied test-statistic, event window or sample. Bondholders experience mean abnormal returns between –0.2% and –0.3% around the announcement date. Comparing the size of the bond market reaction between Panel B and C reveals that forecasting deals also have much stronger negative returns associated with the M&A announcement. This perception is confirmed through Panel D as all the differences in (cumulative) abnormal returns between synergy communicating and non-communicating deals are statistically significant at least at the 5% level. That implies that voluntary synergy disclosure causes stronger negative announcement returns for bondholders.

The following Table 3-6 and Table 3-7 provide the result of the firm level approach regarding bondholder wealth effects on synergy disclosure.

Table 3-6: Bidder's Abnormal Bond Returns and Univariate Comparison for the "Complete Sample" (Firm Level Approach)

Event Window	(C)AAR		t-test	signed rank-test	N	t-test	signed rank-test	N
Panel A: All Issues	**Mean**	**Median**	**Unstandardized AR**			**Standardized AR**		
[-1;0]	-0.048%	-0.033%	-1.255	-1.745*	204	-1.843*	-1.976**	204
[0;0]	-0.053%	-0.020%	-2.185**	-2.150**	205	-1.653*	-2.106**	204
[0;1]	-0.031%	-0.043%	-0.691	-1.316	205	-1.540	-1.764*	204
[-1;1]	-0.028%	-0.052%	-0.496	-1.545	204	-1.773*	-1.854*	204
[-2;2]	-0.070%	-0.057%	-1.009	-2.122**	204	-2.026**	-2.140**	204
[-5;5]	-0.044%	-0.010%	-0.448	-0.525	204	-0.960	-0.851	204
[-10;10]	-0.005%	-0.013%	-0.044	-0.660	204	-1.126	-1.289	204
Panel B: Non-disclosing M&A								
[-1;0]	-0.023%	-0.033%	-0.553	-1.245	171	-1.107	-1.595	171
[0;0]	-0.035%	-0.018%	-1.383	-1.549	172	-1.268	-1.604	171
[0;1]	0.002%	-0.037%	0.032	-0.445	172	-0.844	-1.050	171
[-1;1]	0.012%	-0.031%	0.185	-0.555	171	-0.851	-0.996	171
[-2;2]	-0.013%	-0.050%	-0.162	-1.286	171	-1.173	-1.476	171
[-5;5]	-0.037%	-0.004%	-0.331	-0.423	171	-0.559	-0.477	171
[-10;10]	-0.002%	-0.013%	-0.011	-0.543	171	-0.625	-0.697	171
Panel C: Disclosing M&A								
[-1;0]	-0.173%	-0.028%	-2.120**	-1.546	33	-1.732*	-1.403	33
[0;0]	-0.146%	-0.030%	-2.030*	-1.796*	33	-1.059	-1.420	33
[0;1]	-0.204%	-0.107%	-2.725**	-2.225**	33	-1.898*	-1.885*	33
[-1;1]	-0.236%	-0.120%	-2.543**	-2.618***	33	-2.497**	-2.278**	33
[-2;2]	-0.368%	-0.143%	-2.795***	-2.421**	33	-2.487**	-2.171**	33
[-5;5]	-0.079%	-0.053%	-0.448	-0.420	33	-1.109	-1.135	33
[-10;10]	-0.025%	0.024%	-0.138	-0.473	33	-1.574	-1.760*	33
			t-test	**ranksum-test**		**t-test**	**ranksum-test**	
Panel D: Difference between Panel B and C			**Unstandardized AR**			**Standardized AR**		
[-1;0]	0.150%	-0.005%	1.458	-0.950		1.645	-0.873	
[0;0]	0.112%	0.011%	1.718*	-1.174		0.994	-1.011	
[0;1]	0.206%	0.069%	1.668*	-1.959*		1.420	-1.569	
[-1;1]	0.248%	0.089%	1.618	-2.084**		1.950*	-1.810*	
[-2;2]	0.355%	0.092%	1.893*	-1.800*		1.689*	-1.298	
[-5;5]	0.042%	0.048%	1.270	-0.966		1.095	-0.918	
[-10;10]	0.024%	-0.037%	0.229	-0.370		0.679	-0.670	

This table presents (cumulative) abnormal bond returns of bidding firms over the windows [-1;0], [0;0], [0;1], [-1;1], [-2;2], [-5;5], and [-10;10] surrounding the M&A announcement date for the "Complete Sample", i.e. no adjustments for confounding events are performed. Abnormal bond returns are computed as the bond's return minus the return on a risk and maturity matched portfolio. When a firm has multiple bonds, its abnormal bond return is computed as the market value weighted average of each bond's abnormal return (Firm Level Approach). To check for statistical significance, one parametric and one non-parametric test is used: the one-sample standard t-test and the Wilcoxon sign rank-test. Following Ederington et al. (2012) both test statistics are calculated utilizing standardized bond returns. Standardized abnormal bond returns are computed by dividing the abnormal return by the standard deviation of abnormal returns over the [-10;10] period, excluding returns across event day [0;0]. Panel A reports (cumulative) abnormal bond returns for the complete sample. Panel B reports (cumulative) abnormal bond returns for non-disclosing deals. Panel C reports (cumulative) abnormal bond returns for disclosing deals. Panel D reports the difference in means and difference in medians between Panel B and Panel C. To check for statistical significance, the parametric two-sample standard t-test and the non-parametric Wilcoxon ranksum-test are used. The symbols ***, **, and * denote statistical significance at 1%, 5%, and 10% level, respectively.

Table 3-7: Bidder's Abnormal Bond Returns and Univariate Comparison for the "Control Sample" (Firm Level Approach)

Event Window	(C)AAR		t-test	signed rank-test	N	t-test	signed rank-test	N
Panel A: All Issues	**Mean**	**Median**	**Unstandardized AR**			**Standardized AR**		
[−1;0]	−0.034%	−0.026%	−0.823	−1.135	157	−1.644	−1.473	157
[0;0]	−0.047%	−0.023%	−1.761*	−1.761*	158	−1.950*	−2.051**	157
[0;1]	0.020%	−0.039%	0.374	−0.178	158	−1.125	−1.065	157
[−1;1]	0.031%	−0.031%	0.487	−0.430	157	−1.101	−1.003	157
[−2;2]	0.008%	−0.040%	0.102	−0.737	157	−0.988	−0.984	157
[−5;5]	0.032%	0.040%	0.305	−0.395	157	−0.245	−0.015	157
[−10;10]	−0.025%	−0.013%	−0.179	−0.768	157	−0.725	−0.881	157
Panel B: Non-disclosing M&A								
[−1;0]	0.001%	−0.022%	0.025	−0.227	131	−0.597	−0.733	131
[0;0]	−0.030%	−0.018%	−1.091	−1.038	132	−1.398	−1.378	131
[0;1]	0.060%	−0.011%	0.984	−0.700	132	−0.267	−0.200	131
[−1;1]	0.090%	−0.007%	1.250	−0.783	131	0.069	−0.177	131
[−2;2]	0.069%	−0.026%	0.776	−0.016	131	−0.182	−0.299	131
[−5;5]	0.051%	0.054%	0.426	−0.600	131	0.217	−0.485	131
[−10;10]	−0.009%	−0.013%	−0.055	−0.531	131	−0.232	−0.234	131
Panel C: Disclosing M&A								
[−1;0]	−0.210%	−0.064%	−2.515**	−2.121**	26	−2.182**	−1.943*	26
[0;0]	−0.130%	−0.035%	−1.683	−1.918*	26	−1.369	−1.892*	26
[0;1]	−0.183%	−0.098%	−2.319**	−2.070**	26	−2.283**	−2.222**	26
[−1;1]	−0.270%	−0.124%	−3.100***	−3.086***	26	−3.098***	−3.010***	26
[−2;2]	−0.299%	−0.128%	−2.233**	−2.095**	26	−2.236**	−1.867*	26
[−5;5]	−0.067%	−0.059%	−0.430	−0.546	26	−1.102	−1.130	26
[−10;10]	−0.105%	−0.008%	−0.728	−0.825	26	−1.524	−1.791*	26
			t-test	**ranksum-test**		**t-test**	**ranksum-test**	
Panel D: Difference between Panel B and C			**Unstandardized AR**			**Standardized AR**		
[−1;0]	0.211%	0.042%	1.927*	−1.872*		2.382**	−1.764*	
[0;0]	0.099%	0.017%	1.396	−1.339		1.479	−1.258	
[0;1]	0.242%	0.088%	1.720*	−2.099**		1.885*	−1.929*	
[−1;1]	0.360%	0.117%	2.159**	−2.751***		2.694***	−2.675***	
[−2;2]	0.368%	0.102%	1.766*	−1.792*		1.778*	−1.471	
[−5;5]	0.118%	0.113%	1.002	−0.730		0.984	−0.824	
[−10;10]	0.096%	−0.005%	0.496	−0.692		1.003	−1.051	

This table presents (cumulative) abnormal bond returns of bidding firms over the windows [−1;0], [0;0], [0;1], [−1;1], [−2;2], [−5;5], and [−10;10] surrounding the M&A announcement date for the "Control Sample", i.e. deals with confounding events at the three days surrounding the announcement day are excluded from the sample.

Abnormal bond returns are computed as the bond's return minus the return on a risk and maturity matched portfolio. When a firm has multiple bonds, its abnormal bond return is computed as the market value weighted average of each bond's abnormal return (Firm Level Approach). To check for statistical significance, one parametric and one non-parametric test is used: the one-sample standard t-test and the Wilcoxon sign rank-test. Following Ederington et al. (2012) both test statistics are calculated utilizing standardized bond returns. Standardized abnormal bond returns are computed by dividing the abnormal return by the standard deviation of abnormal returns over the [−10;10] period, excluding returns across event day [0;0]. Panel A reports (cumulative) abnormal bond returns for the complete sample. Panel B reports (cumulative) abnormal bond returns for non-disclosing deals. Panel C reports (cumulative) abnormal bond returns for disclosing deals. Panel D reports the difference in means and difference in medians between Panel B and Panel C. To check for statistical significance, the parametric two-sample standard t-test and the non-parametric Wilcoxon ranksum-test are used. The symbols ***, **, and * denote statistical significance at 1%, 5%, and 10% level, respectively.

As expected, the results of the bond level approach are confirmed, albeit with less statistical significance. Again, weak evidence that acquirer bonds experience a negative announcement effect (Panel A) is found. The mean abnormal return at the announcement day is significantly different from zero for all four test statistics. However, the statistical significance decreases for the unstandardized returns to the 10% level. As predicted earlier, the results in Panel B prove that non-disclosing bidding firms experience no substantial bondholder wealth effect. Not a single parametric or non-parametric test in Table 3-6 and Table 3-7 turns out to be significant. In contrast, synergy disclosing firms generate a statistically significant negative abnormal return. Panel C of Table 3-6 (Table 3-7) demonstrates that energy firms that do communicate synergy estimates experience wealth effects for bondholders of −0.2% (−0.2%) for event window [0;1], −0.2% (−0.4%) for event window [−1;1], and −0.4% (−0.4%) for event window [−2;2]. Furthermore, Panel D shows that the mean and median differences for windows [0;1], [−1;1], and [−2;2] are significantly lower for bonds issued by synergy disclosing energy firms.

Altogether, the results are in line with Billett et al. (2004) who also find a negative mean abnormal return for acquirer bonds, but they differ from research conducted by Asquith and Kim (1982), Eger (1983), and Maquieira et al. (1998). Moreover, this analysis is the first to find evidence that bondholders react differently to M&A announcements depending on management's decision to predict synergies.

3.3.2 Stock Event Study

The following section describes the abnormal stock returns for all deals in the sample, as well as separated by synergy forecast availability. As noted earlier, two different samples ("Complete Sample" and "Control Sample") are used to control for the impact of confounding events. Additionally, two different methodologies are applied to quantify the stock market reactions, i.e. a single-factor model and a four-factor model.

Table 3-8: Bidder's Abnormal Stock Returns and Univariate Comparison for the "Complete Sample" (Market Model)

Event window	(C)AAR		t-test	Boehmer-test	signed rank-test	Corrado-test	N
Panel A: All M&A							
[-1;0]	0.272%	-0.031%	1.571	0.954	-1.117	0.710	205
[0;0]	0.173%	0.005%	1.178	0.199	-0.490	0.239	205
[0;1]	0.275%	0.319%	1.257	0.487	-1.065	1.144	205
[-1;1]	0.375%	0.359%	1.574	1.048	-1.439	1.376	205
[-2;2]	0.271%	0.158%	0.941	0.560	-0.652	0.743	205
[-5;5]	0.185%	-0.355%	0.512	0.044	-0.126	-0.450	205
[-10;10]	-0.477%	-0.952%	-0.917	-1.294	-1.747*	-1.272	205
Panel B: Non-disclosing M&A							
[-1;0]	0.147%	-0.050%	0.807	0.457	-0.576	0.368	172
[0;0]	0.018%	-0.021%	0.130	-0.525	-0.145	-0.268	172
[0;1]	0.078%	0.186%	0.356	-0.019	-0.472	0.431	172
[-1;1]	0.207%	0.062%	0.813	0.657	-0.743	0.808	172
[-2;2]	0.073%	0.133%	0.241	0.157	-0.110	0.198	172
[-5;5]	-0.058%	-0.595%	-0.150	-0.329	-0.610	-0.840	172
[-10;10]	-0.905%	-1.458%	-1.624	-1.995**	-2.466**	-2.135**	172
Panel C: Disclosing M&A							
[-1;0]	0.924%	0.294%	1.853*	1.086	-1.492	0.957	33
[0;0]	0.977%	0.234%	1.914*	1.110	-1.456	1.226	33
[0;1]	1.302%	1.239%	1.827*	0.954	-1.474	1.915*	33
[-1;1]	1.249%	1.152%	1.946*	0.957	-1.742*	1.637	33
[-2;2]	1.306%	2.197%	1.536	0.820	-1.546	1.435	33
[-5;5]	1.449%	2.371%	1.512	0.763	-1.420	0.793	33
[-10;10]	1.756%	1.221%	1.288	1.328	-1.081	1.690*	33
Panel D: Difference between Panel B and C			**t-test**	**ranksum-test**			
[-1;0]	-0.777%	-0.344%	-1.656*	1.190			
[0;0]	-0.958%	-0.255%	-2.431**	1.462			
[0;1]	-1.223%	-1.053%	-2.069**	1.565			
[-1;1]	-1.043%	-1.091%	-1.616	1.552			
[-2;2]	-1.233%	-2.063%	-1.578	1.181			
[-5;5]	-1.507%	-2.966%	-1.780*	1.600			
[-10;10]	-2.662%	-2.679%	-1.628	1.450			

This table presents (cumulative) abnormal stock returns of bidding firms over the windows [-1;0], [0;0], [0;1], [-1;1], [-2;2], [-5;5], and [-10;10] surrounding the M&A announcement date for the "Complete Sample", i.e. no adjustments for confounding events are performed. Abnormal stock returns are computed using the market model based on the S&P 500 Energy Sector index. Panel A reports (cumulative) abnormal stock returns for the complete sample. Panel B reports (cumulative) abnormal stock returns for non-disclosing deals. Panel C reports (cumulative) abnormal stock returns for disclosing deals. To check for statistical significance, two parametric and two non-parametric tests are used: the one-sample standard t-test, the Boehmer-test (Boehmer et al., 1991), the Wilcoxon sign rank-test, and the Corrado-test (Corrado, 1989; Corrado & Zivney, 1992). Panel D reports the difference in means and difference in medians between Panel B and Panel C. To check for statistical significance, the parametric two-sample standard t-test and the non-parametric Wilcoxon ranksum-test are used. The symbols ***, **, and * denote statistical significance at 1%, 5%, and 10% level, respectively.

Table 3-9: Bidder's Abnormal Stock Returns and Univariate Comparison for the "Control Sample" (Market Model)

Event window	(C)AAR		t-test	Boehmer-test	signed rank-test	Corrado-test	N
Panel A: All M&A							
[-1;0]	0.186%	-0.050%	0.950	0.488	-0.671	0.354	158
[0;0]	0.048%	-0.094%	0.303	-0.380	-0.232	-0.727	158
[0;1]	0.262%	0.323%	1.066	0.546	-0.994	1.094	158
[-1;1]	0.399%	0.355%	1.438	1.123	-1.233	1.602	158
[-2;2]	0.164%	-0.216%	0.509	0.403	-0.161	0.564	158
[-5;5]	0.093%	-0.397%	0.237	-0.090	-0.084	-0.806	158
[-10;10]	-0.198%	-0.838%	-0.336	-0.761	-1.405	-1.020	158
Panel B: Non-disclosing M&A							
[-1;0]	0.035%	-0.175%	0.171	-0.039	-0.020	-0.112	132
[0;0]	-0.084%	-0.197%	-0.525	-1.092	-0.809	-1.153	132
[0;1]	0.160%	0.140%	0.616	0.307	-0.645	0.629	132
[-1;1]	0.279%	0.062%	0.924	0.906	-0.668	1.088	132
[-2;2]	-0.002%	-0.142%	-0.007	0.136	-0.189	0.151	132
[-5;5]	-0.095%	-0.627%	-0.229	-0.263	-0.536	-0.941	132
[-10;10]	-0.662%	-1.387%	-1.047	-1.354	-2.094**	-1.816*	132
Panel C: Disclosing M&A							
[-1;0]	0.949%	0.815%	1.763*	0.972	-1.613	1.149	26
[0;0]	0.716%	0.289%	1.414	0.807	-1.130	0.802	26
[0;1]	0.777%	1.624%	1.107	0.515	-1.029	1.325	26
[-1;1]	1.011%	1.444%	1.431	0.660	-1.308	1.557	26
[-2;2]	1.007%	-0.810%	1.135	0.539	-1.156	1.077	26
[-5;5]	1.050%	1.710%	0.933	0.284	-0.775	0.118	26
[-10;10]	2.159%	0.542%	1.403	1.160	-1.054	1.581	26
Panel D: Difference between Panel B and C			**t-test**	**ranksum-test**			
[-1;0]	-0.914%	-0.991%	-1.744*	1.611			
[0;0]	-0.799%	-0.486%	-1.891*	1.344			
[0;1]	-0.617%	-1.484%	-0.933	0.973			
[-1;1]	-0.732%	-1.382%	-0.977	1.067			
[-2;2]	-1.009%	0.667%	-1.167	0.560			
[-5;5]	-1.145%	-2.338%	-0.819	0.617			
[-10;10]	-2.821%	-1.929%	-0.930	0.532			

This table presents (cumulative) abnormal stock returns of bidding firms over the windows [-1;0], [0;0], [0;1], [-1;1], [-2;2], [-5;5], and [-10;10] surrounding the M&A announcement date for the "Control Sample", i.e. deals with confounding events at the three days surrounding the announcement day are excluded from the sample. Abnormal stock returns are computed using the market model based on the S&P 500 Energy Sector index. Panel A reports (cumulative) abnormal stock returns for the complete sample. Panel B reports (cumulative) abnormal stock returns for non-disclosing deals. Panel C reports (cumulative) abnormal stock returns for disclosing deals. To check for statistical significance, two parametric and two non-parametric tests are used: the one-sample standard t-test, the Boehmer-test (Boehmer et al., 1991), the Wilcoxon sign rank-test, and the Corrado-test (Corrado, 1989;

Corrado & Zivney, 1992). Panel D reports the difference in means and difference in medians between Panel B and Panel C. To check for statistical significance, the parametric two-sample standard t-test and the non-parametric Wilcoxon ranksum-test are used. The symbols ***, **, and * denote statistical significance at 1%, 5%, and 10% level, respectively.

Table 3-8 presents the results for the "Complete Sample" and Table 3-9 for the "Control Sample" utilizing the market model. As Panel A in both tables shows, no abnormal return to stockholders can be found for the whole sample. Only the signed rank-test at Table 3-8 for the [−10;10] window provides weak evidence for a negative capital market reaction. This result is in line with previous research that generally finds negative or zero abnormal returns associated with merger announcements for bidder stocks. Moreover, this weak indication for a negative reaction is probably driven by the sample of non-disclosing deals. Both non-parametric tests confirm a statistically significant wealth loss for the stockholders over the 21-day event window. However, all other windows only generate insignificant returns. The disclosing deals in Panel C, on the other hand, provide some evidence for positive abnormal returns due to M&A announcements associated with synergy forecasts, which is also in line with prior research (Fraunhoffer & Schiereck, 2012a). At Table 3-8, one parametric and one non-parametric test turn out to be statistically significant for the [0;1] and the [−1;1] event windows, implying that disclosing deals cause an average wealth gain between 1.2% and 1.3% for bidding firms' stockholders. Compared to prior research for M&A in the energy sector in Europe by Fraunhoffer and Schiereck (2012a), this average abnormal returns turn out to be smaller by approximately 1%. However, the statistical significance disappears for the "Control Sample" revealing that M&A with synergy forecasts do not cause unexpected stock price changes. More interestingly, and in line with the expectations, differences in (cumulative) abnormal returns between disclosing and non-disclosing deals are statistically significant, implying that voluntary synergy disclosure causes higher abnormal stock returns. However, only the t-test indicates statistical significance and the magnitude decreases with controlling for confounding events, leaving only the first event window [−1;0] and the announcement date [0;0] significant.

Replicating the analysis using the four-factor model reveals qualitatively the same results (see Table 3-10 and Table 3-11). Once more, no significant reaction for all deals, some evidence for a wealth loss for non-disclosing M&A, only support for positive abnormal returns for the disclosing deals with the "Complete Sample", and finally, indication for a statistically significant difference between both subsamples are received, implying that abnormal stock returns less negative when management decides to unveil synergy forecast associated with an M&A announcement.

Table 3-10: Bidder's Abnormal Stock Returns and Univariate Comparison for the "Complete Sample" (Four-Factor Model)

Event window	(C)AAR		t-test	Boehmer-test	signed rank-test	Corrado-test	N
Panel A: All M&A							
[-1;0]	0.228%	0.099%	1.296	0.830	-1.001	0.834	205
[0;0]	0.161%	0.027%	1.083	0.227	-0.489	0.376	205
[0;1]	0.225%	0.288%	1.003	0.311	-0.759	1.041	205
[-1;1]	0.292%	0.365%	1.207	0.776	-1.105	1.314	205
[-2;2]	0.217%	0.085%	0.744	0.375	-0.537	0.867	205
[-5;5]	0.162%	0.081%	0.442	0.089	-0.077	-0.312	205
[-10;10]	-0.437%	-0.925%	-0.841	-1.124	-1.672*	-1.144	205
Panel B: Non-disclosing M&A							
[-1;0]	0.111%	0.082%	0.596	0.363	-0.532	0.573	172
[0;0]	0.002%	-0.050%	0.013	-0.485	-0.202	-0.162	172
[0;1]	0.014%	0.178%	0.060	-0.225	-0.102	0.256	172
[-1;1]	0.123%	0.207%	0.473	0.374	-0.442	0.770	172
[-2;2]	0.025%	0.079%	0.082	-0.024	-0.043	0.339	172
[-5;5]	-0.049%	-0.118%	-0.122	-0.222	-0.558	-0.722	172
[-10;10]	-0.775%	-1.270%	-1.378	-1.675*	-2.252**	-1.898*	172
Panel C: Disclosing M&A							
[-1;0]	0.838%	0.197%	1.700*	1.017	-1.456	0.764	33
[0;0]	0.993%	0.386%	1.938*	1.108	-1.563	1.289	33
[0;1]	1.326%	1.274%	1.866*	0.978	-1.510	1.984**	33
[-1;1]	1.171%	1.212%	1.864*	0.927	-1.653*	1.499	33
[-2;2]	1.215%	1.636%	1.462	0.792	-1.474	1.371	33
[-5;5]	1.260%	2.066%	1.422	0.712	-1.331	0.855	33
[-10;10]	1.321%	0.542%	0.989	1.068	-0.956	1.451	33
Panel D: Difference between Panel B and C			**t-test**	**ranksum-test**			
[-1;0]	-0.726%	-0.116%	-1.519	1.049			
[0;0]	-0.991%	-0.436%	-2.474**	1.559			
[0;1]	-1.312%	-1.096%	-2.169**	1.610			
[-1;1]	-1.047%	-1.005%	-1.597	1.533			
[-2;2]	-1.190%	-1.557%	-1.506	1.123			
[-5;5]	-1.309%	-2.184%	-1.502	1.466			
[-10;10]	-2.096%	-1.812%	-1.405	1.318			

This table presents (cumulative) abnormal stock returns of bidding firms over the windows [-1;0], [0;0], [0;1], [-1;1], [-2;2], [-5;5], and [-10;10] surrounding the M&A announcement date for the "Complete Sample", i.e. no adjustments for confounding events are performed. Abnormal stock returns are computed using the four-factor model based on the S&P 500 Energy Sector index. Source for the four factors is the data library provided by Andrea Frazzini (Frazzini, 2014). Panel A reports (cumulative) abnormal stock returns for the complete sample. Panel B reports (cumulative) abnormal stock returns for non-disclosing deals. Panel C reports (cumulative) abnormal stock returns for disclosing deals. To check for statistical significance, two parametric and two non-parametric tests are used: the one-sample standard t-test, the Boehmer-test (Boehmer et al., 1991), the Wilcoxon sign rank-test, and the Corrado-test (Corrado, 1989; Corrado & Zivney, 1992). Panel D reports the difference in means and difference in medians between Panel B and Panel C. To check for statistical significance, the parametric two-sample standard t-test and the non-parametric Wilcoxon ranksum-test are used. The symbols ***, **, and * denote statistical significance at 1%, 5%, and 10% level, respectively.

Table 3-11: Bidder's Abnormal Stock Returns and Univariate Comparison for the "Control Sample" (Four-Factor Model)

Event window	(C)AAR		t-test	Boehmer-test	signed rank-test	Corrado-test	N
Panel A: All M&A							
[-1;0]	0.171%	0.104%	0.844	0.540	-0.612	0.524	158
[0;0]	0.055%	-0.138%	0.334	-0.226	-0.107	-0.501	158
[0;1]	0.218%	0.257%	0.860	0.443	-0.740	0.949	158
[-1;1]	0.334%	0.312%	1.176	0.971	-1.015	1.492	158
[-2;2]	0.108%	-0.072%	0.338	0.326	-0.112	0.737	158
[-5;5]	0.084%	0.126%	0.212	0.031	-0.039	-0.651	158
[-10;10]	-0.252%	-1.053%	-0.432	-0.811	-1.492	-1.157	158
Panel B: Non-disclosing M&A							
[-1;0]	0.032%	0.050%	0.146	0.052	-0.020	0.179	132
[0;0]	-0.086%	-0.203%	-0.520	-0.936	-0.770	-0.979	132
[0;1]	0.094%	0.178%	0.348	0.150	-0.286	0.391	132
[-1;1]	0.212%	0.127%	0.680	0.739	-0.488	1.031	132
[-2;2]	-0.059%	-0.044%	-0.174	0.037	-0.229	0.290	132
[-5;5]	-0.100%	0.054%	-0.235	-0.137	-0.334	-0.855	132
[-10;10]	-0.662%	-1.470%	-1.047	-1.300	-2.071**	-1.885*	132
Panel C: Disclosing M&A							
[-1;0]	0.877%	0.992%	1.629	0.946	-1.613	0.895	26
[0;0]	0.769%	0.497%	1.504	0.874	-1.232	0.971	26
[0;1]	0.849%	1.447%	1.197	0.572	-1.105	1.468	26
[-1;1]	0.956%	1.264%	1.366	0.648	-1.257	1.369	26
[-2;2]	0.953%	-1.081%	1.094	0.562	-1.283	1.173	26
[-5;5]	1.020%	1.151%	0.961	0.329	-0.775	0.319	26
[-10;10]	1.826%	0.091%	1.238	0.950	-0.978	1.391	26
Panel D: Difference between Panel B and C			**t-test**	**ranksum-test**			
[-1;0]	-0.846%	-0.941%	-1.557	1.461			
[0;0]	-0.856%	-0.700%	-1.960*	1.489			
[0;1]	-0.755%	-1.268%	-1.105	1.123			
[-1;1]	-0.745%	-1.138%	-0.972	1.114			
[-2;2]	-1.012%	1.036%	-1.182	0.612			
[-5;5]	-1.121%	-1.097%	-0.661	0.499			
[-10;10]	-2.488%	-1.561%	-0.866	0.382			

This table presents (cumulative) abnormal stock returns of bidding firms over the windows [-1;0], [0;0], [0;1], [-1;1], [-2;2], [-5;5], and [-10;10] surrounding the M&A announcement date for the "Control Sample", i.e. deals with confounding events at the three days surrounding the announcement day are excluded from the sample. Abnormal stock returns are computed using the four-factor model based on the S&P 500 Energy Sector index. Source for the four factors is the data library provided by Andrea Frazzini (Frazzini, 2014). Panel A reports (cumulative) abnormal stock returns for the complete sample. Panel B reports (cumulative) abnormal stock returns for non-disclosing deals. Panel C reports (cumulative) abnormal stock returns for disclosing deals. To check for statistical significance, two parametric and two non-parametric tests are used: the one-sample standard t-test, the Boehmer-test (Boehmer et al., 1991), the Wilcoxon sign rank-test, and the Corrado-test (Corrado, 1989; Corrado & Zivney, 1992). Panel D reports the difference in means and difference in medians between Panel B and Panel C. To check for statistical significance, the parametric two-sample standard t-test and the non-parametric Wilcoxon ranksum-test are used. The symbols ***, **, and * denote statistical significance at 1%, 5%, and 10% level, respectively.

Comparing the weak positive announcement returns for stockholders for disclosing deals with the clear negative returns for bondholders indicates a possible wealth transfer between these two classes of securityholders. This implies that past event studies that focused solely on stock price behavior and suggested erroneously that synergy forecasts have a purely positive effect, neglected the impact on bondholders and therefore the real overall firm value change. The results imply the existence of a link between rising stock prices and dropping bond prices for disclosing deals, indicating that deals with synergy forecasts are interpreted by investors as risk increasing transactions.

3.3.3 Cross Sectional Regression Analysis of Synergy Communication

To obtain more reliable and robust results regarding the impact of synergy disclosure on stock and bond returns, the reasoning by Dutordoir et al. (2014) is considered and a cross sectional regression with a synergy disclosure dummy (Synergy Dummy) performed to capture management's decision to disclose estimated synergies. Table 3-12 and Table 3-13 report the regression results. Again, confounding events are controlled for by computing regression analysis for two different samples ("Complete Sample" and "Control Sample"). Several explanatory variables are included that may be related to the market reaction to control for deal, industry and company specific characteristics.

Ln(Market Cap) and Ln(Deal Size) present the natural logarithm of market capitalization as well as the amount paid for the target firm. These variables are added to control for a possible size effect. Further explanatory variables are included to control for a company's liquidity, profitability and leverage. The ratio of current assets and current liabilities (Current Ratio), return on assets (RoA) and the ratio of total debt and the market value of equity (Bidder Leverage) are chosen, all measured at fiscal year-end prior to the announcement. Market to Book presents the ratio of the market price and the book value per share, also measured at fiscal year-end prior to the announcement. The data is winsorized at the 0.5% and 99.5% level, due to a single but heavy outlier associated with this variable.[39] Policy Act 2005- and Policy Act 2007-Dummy are dummy variables

---

39 One company has a market to book ratio of 144.99 compared to a mean (median) value of 3.67 (2.15). The second largest value is 33.46.

equal to one for deals announced after the Energy Policy Act of 2005 and the Energy Independence and Security Act of 2007 was signed into law, respectively. Adding these variables accounts for major regulatory changes in the US Energy sector during the investigation period. For instance, part of the Energy Policy Act of 2005 was the repeal of the Public Utility Holding Company Act of 1935 (PUHCA), which eliminated several obstacles to consolidation of the electric industry.[40] Thakar (2008) concludes that this will encourage investments and lead to an increased M&A activity in the energy sector, which could also have an effect on the stock price changes due to M&A. The Energy Independence and Security Act of 2007 consists mainly of provisions designed to increase the availability of renewable energy and reduce US dependence on oil imports (Sissine, 2007). Despite the fact that an impact on abnormal returns is not to be expected, this variable is also included into the regression as the possibility of a connection cannot be ruled out for certain. An Industry-Dummy is included as a dummy variable equal to one if the bidder's and target's two-digit SIC code match to control for a conglomerate effect. SIC-49-, -13- and -29-Dummy are dummy variables equal to one if the bidding firm's primary two-digit SIC code is 49, 13 and 29, respectively. Abnormal bond returns in basis points (Panel A) and abnormal stock returns[41] in percent (Panel B) over the event windows [0;0], [0;1], and [−1;1] are utilized as dependent variables.

Following Dutordoir et al. (2014) another five variables are included. Percentage of Stock presents the percentage equity financing of the deal. They argue in line with prior research that equity financed deals induce more negative abnormal returns than purely cash financed mergers. The Industry Liquidity Index following Schlingemann, Stulz, and Walkling (2002) is computed as a proxy for market liquidity. The variable presents the ratio of the value of M&A transactions in the Energy Industry (excluding minority stake purchases, leveraged buyouts, spin-offs, recapitalizations, self-tenders, exchange offers, repurchases and the sample deals) in a year and the total book value of assets of firms in the same two-digit SIC code for that year. Schlingemann et al. (2002) argue that in more active asset markets assets can be sold without a discount. Dutordoir et al. (2014) argue that a higher Industry Liquidity Index simplifies accurate synergy estimates for managers. Shareholder Approval-Dummy is a dummy variable equal

40 First, utilities are no longer confined to a single integrated system and second, non-utility-related companies have the permission to invest in public utilities without the requirement to divest unrelated holdings (Thakar, 2008).

41 Since both procedures (market model vs. four-factor model) yield qualitatively the same results, the abnormal returns of the second approach are used.

to one if shareholders of the bidding firm have to approve the deal, which is the case when the acquirer plans to issue more than 20% of the pre-bid outstanding shares to finance the deal (Bethel, Hu, & Wang, 2009; Dutordoir et al., 2014). Dutordoir et al. (2014) identify a negative impact on bidder stock returns. Takeover Premium presents the premium paid by the bidding firm.[42]

Finally, to account for the potential endogeneity of management's decision of whether to disclose synergy forecasts, the inverse Mill's ratio (Mill's Ratio) is added in the cross sectional regression. This is in line with prior research by Bernile and Lyandres (2013) and Dutordoir et al. (2014). Following the two step procedure described by Heckman (1979), first a probit regression is run with the Synergy-Dummy as dependent variable and the remaining explanatory variables described earlier. Secondly, the cross sectional regression is estimated and the inverse Mill's ratio from the probit regression included. The inverse Mill's ratio allows to control for possible selection bias causing correlation between the error term in the probit regression and the cross sectional regression (Bernile & Lyandres, 2013; Dutordoir et al., 2014). Four different regression models are estimated: Model I contains the dummy for management's decision to publicly disclose a synergy forecast, the variables for firm and deal size, and the variables controlling for a company's liquidity, profitability, leverage, and growth opportunity. Model II adds several dummies controlling for changes in sector regulations, conglomerate merger, and industry differences. The variables added in Model III are deemed necessary as a result of the review of prior literature on synergy disclosure, while Model IV only adds the variable to control for possible endogeneity. Moreover, variance inflation factors (VIF) are computed to detect the presence of multicollinearity. Whenever a regression model exhibits a VIF of five, which is a common threshold value (Craney & Surles, 2002), the variables causing the multicollinearity are excluded, with the exception of Mill's Ratio. The results of the impact of synergy disclosure on abnormal stock and bond returns are reported in Table 3-12 ("Complete Sample") and Table 3-13 ("Control Sample").

The results for abnormal bond return as the dependent variable are presented in Panel A. Examining the results of the "Complete Sample" (Table 3-12), presents only negative coefficients for the dummy indicating synergy disclosures, which implies that bondholders experience a wealth loss when management decides to publish synergy forecasts along with an M&A announcement. However, only

42 Following Dutordoir et al. (2014) Takeover Premium is calculated as percentage premium paid by the bidding firm multiplied by the target market capitalization measured four days prior to the takeover announcement. Since it is not required for the target to be publicly listed, this figure is only attained for 22 sample targets.

Model III and Model IV of the two-day [0;1] and three-day [1;1] event windows exhibit statistically significant values at the 10% level. Nonetheless, this can be considered as a first indication that synergy disclosure harms bondholders of the respective company. Furthermore, after accounting for the coinciding of other firm relevant events in Table 3-13 results reveal much more significant results. Models II to IV of the [0;1] event window and Models I to IV of the [–1;1] window present negative coefficients significant at all three levels (i.e. 10%, 5%, and 1%). Apparently, bondholders experience a loss of wealth between -20bps and -40bps with the disclosure of synergies, making it clear that the decision to publicly announce synergy expectations can no longer be seen as a purely wealth enhancing action. Interestingly, the effect seems to spread over several days, as the synergy dummy for the event day regression turns out to be insignificant for every model. An explanation for this result might be provided by the inherent illiquidity of bond markets, causing slower price reactions compared to stock markets.

Browsing Panel A of Table 3-12 shows a statistically significant negative coefficient for Return on Assets, implying that firms that were more profitable in the year before the merger announcement are exposed to stronger negative bond returns. An explanation could be that bond investors assess the deal as a risk increasing event because management needs to increase the overall risk to maintain the high past profitability. Moreover, focusing on the event day [0;0] regression analysis, displays weak evidence of a positive impact of the current ratio and a negative impact of leverage. Apparently, higher liquidity leads to weaker bond price changes while a higher level of debt causes stronger negative bond returns. However, including the inverse Mill's ratio nullifies this effect. Comparing the results after adjustment for confounding events (Table 3-13) with the results of Table 3-12, offers two major changes. First, Bidder Leverage loses all explanatory power as no variable is statistically significant. Second, the market to book ratio becomes highly significant and negative, indicating that bidders with high growth opportunities experience more negative abnormal bond returns at an M&A announcement. Once more, bondholders' expectations to risk increasing behavior could be the reason for the negative impact.

Table 3-12: Cross Sectional Regression Analysis of Synergy Disclosure on Bidder Bond and Stock Returns for the "Complete Sample"

Panel A: Abnormal Bond Returns [bps]	I [0;0]	II [0;0]	III [0;0]	IV [0;0]	I [0;1]	II [0;1]	III [0;1]	IV [0;1]	I [–1;1]	II [–1;1]	III [–1;1]	IV [–1;1]
Intercept	0.036	0.049	0.020	–0.697	0.408	0.274	0.365	–0.573	0.167	–0.035	0.003	–0.754
Synergy-Dummy	–0.084	–0.081	–0.095	–0.095	–0.185	–0.170	–0.232*	–0.233*	–0.251	–0.239	–0.298*	–0.299*
Ln(Market Cap)	0.003	0.013	0.020	–0.015	–0.026	–0.016	–0.011	–0.056	–0.005	0.008	0.018	–0.019
Ln(Deal Size)	–0.011	–0.007	–0.020	0.039	–0.032	–0.033	–0.056*	0.020	–0.044	–0.050	–0.077**	–0.015
Current Ratio	0.100*	0.130*	0.135*	0.279	0.238*	0.216	0.214	0.402	0.312**	0.226	0.229	0.380
ROA	–0.011*	–0.012	–0.011	–0.008	–0.024**	–0.026**	–0.025**	–0.021*	–0.022*	–0.022	–0.022	–0.018
Bidder Leverage	–0.136**	–0.128*	–0.122*	–0.052	–0.134	–0.077	–0.067	0.026	–0.040	0.052	0.065	0.140
Market to Book	0.005	0.004	0.001	–0.004	–0.003	–0.003	–0.009	–0.016	–0.008	–0.007	–0.014	–0.020
Policy Act 2005-Dummy	–	–0.017	–0.013	–0.148	–	0.043	0.040	–0.137	–	0.123	0.128	–0.014
Policy Act 2007-Dummy	–	–0.019	–0.008	0.090	–	0.003	0.020	0.148	–	0.037	0.059	0.162
Industry-Dummy	–	–0.057	–0.082	–0.063	–	–0.026	–0.063	–0.039	–	0.074	0.024	0.044
SIC-49-Dummy	–	–0.105	–0.086	–0.136	–	–0.047	–0.047	–0.113	–	–0.107	–0.095	–0.148
SIC-13-Dummy	–	–0.053	–0.011	–0.105	–	0.098	0.141	0.018	–	0.038	0.105	0.005
SIC-29-Dummy	–	–0.136	–0.122	–0.191	–	0.056	0.064	–0.027	–	0.117	0.125	0.052
Percentage of Stock	–	–	–0.154	–0.143	–	–	–0.131	–0.117	–	–	–0.237	–0.226
Industry Liquidity Index	–	–	1.069**	0.387	–	–	0.935	0.042	–	–	1.951	1.230
Shareholder Approval Dummy	–	–	0.281*	0.355**	–	–	0.240	0.337	–	–	0.382	0.460
Takeover Premium	–	–	0.000	0.000	–	–	0.000	0.001	–	–	0.000	0.001
Mill's Ratio	–	–	–	0.319	–	–	–	0.417	–	–	–	0.336

Panel A: Abnormal Bond Returns [bps]	I [0;0]	II [0;0]	III [0;0]	IV [0;0]	I [0;1]	II [0;1]	III [0;1]	IV [0;1]	I [−1;1]	II [−1;1]	III [−1;1]	IV [−1;1]
N	204	204	204	204	204	204	204	204	203	203	203	203
max. VIF	1.29	4.24	4.33	90.02	1.29	4.24	4.33	90.02	1.29	4.23	4.32	90.01
R^2	9.63%	10.83%	13.40%	13.65%	9.72%	10.49%	11.87%	11.99%	8.19%	9.53%	11.05%	11.11%
adj. R^2	6.40%	4.73%	5.48%	5.25%	6.49%	4.37%	3.81%	3.43%	4.89%	3.31%	2.88%	2.41%
F-statistic	1.89*	1.35	1.31	1.25	2.41**	1.35	1.39	1.47	2.86***	1.60*	1.62*	1.67**
Panel B: Abnormal Stock Returns [%]	**I [0;0]**	**II [0;0]**	**III [0;0]**	**IV [0;0]**	**I [0;1]**	**II [0;1]**	**III [0;1]**	**IV [0;1]**	**I [−1;1]**	**II [−1;1]**	**III [−1;1]**	**IV [−1;1]**
Intercept	0.002	−0.010	−0.009	−0.121***	0.019	0.003	−0.010	−0.249***	0.028	0.015	0.001	−0.269***
Synergy-Dummy	0.010**	0.011**	0.014***	0.014***	0.013*	0.015*	0.023***	0.023***	0.011	0.013*	0.021***	0.021***
Ln(Market Cap)	0.000	0.000	−0.001	−0.006***	−0.002	−0.002	−0.003	−0.014***	−0.003	−0.003	−0.004	−0.017***
Ln(Deal Size)	−0.001	−0.002	0.001	0.010***	−0.002	−0.002	0.001	0.021***	−0.002	−0.002	0.001	0.023***
Current Ratio	0.001	−0.002	−0.002	0.020**	0.008	0.005	0.006	0.053***	0.005	0.003	0.004	0.058***
ROA	0.000	0.000	0.000*	0.000	0.000	0.000	0.000	0.001	0.000	0.000	−0.001	0.001
Bidder Leverage	0.003	0.007	0.006	0.017**	0.001	0.005	0.004	0.028***	0.000	0.003	0.002	0.028***
Market to Book	0.001***	0.002***	0.002***	0.001**	0.001	0.001*	0.001**	0.000	0.001**	0.001***	0.002***	0.000
Policy Act 2005-Dummy	–	0.011**	0.011***	−0.010	–	0.007	0.009	−0.036***	–	0.008	0.010	−0.041***
Policy Act 2007-Dummy	–	−0.004	−0.006	0.009	–	−0.004	−0.006	0.026***	–	−0.006	−0.008	0.029***
Industry-Dummy	–	0.000	0.001	0.004	–	0.001	0.004	0.010*	–	−0.001	0.002	0.009
SIC-49-Dummy	–	0.005	0.002	−0.006	–	0.008	0.006	−0.010	–	0.013	0.012	−0.007
SIC-13-Dummy	–	0.011*	0.007	−0.007	–	0.018*	0.014	−0.018*	–	0.021*	0.016*	−0.019*
SIC-29-Dummy	–	0.012*	0.007	−0.004	–	0.019*	0.014	−0.009	–	0.022*	0.018*	−0.008
Percentage of Stock	–	–	−0.004	−0.003	–	–	−0.006	−0.002	–	–	−0.006	−0.002
Industry Liquidity Index	–	–	−0.034	−0.140*	–	–	−0.009	−0.236**	–	–	0.002	−0.255***
Shareholder Approval Dummy	–	–	−0.030***	−0.018***	–	–	−0.027**	−0.003	–	–	−0.027*	0.001
Takeover Premium	–	–	0.000	0.000***	–	–	0.000	0.000***	–	–	0.000	0.000***
Mill's Ratio	–	–	–	0.050***	–	–	–	0.106***	–	–	–	0.120***

Panel B: Abnormal Stock Returns [%]	I [0;0]	II [0;0]	III [0;0]	IV [0;0]	I [0;1]	II [0;1]	III [0;1]	IV [0;1]	I [−1;1]	II [−1;1]	III [−1;1]	IV [−1;1]
N	204	204	204	204	204	204	204	204	204	204	204	204
max. VIF	1.29	4.24	4.33	90.02	1.29	4.24	4.33	90.02	1.29	4.24	4.33	90.02
R^2	10.75%	16.05%	26.35%	27.98%	6.35%	10.07%	18.74%	22.04%	5.35%	8.56%	15.86%	19.48%
adj. R^2	7.56%	10.31%	19.62%	20.98%	3.01%	3.91%	11.32%	14.46%	1.97%	2.30%	8.17%	11.64%
F-statistic	2.29**	2.62***	3.37***	3.99***	1.82*	1.29	2.03**	3.42***	3.24***	2.96***	2.12***	3.96***

This table presents the results of a cross sectional regression analysis of (cumulative) abnormal stock returns (Panel A) and of (cumulative) abnormal bond returns (Panel B) over the windows [0;+0], [0;+1], and [−1;+1] surrounding the M&A announcement date for the "Complete Sample", i.e. no adjustments for confounding events are performed. Due to missing data, one observation had to be removed from the sample. Moreover, due to missing price data, another observation had to be removed from the [−1;1] regression of Panel B. Regressions with a maximum VIF of five or higher are recalculated only containing variables with a maximum VIF under five. Variables are defined as follows (in table order): Synergy-Dummy is a dummy variable equal to one for deals, in which bidding-firm managers publicly disclose a forecast of the value of synergies they expect to achieve. Ln(Market Cap) presents the natural logarithm of market capitalization measured at fiscal year-end prior to the announcement. Ln(Deal Size) presents the natural logarithm of the amount paid for the target firm in the merger transaction. Current Ratio presents the ratio of current assets and current liabilities measured at fiscal year-end prior to the announcement. ROA is the return on assets measured at fiscal year-end prior to the announcement. Bidder Leverage presents the ratio of total debt and the market value of equity measured at fiscal year-end prior to the announcement. Market to Book presents the ratio of the market price and the book value per share measured at fiscal year-end prior to the announcement. Due to outlier, the variable Market to Book was winsorized at the 0.5% and 99.5% level. Policy Act 2005- (2007-) Dummy is a dummy variable equal to one for deals, announced after the Energy Policy Act of 2005 (Energy Independence and Security Act of 2007) was signed into law. Industry-Dummy is a dummy variable equal to one, if the bidder's and target's two-digit SIC code are the same. SIC-49- (13-) (29-) Dummy is a dummy variable equal to one, if the bidding firm's two-digit SIC code is 49 (13) (29). Percentage of Stock presents the percentage equity financing of the deal. The Industry Liquidity Index is computed following Schlingemann et al. (2002), which represents the ratio of the value of M&A transactions in the energy industry (excluding minority stake purchases, leveraged buyouts, spin-offs, recapitalizations, self-tenders, exchange offers, repurchases and the sample deals) in a year and the total book value of assets of firms in the same two-digit SIC code for that year. Shareholder Approval-Dummy is a dummy variable equal to one, if shareholders of the bidding firm have to approve the deal. Takeover Premium presents the premium paid by the bidding firm. Mill's Ratio is computed from a probit regression to control for possible endogeneity of the disclosure decision. T-statistics are computed using robust standard errors adjusted for heteroskedasticity. The symbols ***, **, and * denote statistical significance at 1%, 5%, and 10% level, respectively. Abnormal stock returns are in percent and calculated using the four-factor model. Abnormal bond returns are in basis points and calculated using the firm level approach.

Table 3-13: Cross Sectional Regression Analysis of Synergy Disclosure on Bidder Bond and Stock Returns for the "Control Sample"

Panel A: Abnormal Bond Returns [bps]	I	II	III		IV	I	II	III		IV	I	II	III		IV
	[0;0]	[0;0]	[0;0]	[0;0]	[0;0]	[0;1]	[0;1]	[0;1]	[0;1]	[0;1]	[−1;1]	[−1;1]	[−1;1]	[−1;1]	[−1;1]
Intercept	−0.045	−0.131	−0.143	−0.160	0.896	0.533	0.209	0.384	0.365	0.936	0.353	0.030	0.156	–	−0.510
Synergy-Dummy	−0.067	−0.072	−0.091	−0.084	−0.085	−0.214	−0.194*	−0.267**	−0.260**	−0.260**	−0.324**	−0.304**	−0.382***	–	−0.385***
Ln(Market Cap)	0.020	0.044	0.050	0.038	0.087*	−0.030	0.004	0.009	−0.005	0.021	−0.003	0.033	0.042	–	0.015
Ln(Deal Size)	−0.019	−0.014	−0.024	−0.026	−0.106*	−0.033	−0.032	−0.055*	−0.057*	−0.101	−0.041	−0.043	−0.069**	–	−0.016
Current Ratio	0.086	0.145*	0.150*	0.153*	−0.074	0.274*	0.278*	0.260	0.262	0.140	0.346**	0.288*	0.273	–	0.417
ROA	−0.008	−0.011	−0.010	−0.010	−0.014	−0.028**	−0.031*	−0.030*	−0.030*	−0.032*	−0.032**	−0.033**	−0.032*	–	−0.030*
Bidder Leverage	−0.076	−0.034	−0.031	−0.056	−0.097	−0.112	0.032	0.040	0.012	−0.010	−0.094	0.078	0.088	–	0.123
Market to Book	−0.010	−0.013**	−0.017**	−0.014	−0.015*	−0.021**	−0.022**	−0.035***	−0.031**	−0.032**	−0.033***	−0.034***	−0.048***	–	−0.049***
Policy Act 2005-Dummy	–	−0.065	−0.066	−0.065	0.123	–	−0.086	−0.106	−0.104	−0.003	–	−0.031	−0.043	–	−0.166
Policy Act 2007-Dummy	–	−0.052	−0.039	−0.040	−0.143	–	0.041	0.067	0.066	0.010	–	0.072	0.101	–	0.164
Industry-Dummy	–	−0.053	−0.076	−0.079	−0.062	–	−0.054	−0.083	−0.087	−0.078	–	0.025	−0.005	–	−0.014
SIC-49-Dummy	–	−0.174*	−0.166	–	–	–	−0.145	−0.189	–	–	–	−0.235	−0.278	–	−0.344
SIC-13-Dummy	–	−0.040	−0.010	0.116*	0.223**	–	0.198	0.187	0.331*	0.389*	–	0.095	0.092	–	−0.021
SIC-29-Dummy	–	−0.161	−0.156	−0.017	0.048	–	0.028	0.005	0.162	0.198	–	0.067	0.038	–	−0.062
Percentage of Stock	–	–	−0.133	−0.126	−0.239*	–	–	0.028	0.036	−0.025	–	–	0.063	–	0.128
Industry Liquidity Index	–	–	0.889	1.014**	1.556**	–	–	0.336	0.479	0.772	–	–	1.318	–	0.905
Shareholder Approval Dummy	–	–	0.190	0.218	0.154	–	–	−0.005	0.027	−0.007	–	–	−0.032	–	−0.007
Takeover Premium	–	–	0.000	0.000	0.000	–	–	0.001***	0.001***	0.000	–	–	0.001***	–	0.001
Mill's Ratio	–	–	–	–	−0.482	–	–	–	–	−0.260	–	–	–	–	0.303

Panel A: Abnormal Bond Returns [bps]	I	II	III		IV	I	II	III		IV	I	II	III		IV
	[0;0]	[0;0]	[0;0]	[0;0]	[0;0]	[0;1]	[0;1]	[0;1]	[0;1]	[0;1]	[−1;1]	[−1;1]	[−1;1]	[−1;1]	[−1;1]
N	157	157	157	157	157	157	157	157	157	157	156	156	156	–	156
max. VIF	1.30	4.71	5.01	2.35	68.30	1.30	4.71	5.01	2.35	68.30	1.30	4.69	4.99	–	175.40
R^2	6.91%	11.11%	13.20%	11.99%	12.74%	13.46%	16.87%	18.69%	18.29%	18.35%	15.58%	18.36%	20.15%	–	20.17%
adj. R^2	2.54%	3.03%	2.58%	1.93%	2.07%	9.39%	9.32%	8.74%	8.95%	8.36%	11.59%	10.89%	10.32%	–	9.69%
F-statistic	1.32	1.60*	1.54*	1.13	2.12***	2.82***	1.59*	1.58*	1.61*	1.73**	5.16***	2.98***	2.76***	–	2.19***
Panel B: Abnormal Stock Returns [%]	**I**	**II**	**III**		**IV**	**I**	**II**	**III**		**IV**	**I**	**II**	**III**		**IV**
	[0;0]	[0;0]	[0;0]	[0;0]	[0;0]	[0;1]	[0;1]	[0;1]	[0;1]	[0;1]	[−1;1]	[−1;1]	[−1;1]	[−1;1]	[−1;1]
Intercept	0.024	0.014	0.020	0.021	−0.103*	0.050**	0.033	0.016	0.017	−0.207***	0.056**	0.038	0.019	0.021	−0.239***
Synergy-Dummy	0.009*	0.011**	0.014***	0.013***	0.013***	0.007	0.009	0.019**	0.018**	0.018**	0.007	0.009	0.019**	0.019**	0.019**
Ln(Market Cap)	−0.002	−0.002*	−0.004***	−0.003***	−0.009***	−0.005**	−0.006**	−0.007***	−0.006***	−0.016***	−0.006**	−0.007**	−0.008***	−0.006**	−0.018***
Ln(Deal Size)	−0.001	−0.002	0.001	0.001	0.011**	−0.001	−0.001	0.004**	0.004**	0.021***	−0.001	−0.001	0.004*	0.004*	0.024***
Current Ratio	0.001	−0.002	−0.003	−0.003	0.024**	0.009	0.009	0.010	0.010	0.058***	0.009	0.009	0.011	0.011	0.067***
ROA	0.000	−0.001	−0.001**	−0.001**	0.000	−0.001*	−0.001*	−0.001**	−0.001**	0.000	−0.001	−0.001*	−0.001**	−0.001**	0.000
Bidder Leverage	−0.004	−0.001	−0.002	−0.002	0.003	−0.008*	−0.004	−0.005	−0.003	0.006	−0.007	−0.003	−0.004	−0.001	0.009
Market to Book	0.001	0.002**	0.002**	0.002*	0.002***	0.001	0.001***	0.003***	0.002***	0.002***	0.001	0.001***	0.003***	0.002***	0.003***
Policy Act 2005-Dummy	–	0.012**	0.012***	0.012***	−0.009	–	0.006	0.009	0.009	−0.031**	–	0.008	0.011	0.011	−0.036***
Policy Act 2007-Dummy	–	−0.005	−0.007	−0.007	0.005	–	−0.005	−0.010	−0.010	0.012	–	−0.008	−0.012	−0.012	0.013
Industry-Dummy	–	0.000	0.002	0.002	0.000	–	−0.004	0.000	0.001	−0.003	–	−0.008	−0.003	−0.003	−0.007
SIC-49-Dummy	–	0.011	0.004	–	–	–	0.017	0.016*	–	–	–	0.023*	0.022**	–	–
SIC-13-Dummy	–	0.014	0.006	0.003	−0.009	–	0.028**	0.023**	0.011	−0.012	–	0.035**	0.031***	0.014	−0.013
SIC-29-Dummy	–	0.013	0.003	0.000	−0.008	–	0.023	0.016	0.003	−0.011	–	0.028*	0.021*	0.003	−0.013
Percentage of Stock	–	–	−0.009	−0.009	0.004	–	–	−0.005	−0.006	0.018	–	–	−0.006	−0.007	0.021
Industry Liquidity Index	–	–	−0.083	−0.085	−0.149**	–	–	−0.049	−0.061	−0.176	–	–	−0.022	−0.039	−0.173*
Shareholder Approval Dummy	–	–	−0.031***	−0.032***	−0.024***	–	–	−0.029**	−0.032**	−0.019	–	–	−0.028*	−0.032**	−0.016
Takeover Premium	–	–	0.000	0.000	0.000***	–	–	0.000***	0.000***	0.000	–	–	0.000***	0.000***	0.000*
Mill's Ratio	–	–	–	–	0.056**	–	–	–	–	0.102***	–	–	–	–	0.119***

Panel B: Abnormal Stock Returns [%]	I	II	III		IV	I	II	III		IV	I	II	III		IV
	[0;0]	[0;0]	[0;0]	[0;0]	[0;0]	[0;1]	[0;1]	[0;1]	[0;1]	[0;1]	[−1;1]	[−1;1]	[−1;1]	[−1;1]	[−1;1]
N	157	157	157	157	157	157	157	157	157	157	157	157	157	157	157
max. VIF	1.30	4.71	5.01	2.35	68.30	1.30	4.71	5.01	2.35	68.30	1.30	4.71	5.01	2.35	68.30
R^2	9.96%	16.43%	33.39%	33.24%	35.92%	8.40%	13.38%	28.20%	26.94%	30.63%	7.36%	13.30%	25.27%	23.40%	27.37%
adj. R^2	5.73%	8.83%	25.24%	25.61%	28.09%	4.09%	5.51%	19.42%	18.59%	22.15%	3.01%	5.42%	16.13%	14.65%	18.49%
F-statistic	1.56	1.94**	3.61***	3.57***	4.67***	2.77***	2.09**	4.13***	3.93***	5.47***	2.54**	2.07**	3.43***	3.22***	4.91***

This table presents the results of a cross sectional regression analysis of (cumulative) abnormal stock returns (Panel A) and of (cumulative) abnormal bond returns (Panel B) over the windows [0;+0], [0;+1], and [−1;+1] surrounding the M&A announcement date for the "Control Sample", i.e. deals with confounding events at the three days surrounding the announcement day are excluded from the sample. Due to missing data, one observation had to be removed from the sample. Moreover, due to missing price data, another observation had to be removed from the [−1;1] regression of Panel B. Regressions with a maximum VIF of five or higher are recalculated only containing variables with a maximum VIF under five. Variables are defined as follows (in table order): Synergy-Dummy is a dummy variable equal to one for deals, in which bidding-firm managers publicly disclose a forecast of the value of synergies they expect to achieve. Ln(Market Cap) presents the natural logarithm of market capitalization measured at fiscal year-end prior to the announcement. Ln(Deal Size) presents the natural logarithm of the amount paid for the target firm in the merger transaction. Current Ratio presents the ratio of current assets and current liabilities measured at fiscal year-end prior to the announcement. ROA is the return on assets measured at fiscal year-end prior to the announcement. Bidder leverage presents the ratio of total debt and the market value of equity measured at fiscal year-end prior to the announcement. Market to Book presents the ratio of the market price and the book value per share measured at fiscal year-end prior to the announcement. Due to outlier, the variable Market to Book was winsorized at the 0.5% and 99.5% level. Policy Act 2005- (2007-) Dummy is a dummy variable equal to one for deals, announced after the Energy Policy Act of 2005 (Energy Independence and Security Act of 2007) was signed into law. Industry-Dummy is a dummy variable equal to one, if the bidder's and target's two-digit SIC code are the same. SIC-49- (13-) (29-) Dummy is a dummy variable equal to one, if the bidding firm's two-digit SIC code is 49 (13) (29). Percentage of Stock presents the percentage equity financing of the deal. The Industry Liquidity Index is computed following Schlingemann et al. (2002), which represents the ratio of the value of M&A transactions in the energy industry (excluding minority stake purchases, leveraged buyouts, spin-offs, recapitalizations, self-tenders, exchange offers, repurchases and the sample deals) in a year and the total book value of assets of firms in the same two-digit SIC code for that year. Shareholder Approval-Dummy is a dummy variable equal to one, if shareholders of the bidding firm have to approve the deal. Takeover Premium presents the premium paid by the bidding firm. Mill's Ratio is computed from a probit regression to control for possible endogeneity of the disclosure decision. T-statistics are computed using robust standard errors adjusted for heteroskedasticity. The symbols ***, **, and * denote statistical significance at 1%, 5%, and 10% level, respectively. Abnormal stock returns are in percent and calculated using the four-factor model. Abnormal bond returns in basis points and calculated using the firm level approach.

Panel B of Table 3-12 and Table 3-13 present the results for the abnormal stock returns. Consistent with the expectations and prior research, tables almost always present a positive and statistically significant coefficient for the Synergy-Dummy regardless of the investigated event window, chosen regression model and utilized sample. The results suggest that a management's decision to disclose synergy estimates increases the bidder announcements returns by approximately 1.0%–2.3%, depending on the examined event period. However, the impact of synergy disclosure on stock returns turns out to be weaker compared to prior research.[43] Taken together with the negative coefficient for bond returns, the results imply the existence of a transfer of wealth from bondholders to stockholders for disclosing deals.

In line with Dutordoir et al. (2014) firm size affects abnormal stock returns negatively, but only after accounting for confounding events. A robust positive impact of the market to book ratio is found, indicating that acquirers with higher growth opportunities experience weaker negative announcement effects. This is consistent with the risk increasing hypothesis explaining the negative impact on bondholder wealth. The introduction of the Policy Act 2005 offers conflicting results. On the one hand, the coefficient is highly significant and negative for the announcement day (Model II and Model III), but loses all explanatory power when the model controls for endogeneity (Model IV). On the other hand, the two-day and three-day event window regressions exhibit a significant value only in Model IV, and it turns out to be negative thereby contradicting the result of the other regressions. A reason for this inconsistence could be the strong multicollinearity associated with adding the inverse mill's ratio. Consistent with Dutordoir et al. (2014) a negative coefficient for the Shareholder Approval-Dummy is detected suggesting that a necessary deal approval by the bidder's shareholders causes stronger announcement effects.

3.3.4 Analysis of the Transfer of Wealth between Bondholders and Stockholders

As discussed earlier, signs for a possible wealth transfer between bondholders and stockholders are found, but only for the subsample of disclosing deals. Prior research provides ways to further investigate this relationship (e.g. Baran & King, 2010; Kitsabunnarat-Chatjuthamard et al., 2010; Maxwell & Rao, 2003; Maxwell & Stephens, 2003). Two different approaches are utilized: 1) Pearson correlation coefficient and 2) cross sectional regression analysis. Both procedures are applied on two different sets of variables which measure the impact

---

43 See Dutordoir et al. (2014); Fraunhoffer and Schiereck (2012a).

of M&A announcements on bondholder and stockholder wealth. In a first step, the abnormal value change is calculated by multiplying the abnormal return[44] with the respective market value measured at fiscal year-end prior to the announcement (FY-1), labeled "Yearly Data". More specifically, the abnormal change in the market value of equity (ACMVE) on day t is computed as the product of a company's market capitalization at FY-1 and the abnormal stock return on trading day t. Similarly, a firm's total debt at FY-1 is multiplied with the abnormal bond return (firm level) on trading day t to obtain the abnormal change in the market value of debt (ACMVD). This approach is advantageous, as it considers all interest bearing short- and long-term obligations for analysis. However, per definition both Dollar values, i.e. Market Capitalization and Total Debt, are constant over the event window, thus not reflecting the actual wealth changes for both stakeholders.

A second set of variables with daily data is utilized to address this issue. This time ACMVE is calculated as the multiplication of a firm's Market Capitalization on trading day t-1 and the abnormal stock return on trading day t. To obtain ACMVD a two step procedure is followed: First, each abnormal bond return on trading day t is multiplied with the bond's respective market value on trading day t-1. Second, a firm value is created by equally weighting a company's numbers. This time, the daily market value change of equity and debt is considered. However, only debt attributed to sample bonds is utilized leading to the disregard of other firms' debt. Both approaches have their benefits and shortcomings. Consequently, using them both provides the estimation of a range of the actual wealth effect.

Table 3-14 presents the Pearson correlation between ACMVE and ACMVD with yearly data, while Table 3-15 displays the same figures using the daily dataset. First, the results of the "Complete Sample" (Panel A) are examined. The figures confirm the expectations. Both tables show a statistically significant and negative coefficient only for the disclosing M&A. Neither the full sample, nor the non-disclosing deals exhibit a single significant value, thus illustrating that a redistribution of wealth from bondholders to stockholders only occurs when management decides to unveil synergy forecasts together with an M&A announcement.

The next analysis focuses on the adjusted sample (Panel B) of Table 3-14 and Table 3-15. Accounting for confounding events not only confirms the results of the "Complete Sample", but also leads to stronger effects. Table 3-14 (Table 3-15)

44 Again, the abnormal returns yielded by the four-factor model is utilized.

detects three (four) different event windows that point to a transfer of wealth with the highest coefficient being almost (over) 50% and significant at the 5% (1%) level. Additionally, both tables present a significant coefficient for the full sample on the event day [0;0]. However, the assumption is that this effect is largely driven by the disclosing deals as the deals that lack synergy forecasts present only insignificant values.

Table 3-14: Pearson Correlation between Abnormal Change in the Market Value of Equity and Debt (Yearly Data)

	All M&A		Non-disclosing M&A		Disclosing M&A	
	Correlation	p-value	Correlation	p-value	Correlation	p-value
Panel A: Complete Sample						
[−1;0]	−0.055	0.432	−0.051	0.513	−0.224	0.210
[0;0]	−0.089	0.207	0.016	0.838	−0.383**	0.027
[0;1]	−0.061	0.390	−0.030	0.692	−0.215	0.229
[−1;1]	−0.107	0.130	−0.106	0.168	−0.094	0.603
[−5;0]	0.075	0.290	−0.023	0.763	−0.224	0.211
[0;5]	−0.016	0.815	−0.020	0.797	−0.013	0.944
[−10;0]	0.006	0.932	−0.001	0.994	−0.183	0.309
[0;10]	−0.022	0.755	−0.029	0.710	0.065	0.721
Panel B: Control Sample						
[−1;0]	−0.089	0.269	−0.037	0.674	−0.481**	0.013
[0;0]	−0.159**	0.047	−0.082	0.350	−0.421**	0.032
[0;1]	−0.106	0.184	−0.094	0.287	−0.200	0.326
[−1;1]	−0.119	0.138	−0.094	0.287	−0.355*	0.075
[−5;0]	−0.054	0.507	−0.019	0.828	−0.289	0.151
[0;5]	−0.047	0.556	−0.039	0.662	−0.152	0.458
[−10;0]	−0.028	0.731	−0.023	0.798	−0.156	0.446
[0;10]	−0.089	0.269	−0.086	0.331	−0.096	0.640

This table presents the Pearson Correlation Coefficient and p-value between the abnormal change in the market value of equity (ACMVE) and the abnormal change in the market value of debt (ACMVD) for various event windows surrounding the event day. ACMVE on day t is calculated as the multiplication of a firm's market capitalization at fiscal year-end prior to the announcement and the abnormal stock return on day t. ACMVD on day t is calculated by multiplying each abnormal bond return (firm level) on day t with Total Debt at fiscal year-end prior to the announcement. Panel A reports the results for the "Complete Sample", while Panel B reports the result for the "Control Sample". The symbols ***, **, and * denote statistical significance at 1%, 5%, and 10% level, respectively.

Table 3-15: Pearson Correlation between Abnormal Change in the Market Value of Equity and Debt (Daily Data)

	All M&A		Non-disclosing M&A		Disclosing M&A	
	Correlation	**p-value**	**Correlation**	**p-value**	**Correlation**	**p-value**
Panel A: Complete Sample						
[−1;0]	−0.077	0.274	−0.076	0.327	−0.294	0.096
[0;0]	−0.088	0.210	−0.015	0.846	−0.315*	0.074
[0;1]	−0.040	0.566	−0.007	0.931	−0.166	0.355
[−1;1]	−0.057	0.423	−0.050	0.516	−0.154	0.392
[−5;0]	−0.015	0.827	−0.057	0.456	−0.330*	0.061
[0;5]	−0.006	0.928	−0.017	0.821	0.044	0.807
[−10;0]	−0.015	0.829	−0.018	0.817	−0.250	0.160
[0;10]	0.043	0.544	0.022	0.777	0.200	0.264
Panel B: Control Sample						
[−1;0]	−0.108	0.179	−0.045	0.614	−0.515***	0.007
[0;0]	−0.176**	0.028	−0.074	0.402	−0.527***	0.006
[0;1]	−0.086	0.284	−0.044	0.619	−0.251	0.216
[−1;1]	−0.065	0.419	−0.031	0.724	−0.238	0.241
[−5;0]	−0.071	0.377	−0.019	0.828	−0.403**	0.041
[0;5]	−0.027	0.734	−0.016	0.856	−0.156	0.447
[−10;0]	−0.054	0.507	−0.033	0.712	−0.354*	0.076
[0;10]	0.011	0.888	0.006	0.950	0.095	0.645

This table presents the Pearson Correlation Coefficient and p-value between the abnormal change in the market value of equity (ACMVE) and the abnormal change in the market value of debt (ACMVD) for various event windows surrounding the event day. ACMVE on day t is calculated as the multiplication of a firm's market capitalization on day t-1 and the abnormal stock return on day t. ACMVD on day t is calculated by first, multiplying each abnormal bond return on day t with the bond's respective market value on day t-1. Second, the equally weighted average is computed for every firm in the sample. Panel A reports the results for the "Complete Sample", while Panel B reports the result for the "Control Sample". The symbols ***, **, and * denote statistical significance at 1%, 5%, and 10% level, respectively.

Altogether, Pearson correlation analysis reveals that stockholders gain at the expense of the same firm's bondholders, when management decides to disclose synergies along with the M&A announcement. A reason for the restriction of the redistribution effects to the disclosing deals could be that the concurrent forecasting of expected synergies unveils that the M&A is actually a risk increasing venture, as management is obliged to achieve the projected numbers. This rise in risk would lead to negative bondholder returns and, at the same time, cause a wealth appreciation to the stockholders. This type of wealth redistribution is in line with the incentive hypothesis (Asquith & Kim, 1982; Jensen & Meckling, 1976).

Next, several cross sectional regressions are utilized to further examine the connection between stockholder and debtholder wealth at M&A announcements. Both Samples ("Complete Sample" versus "Control Sample") and both datasets ("Yearly Data" versus "Daily Data") are applied, leading to four different tables (Table 3-16, Table 3-17, Table 3-18, and Table 3-19). Each table consists of three panels (Panel A, Panel B, and Panel C) describing the results for all M&A, non-disclosing M&A, and disclosing M&A, respectively. Moreover, five different models are computed, depicted as I, II, III, IV, and V, which include different sets of variables. The utilization of various models is the result of the small sample size in Panel C and its impact on the regression's validity. The statistical power of regression analyses highly depends on the number of observations or more specifically on the ratio of sample size and independent variables. This interrelation leads to several rules of thumb to achieve a reasonable sample size (see VanVoorhis and Morgan (2007) for further information) underlining the need to account for this factor. Thus, this challenge is addressed by computing regressions with alternating varieties of variables, starting with rather small models.

Model I includes, like every other model, the variable of interest ACMVD, and the variable for firm size Ln(Market Cap) as well as for deal size Ln(Deal Size). Model II adds the variables Current Ratio, ROA, Bidder Leverage, and Market to Book, which control for a firm's liquidity, profitability, level of debt, and growth opportunity. Only industry specific Dummy variables (i.e. Policy Act 2005-, Policy Act 2007-, Industry-, SIC-49-, SIC-13-, and SIC-29-Dummy) are added with Model III, and Model IV only adds the remaining variables. Finally, a regression is computed that includes all variables with Model V. All models are applied to the event day window [0;0] and the three-day window [−1;1]. Again, regressions with variance inflation factors of five or higher are recalculated and the causing variables are removed from the model.

Other control variables are not analyzed, since the prime interest lies in the sign and statistical significance of the variable ACMVD. Examining the yearly data (Table 3-16 and Table 3-17) offers evidence consistent with a redistribution of wealth from bondholders to stockholders for the disclosing deals (Panel C). Repeatedly, the coefficient for ACMVD is negative and statistically significant up to the 1% level, which is in line with the expectations. However, the results also show some inconsistencies about the significant models. Panel C of Table 3-16 only presents significant coefficients for event day regressions (i.e. Model I through IV on the left hand side), while Table 3-17 exhibits much stronger results utilizing abnormal returns over the three-day event window (i.e. Model I through

IV on the right hand side). The data in Panel A and Panel B, presents statistically significant values only for the full sample after accounting for confounding events. The non-disclosing deals reveal no notable wealth redistribution.[45] At first glance, the observer could be inclined to infer that the significant effects of the full sample (Panel A) are driven by disclosing deals. However, a closer look at the numbers reveals that for some models the significance of the variable ACMVD turns out to be higher for the full sample than for disclosing deals. Apparently, some evidence is found, albeit weak, that M&A generally experience a transfer of wealth. Nevertheless, the higher absolute value in Panel C confirms a stronger redistribution effect for the synergy communicating announcements.

Next, the results of the daily data approach are evaluated in Table 3-18 and Table 3-19. Browsing the first spreadsheet identifies not a single model with a statistically significant coefficient for ACMVD, contradicting the results of the preceding regressions. Results do not confirm the expectations of a redistribution of wealth, irrespective of the applied sample (all M&A, non-disclosing M&A, or disclosing M&A), model (I, II, III, IV, or V), or event window ([0;0] or [−1;1]). The only indication for this wealth transfer is that the variable ACMVD constantly has a negative coefficient. However, this holds for all three panels, thus not confirming the hypothesis of a unique effect for disclosing deals. Even so, after controlling for confounding events in Table 3-19 once more presents evidence for the expropriation of wealth between stakeholders. All three samples exhibit a negative and statistically significant coefficient for the event day regressions. This is again an indication that all announcements experience a wealth transfer to some degree. Nevertheless, analyzing the results of the disclosing deals reveals two reasons why the effect is strongest with this subsample. First, the disclosing deals are the only M&A with statistically significant coefficients for the regressions that utilize abnormal returns over the three day event window [−1;1]. Second, the absolute value of the figures is by far the largest.

Taken together, the analysis of the existence of a wealth expropriation from bondholders to stockholders yields two results. First, the Pearson correlation coefficient strongly confirms the expectations of the wealth transfer for disclosing deals. Table 3-14 and Table 3-15 present statistically significant and negative correlation coefficients, particularly strong after controlling for confounding

45 Model I in Panel B of Table 3-17 using event window [0;0] exhibits a negative and statistically significant coefficient for the variable ACMVD. However, since it is the only significant model and only significant at the 10% level, it is deduced that deal announcements without synergy forecasts do not experience a transfer of wealth between bondholders and stockholders.

events. Second, several cross sectional regressions also provide evidence for this synergy related redistribution effect, although not as robust as with the bivariate approach. Some models detect the expected relationship while others do not. Nevertheless, almost all coefficients turn out to be negative thereby pointing to the existence of the wealth transfer. Reason for the partially inconclusive results of the regression could be the rather small number of observations. Small sample sizes represent an undesired hindrance for multiple regression analysis that makes it hard to establish the actual causal connection between variables. The attempt to address this tradeoff between appropriate ratio of sample size and independent variables and including all the necessary variables was to utilize several different models with changing sets of variables. In the end, it is deduced that the results provide some, albeit only weak evidence for a wealth transfer from bondholders to stockholders primarily for synergy disclosing M&A. To validate this result, future research might repeat this analysis with an extended sample.

Table 3-16: Cross Sectional Regression Analysis of Wealth Transfer between Bidders' Market Value of Equity and Market Value of Debt for the "Complete Sample" (Yearly Data)

Panel A: All M&A	I	II	III		IV	V		I	II	III		IV	V	
	[0;0]	[0;0]	[0;0]	[0;0]	[0;0]	[0;0]	[0;0]	[-1;1]	[-1;1]	[-1;1]	[-1;1]	[-1;1]	[-1;1]	[-1;1]
Intercept	271.52	266.42	211.18	–	333.50	231.52	–	334.82	339.44	297.11	–	281.62	149.67	–
ACMVD	-0.992	-1.044	-1.131	–	-0.868	-0.895	–	-0.917	-0.850	-0.971	–	-0.951	-0.938	–
Ln(Market Cap)	-32.682	-32.026	-31.065	–	-40.533	-35.848	–	-36.731	-36.504	-37.108	–	-43.569	-37.841	–
Ln(Deal Size)	-0.388	-3.894	0.804	–	1.405	3.822	–	-5.575	-7.489	-7.405	–	17.730	13.967	–
Current Ratio	–	-6.946	–	–	–	-14.407	–	–	-9.742	–	–	–	-25.086	–
ROA	–	0.641	–	–	–	-1.820	–	–	0.322	–	–	–	-0.239	–
Bidder Leverage	–	-6.178	–	–	–	5.911	–	–	-2.892	–	–	–	33.857	–
Market to Book	–	8.904	–	–	–	9.076**	–	–	5.053	–	–	–	9.736	–
Policy Act 2005-Dummy	–	–	50.650	–	–	65.539	–	–	–	-48.843	–	–	-20.895	–
Policy Act 2007-Dummy	–	–	-29.599	–	–	-36.998	–	–	–	64.421	–	–	61.290	–
Industry-Dummy	–	–	-8.187	–	–	-9.084	–	–	–	-19.630	–	–	-5.908	–
SIC-49-Dummy	–	–	18.913	–	–	15.255	–	–	–	22.439	–	–	23.378	–
SIC-13-Dummy	–	–	57.665**	–	–	60.357*	–	–	–	111.99**	–	–	110.66**	–
SIC-29-Dummy	–	–	-54.405	–	–	-61.027	–	–	–	86.512	–	–	88.727	–
Percentage of Stock	–	–	–	–	19.218	10.113	–	–	–	–	–	-119.29	-121.87	–
Industry Liquidity Index	–	–	–	–	-248.35	54.325	–	–	–	–	–	100.79	264.83	–
Shareholder Approval Dummy	–	–	–	–	-206.61**	-228.70**	–	–	–	–	–	-63.406	-62.983	–
Takeover Premium	–	–	–	–	0.340	0.315	–	–	–	–	–	-0.158	-0.178	–

Panel A: All M&A	I	II	III		IV	V		I	II	III		IV	V	
	[0;0]	[0;0]	[0;0]	[0;0]	[0;0]	[0;0]	[0;0]	[−1;1]	[−1;1]	[−1;1]	[−1;1]	[−1;1]	[−1;1]	[−1;1]
N	204	204	204	–	204	204	–	203	203	203	–	203	203	–
max. VIF	1.13	1.63	3.96	–	2.26	4.32	–	1.14	1.23	3.94	–	2.26	4.35	–
R^2	2.89%	4.70%	5.29%	–	7.46%	11.95%	–	2.60%	2.88%	4.17%	–	4.90%	7.06%	–
adj. R^2	1.44%	1.29%	0.90%	–	4.15%	3.90%	–	1.13%	−0.60%	−0.30%	–	1.49%	−1.48%	–
F-statistic	0.73	0.72	1.35	–	1.92*	1.47	–	0.86	0.6	1.48	–	1.12	1.08	–

Panel B: Non-disclosing M&A	I	II	III		IV	V		I	II	III		IV	V	
	[0;0]	[0;0]	[0;0]	[0;0]	[0;0]	[0;0]	[0;0]	[−1;1]	[−1;1]	[−1;1]	[−1;1]	[−1;1]	[−1;1]	[−1;1]
Intercept	319.77	413.15	252.94	–	339.48	300.99	–	292.99	385.78	280.82	–	306.31	311.30	–
ACMVD	0.159	−0.157	0.058	–	0.228	−0.155	–	−0.865	−0.918	−0.903	–	−0.859	−0.900	–
Ln(Market Cap)	−32.718	−37.463	−28.545	–	−41.382	−39.544	–	−32.312	−39.387	−31.188	–	−42.634	−42.628	–
Ln(Deal Size)	−8.696	−10.789	−7.854	–	1.745	4.134	–	−4.666	−6.594	−9.387	–	11.713	7.118	–
Current Ratio	–	−14.622	–	–	–	9.258	–	–	15.326	–	–	–	13.238	–
ROA	–	−0.353	–	–	–	−2.498	–	–	−0.038	–	–	–	−1.052	–
Bidder Leverage	–	−40.078	–	–	–	−46.724	–	–	−62.851	–	–	–	−31.590	–
Market to Book	–	1.041	–	–	–	5.156	–	–	1.206	–	–	–	4.442	–
Policy Act 2005-Dummy	–	–	38.316	–	–	45.587	–	–	–	−41.380	–	–	−47.309	–
Policy Act 2007-Dummy	–	–	−38.675	–	–	−44.473	–	–	–	10.882	–	–	14.767	–
Industry-Dummy	–	–	−14.691	–	–	−0.033	–	–	–	−18.833	–	–	−9.857	–
SIC-49-Dummy	–	–	23.297	–	–	23.477	–	–	–	11.342	–	–	15.320	–
SIC-13-Dummy	–	–	65.371**	–	–	46.487	–	–	–	112.23**	–	–	90.399	–
SIC-29-Dummy	–	–	−68.528	–	–	−95.198	–	–	–	106.79	–	–	70.254	–
Percentage of Stock	–	–	–	–	54.198	51.639	–	–	–	–	–	−98.566	−117.14	–
Industry Liquidity Index	–	–	–	–	37.594	347.24	–	–	–	–	–	−26.265	15.123	–
Shareholder Approval Dummy	–	–	–	–	−329.41*	−373.43*	–	–	–	–	–	−93.114	−109.76	–
Takeover Premium	–	–	–	–	0.544	0.619	–	–	–	–	–	−0.442	−0.255	–

Panel B: Non-disclosing M&A	I	II	III		IV	V		I	II	III		IV	V	
	[0;0]	[0;0]	[0;0]	[0;0]	[0;0]	[0;0]	[0;0]	[−1;1]	[−1;1]	[−1;1]	[−1;1]	[−1;1]	[−1;1]	[−1;1]
N	171	171	171	–	171	171	–	170	170	170	–	170	170	–
max. VIF	1.10	1.40	4.06	–	2.28	4.50	–	1.10	1.27	4.03	–	2.29	4.50	–
R^2	2.57%	3.22%	5.33%	–	6.05%	10.24%	–	2.32%	3.10%	4.11%	–	4.58%	6.29%	–
adj. R^2	0.82%	−0.93%	0.04%	–	2.02%	0.27%	–	0.55%	−1.09%	−1.28%	–	0.45%	−4.19%	–
F-statistic	0.32	0.86	0.83	–	1.12	0.99	–	0.68	0.69	1.4	–	1.98*	1.32	–

Panel C: Disclosing M&A	I	II	III		IV	V		I	II	III		IV	V	
	[0;0]	[0;0]	[0;0]	[0;0]	[0;0]	[0;0]	[0;0]	[−1;1]	[−1;1]	[−1;1]	[−1;1]	[−1;1]	[−1;1]	[−1;1]
Intercept	184.44	5.227	−117.15	−50.016	441.88	502.07	55.269	522.653	924.01	355.20	459.62	234.94	−218.35	1,327.5
ACMVD	−2.536***	−1.717	−3.203**	−2.946**	−2.482***	−1.192	−1.080	−1.477	−3.506	0.888	0.434	−1.213	3.576	0.514
Ln(Market Cap)	−48.926	−35.877	−28.393	−49.781	−71.830*	−65.872	−53.982	−63.007	−94.282	−62.837	−94.905	−61.930	−33.400	−144.94
Ln(Deal Size)	31.851	16.571	31.420	36.145	22.328	8.561	22.269	−1.983	−3.840	39.649	43.676	52.972	65.450	–
Current Ratio	–	−7.175	–	–	–	−202.44	−87.437	–	−264.53	–	–	–	−196.12	−514.71*
ROA	–	11.314	–	–	–	4.731	5.517	–	7.168	–	–	–	−15.980	−2.621
Bidder Leverage	–	49.588	–	–	–	105.55	85.350	–	162.59	–	–	–	78.448	107.40
Market to Book	–	20.621***	–	–	–	14.160	23.434***	–	0.656	–	–	–	37.201	9.131
Policy Act 2005-Dummy	–	–	171.77	158.12	–	115.59	–	–	–	−284.42	−299.67	–	−83.722	–
Policy Act 2007-Dummy	–	–	107.09	54.479	–	185.61	189.00	–	–	658.72	564.58	–	872.04*	572.54**
Industry-Dummy	–	–	96.671	46.738	–	20.576	18.200	–	–	−75.782	−133.82	–	165.82	27.620
SIC-49-Dummy	–	–	−202.64	–	–	−221.30	–	–	–	−301.57	–	–	−510.36	–
SIC-13-Dummy	–	–	−142.51	37.179	–	−126.68	56.376	–	–	−203.76	67.502	–	−321.93	97.220
SIC-29-Dummy	–	–	41.306	160.98	–	11.234	143.55	–	–	−125.50	53.734	–	34.490	223.49
Percentage of Stock	–	–	–	–	−54.609	55.438	221.82	–	–	–	–	−174.21	374.27	−52.257
Industry Liquidity Index	–	–	–	–	−2,136.9*	−1,649.4	−788.70	–	–	–	–	519.15	2,291.5	824.81
Shareholder Approval Dummy	–	–	–	–	−103.88	−78.021	−132.40	–	–	–	–	−14.873	−52.713	136.73
Takeover Premium	–	–	–	–	0.377*	0.286	–	–	–	–	–	−0.239	−0.666	–

Panel C: Disclosing M&A	I	II	III		IV	V		I	II	III		IV	V	
	[0;0]	[0;0]	[0;0]	[0;0]	[0;0]	[0;0]	[0;0]	[−1;1]	[−1;1]	[−1;1]	[−1;1]	[−1;1]	[−1;1]	[−1;1]
N	33	33	33	33	33	33	33	33	33	33	33	33	33	33
max. VIF	1.63	3.14	5.78	3.97	2.96	7.17	4.09	1.70	2.59	5.77	3.90	3.23	7.31	3.63
R^2	19.39%	40.84%	35.32%	32.15%	36.90%	63.06%	54.77%	4.50%	14.85%	22.64%	20.36%	9.88%	50.68%	39.00%
adj. R^2	11.05%	24.28%	10.01%	9.53%	19.23%	21.19%	19.58%	−5.38%	−9.00%	−7.63%	−6.19%	−15.35%	−5.22%	−2.74%
F-statistic	2.84*	24.93***	1.11	1.18	3.30**	14.00***	21.96***	0.30	1.86	0.77	0.79	0.22	2.51**	1.92*

This table presents the results of a cross sectional regression analysis of abnormal change in the market value of equity (ACMVE) over the windows [0;+0] and [−1;+1] surrounding the M&A announcement date for the "Complete Sample", i.e. no adjustments for confounding events are performed. ACMVE on day t is calculated as the multiplication of a firm's market capitalization at fiscal year-end prior to the announcement and the abnormal stock return on day t. Panel A displays the results for the full sample, Panel B for the non-disclosing deals, and Panel C for the disclosing deals. Due to missing data, one observation had to be removed from the sample. Moreover, due to missing price data, another observation had to be removed from the [−1;1] regression of Panel A and B. Regressions with a maximum VIF of five or higher are recalculated only containing variables with a maximum VIF under five. Variables are defined as follows (in table order): Abnormal change in the market value of debt (ACMVD) on day t is calculated by first multiplying each abnormal bond return on day t with Total Debt at fiscal year-end prior to the announcement. Second, the equally weighted average is computed for every firm in the sample. Ln(Market Cap) presents the natural logarithm of market capitalization measured at fiscal year-end prior to the announcement. Ln(Deal Size) presents the natural logarithm of the amount paid for the target firm in the merger transaction. Current Ratio presents the ratio of current assets and current liabilities measured at fiscal year-end prior to the announcement. ROA is the return on assets measured at fiscal year-end prior to the announcement. Bidder leverage presents the ratio of total debt and the market value of equity measured at fiscal year-end prior to the announcement. Market to Book presents the ratio of the market price and the book value per share measured at fiscal year-end prior to the announcement. Due to outlier the variable Market to Book was winsorized at the 0.5% and 99.5% level. Policy Act 2005- (2007-) Dummy is a dummy variable equal to one for deals announced after the Energy Policy Act of 2005 (Energy Independence and Security Act of 2007) was signed into law. Industry-Dummy is a dummy variable equal to one, if the bidder's and target's two-digit SIC code are the same. SIC-49- (13-) (29-) Dummy is a dummy variable equal to one, if the bidding firm's two-digit SIC code is 49 (13) (29). Percentage of Stock presents the percentage equity financing of the deal. The Industry Liquidity Index is computed following Schlingemann et al. (2002), which represents the ratio of the value of M&A transactions in the energy industry (excluding minority stake purchases, leveraged buyouts, spin-offs, recapitalizations, self-tenders, exchange offers, repurchases and the sample deals) in a year and the total book value of assets of firms in the same two-digit SIC code for that year. Shareholder Approval-Dummy is a dummy variable equal to one, if shareholders of the bidding firm have to approve the deal. Takeover Premium presents the premium paid by the bidding firm. T-statistics are computed using robust standard errors adjusted for heteroskedasticity. The symbols ***, **, and * denote statistical significance at 1%, 5%, and 10% level, respectively.

Table 3-17: Cross Sectional Regression Analysis of Wealth Transfer between Bidders' Market Value of Equity and Market Value of Debt for the "Control Sample" (Yearly Data)

Panel A: All M&A	I	II	III		IV	V		I	II	III		IV	V	
	[0;0]	[0;0]	[0;0]	[0;0]	[0;0]	[0;0]	[0;0]	[−1;1]	[−1;1]	[−1;1]	[−1;1]	[−1;1]	[−1;1]	[−1;1]
Intercept	632.32**	739.57**	553.78**	–	690.02**	651.67*	659.54*	739.30**	845.88**	732.68**	–	661.41*	557.60	567.884
ACMVD	−2.299**	−1.892**	−2.290**	–	−1.915**	−1.44*	−1.505*	−1.012	−0.840	−1.053	–	−1.106	−0.875	−0.925
Ln(Market Cap)	−72.735**	−77.549**	−69.997**	–	−80.369**	−84.544	−79.194**	−84.265*	−90.336**	−89.858*	–	−92.11**	−100.36*	−91.695*
Ln(Deal Size)	−8.044	−11.855	−6.475	–	−5.019	2.096	2.757	−9.065	−11.108	−7.815	–	21.321	23.802	25.019
Current Ratio	–	−66.397	–	–	–	−57.083	−58.090	–	−43.321	–	–	–	−36.764	−38.443
ROA	–	−3.319	–	–	–	−6.412**	−6.444**	–	−2.923	–	–	–	−4.616	−4.702
Bidder Leverage	–	6.995	–	–	–	4.736	15.296	–	−13.708	–	–	–	26.381	43.851
Market to Book	–	15.643***	–	–	–	17.047***	15.683**	–	11.192**	–	–	–	25.981***	23.778***
Policy Act 2005-Dummy	–	–	21.834	–	–	70.122	69.501	–	–	−65.504	–	–	−5.002	−5.834
Policy Act 2007-Dummy	–	–	−45.363	–	–	−60.934	−60.835	–	–	56.442	–	–	26.369	26.837
Industry-Dummy	–	–	6.824	–	–	16.585	17.701	–	–	−52.379	–	–	−22.099	−19.518
SIC-49-Dummy	–	–	59.012	–	–	72.720	–	–	–	63.806	–	–	116.353	–
SIC-13-Dummy	–	–	81.104**	–	–	87.985**	32.975	–	–	157.45***	–	–	191.28***	103.212
SIC-29-Dummy	–	–	−71.392	–	–	−56.986	−117.388	–	–	127.667	–	–	170.746	74.476
Percentage of Stock	–	–	–	–	13.509	27.629	23.991	–	–	–	–	−98.71	−69.85	−75.683
Industry Liquidity Index	–	–	–	–	−517.38	−351.422	−402.411	–	–	–	–	−19.35	83.93	1.795
Shareholder Approval Dummy	–	–	–	–	−193.48**	−235.71***	−247.54***	–	–	–	–	−71.373	−63.545	−83.325
Takeover Premium	–	–	–	–	0.324	0.192	0.214	–	–	–	–	−0.351	−0.560*	−0.524*

Panel A: All M&A	I	II	III		IV	V		I	II	III		IV	V	
	[0;0]	[0;0]	[0;0]	[0;0]	[0;0]	[0;0]	[0;0]	[−1;1]	[−1;1]	[−1;1]	[−1;1]	[−1;1]	[−1;1]	[−1;1]
N	157	157	157	–	157	157	157	156	156	156	–	156	156	156
max. VIF	1.14	1.31	4.23	–	2.18	5.02	2.35	1.12	1.28	4.2	–	2.16	5.01	2.33
R^2	14.31%	20.62%	18.26%	–	18.93%	29.23%	28.83%	8.21%	9.64%	10.00%	–	12.30%	17.61%	17.17%
adj. R^2	12.63%	16.89%	13.25%	–	15.12%	20.57%	20.69%	6.40%	5.37%	4.45%	–	8.15%	7.46%	7.64%
F-statistic	2.76**	2.36**	1.73*	–	2.78***	2.49***	2.52***	1.95	1.47	2.09**	–	1.91*	1.99**	1.92**
Panel B: Non-disclosing M&A	I	II	III		IV	V		I	II	III		IV	V	
	[0;0]	[0;0]	[0;0]	[0;0]	[0;0]	[0;0]	[0;0]	[−1;1]	[−1;1]	[−1;1]	[−1;1]	[−1;1]	[−1;1]	[−1;1]
Intercept	738.10*	855.05**	618.89**	–	758.38**	732.49**	749.49**	757.00*	793.21**	749.54*	–	776.65*	720.88	741.223
ACMVD	−1.242*	−1.162	−1.017	–	−1.114	−0.861	−0.888	−0.683	−0.643	−0.656	–	−0.647	−0.604	−0.619
Ln(Market Cap)	−78.333*	−80.245**	−71.542**	–	−86.674**	−85.443**	−82.231**	−84.589*	−88.204*	−87.131	–	−96.209*	−96.418	−92.259
Ln(Deal Size)	−18.433	−20.870	−14.788	–	−7.974	−2.784	−1.507	−11.201	−10.636	−11.840	–	6.352	5.228	7.006
Current Ratio	–	−78.618	–	–	–	−39.899	−39.120	–	−5.300	–	–	–	0.348	1.509
ROA	–	−3.796	–	–	–	−5.210*	−5.101*	–	−2.605	–	–	–	−3.511	−3.390
Bidder Leverage	–	3.700	–	–	–	−27.970	−23.450	–	−23.907	–	–	–	4.262	10.312
Market to Book	–	6.962	–	–	–	8.127	5.997	–	10.580	–	–	–	13.285	10.563
Policy Act 2005-Dummy	–	–	8.628	–	–	38.520	34.594	–	–	−59.532	–	–	−37.776	−43.043
Policy Act 2007-Dummy	–	–	−53.798	–	–	−65.182	−66.689	–	–	−9.096	–	–	−20.962	−22.850
Industry-Dummy	–	–	23.643	–	–	48.794	50.581	–	–	−35.263	–	–	−22.568	−19.924
SIC-49-Dummy	–	–	65.960	–	–	56.851	–	–	–	69.061	–	–	72.853	–
SIC-13-Dummy	–	–	66.626*	–	–	40.712	−3.991	–	–	151.12***	–	–	141.92*	84.870
SIC-29-Dummy	–	–	−97.717	–	–	−99.384	−149.046	–	–	135.35	–	–	112.981	49.386
Percentage of Stock	–	–	–	–	65.724	57.300	59.165	–	–	–	–	−27.677	−52.12	−50.200
Industry Liquidity Index	–	–	–	–	−255.081	−204.40	−252.259	–	–	–	–	−352.626	−405.087	−466.940
Shareholder Approval Dummy	–	–	–	–	−364.12*	−354.837	−372.925	–	–	–	–	−170.963	−121.64	−144.831
Takeover Premium	–	–	–	–	0.654	0.507	0.523	–	–	–	–	−0.351	−0.336	−0.315

Panel B: Non-disclosing M&A	I	II	III		IV	V		I	II	III		IV	V	
	[0;0]	[0;0]	[0;0]	[0;0]	[0;0]	[0;0]	[0;0]	[−1;1]	[−1;1]	[−1;1]	[−1;1]	[−1;1]	[−1;1]	[−1;1]
N	131	131	131	–	131	131	131	130	130	130	–	130	130	130
max. VIF	1.11	1.29	4.61	–	2.45	5.96	2.63	1.10	1.26	4.56	–	2.45	5.95	2.63
R^2	15.26%	18.24%	20.63%	–	20.00%	27.32%	27.12%	7.92%	8.61%	9.81%	–	10.21%	12.25%	12.10%
adj. R^2	13.25%	13.59%	14.72%	–	15.45%	16.39%	16.89%	5.73%	3.37%	3.05%	–	5.06%	−1.07%	−0.35%
F-statistic	2	1.46	1.62	–	1.75	1.32	1.45	1.52	0.95	1.78*	–	2.09**	1.47	1.38

Panel C: Disclosing M&A	I	II	III		IV	V		I	II	III		IV	V	
	[0;0]	[0;0]	[0;0]	[0;0]	[0;0]	[0;0]	[0;0]	[−1;1]	[−1;1]	[−1;1]	[−1;1]	[−1;1]	[−1;1]	[−1;1]
Intercept	367.03	381.181	−7.36	127.155	466.35	337.31	561.309*	911.460	1,803.7*	578.97	798.56	231.31	−208.87	2,116.6**
ACMVD	−4.252**	−3.159*	−4.111	−4.136	−3.724*	−1.004	−2.242	−6.992**	−8.596*	−5.844**	−6.124**	−8.592***	−1.935	−5.952
Ln(Market Cap)	−70.875*	−74.092*	−47.990*	−76.062**	−87.251*	−115.02**	−130.84***	−119.459	−177.474*	−104.525	−149.290	−119.116	−120.163	−262.38**
Ln(Deal Size)	28.056	15.073	38.068	38.963	41.503	99.443**	80.685***	−4.331	−7.822	35.530	35.764	120.786	176.434*	82.326
Current Ratio	–	−166.122	–	–	–	−87.12	−187.29*	–	−519.71*	–	–	–	−49.98	−637.94**
ROA	–	25.058**	–	–	–	−10.053	8.642	–	20.407	–	–	–	−42.026	–
Bidder Leverage	–	78.132	–	–	–	−36.28	−15.888	–	176.38	–	–	–	−76.477	62.34
Market to Book	–	21.409***	–	164.699	–	28.946***	21.561***	–	−11.213	–	–	–	40.972	−8.566
Policy Act 2005-Dummy	–	–	183.48	164.70	–	272.13**	261.72**	–	–	−202.01	−231.38	–	229.354	107.518
Policy Act 2007-Dummy	–	–	110.45	30.691	–	−12.43	−48.19	–	–	586.21	455.19	–	397.443	299.647
Industry-Dummy	–	–	75.973	18.601	–	−5.743	−19.534	–	–	−29.924	−117.61	–	172.70	−34.037
SIC-49-Dummy	–	–	−251.22*	–	–	−87.57	–	–	–	−397.72	–	–	−306.56	–
SIC-13-Dummy	–	–	−63.32	153.69*	–	99.14	108.090	–	–	−82.73	263.150	–	142.80	276.165
SIC-29-Dummy	–	–	130.933	256.19**	–	236.447	313**	–	–	80.01	279.821	–	388.875	391.67
Percentage of Stock	–	–	–	–	−157.734	−74.509	−268.85**	–	–	–	–	−266.26	79.76	−527.057
Industry Liquidity Index	–	–	–	–	−1,772.855	−2,000.6	−2,571.0**	–	–	–	–	2,495.99	2,792.3	−1,059.71
Shareholder Approval Dummy	–	–	–	–	−57.77	−226.861	–	–	–	–	–	−12.987	−231.717	150.46
Takeover Premium	–	–	–	–	0.226	−0.121	–	–	–	–	–	−0.846***	−1.253**	–

Panel C: Disclosing M&A	I	II	III		IV	V		I	II	III		IV	V	
	[0;0]	[0;0]	[0;0]	[0;0]	[0;0]	[0;0]	[0;0]	[−1;1]	[−1;1]	[−1;1]	[−1;1]	[−1;1]	[−1;1]	[−1;1]
N	26	26	26	26	26	26	26	26	26	26	26	26	26	26
max. VIF	1.42	2.26	5.04	3.21	2.78	7.98	4.97	1.41	2.26	5.06	3.20	2.73	7.27	4.90
R^2	27.86%	62.84%	52.11%	46.53%	37.87%	89.02%	85.75%	23.96%	36.40%	43.99%	40.03%	54.78%	84.13%	61.65%
adj. R^2	18.03%	48.38%	25.18%	21.37%	13.71%	65.67%	67.61%	13.59%	11.67%	12.49%	11.81%	37.20%	50.41%	12.84%
F-statistic	2.41*	30.75***	2.26*	2.20*	2.46*	112.79***	136.20***	2.57*	2.22*	1.26	1.35	4.07***	26.36***	3.14**

This table presents the results of a cross sectional regression analysis of abnormal change in the market value of equity (ACMVE) over the windows [0;+0] and [−1;+1] surrounding the M&A announcement date for the "Control Sample", i.e. deals with confounding events at the three days surrounding the announcement day are excluded from the sample. ACMVE on day t is calculated as the multiplication of a firm's market capitalization at fiscal year-end prior to the announcement and the abnormal stock return on day t. Panel A displays the results for the full sample, Panel B for the non-disclosing deals, and Panel C for the disclosing deals. Due to missing data, one observation had to be removed from the sample. Moreover, due to missing price data, another observation had to be removed from the [−1;1] regression of Panel A and B. Regressions with a maximum VIF of five or higher are recalculated only containing variables with a maximum VIF under five. Variables are defined as follows (in table order): Abnormal change in the market value of debt (ACMVD) on day t is calculated by first multiplying each abnormal bond return on day t with Total Debt at fiscal year-end prior to the announcement. Second, the equally weighted average is computed for every firm in the sample. Ln(Market Cap) presents the natural logarithm of market capitalization measured at fiscal year-end prior to the announcement. Ln(Deal Size) presents the natural logarithm of the amount paid for the target firm in the merger transaction. Current Ratio presents the ratio of current assets and current liabilities measured at fiscal year-end prior to the announcement. ROA is the return on assets measured at fiscal year-end prior to the announcement. Bidder leverage presents the ratio of total debt and the market value of equity measured at fiscal year-end prior to the announcement. Market to Book presents the ratio of the market price and the book value per share measured at fiscal year-end prior to the announcement. Due to outlier the variable Market to Book was winsorized at the 0.5% and 99.5% level. Policy Act 2005- (2007-) Dummy is a dummy variable equal to one for deals announced after the Energy Policy Act of 2005 (Energy Independence and Security Act of 2007) was signed into law. Industry-Dummy is a dummy variable equal to one, if the bidder's and target's two-digit SIC code are the same. SIC-49- (13-) (29-) Dummy is a dummy variable equal to one if the bidding firm's two-digit SIC code is 49 (13) (29). Percentage of Stock presents the percentage equity financing of the deal. The Industry Liquidity Index is computed following Schlingemann et al. (2002), which represents the ratio of the value of M&A transactions in the energy industry (excluding minority stake purchases, leveraged buyouts, spin-offs, recapitalizations, self-tenders, exchange offers, repurchases and the sample deals) in a year and the total book value of assets of firms in the same two-digit SIC code for that year. Shareholder Approval-Dummy is a dummy variable equal to one, if shareholders of the bidding firm have to approve the deal. Takeover Premium presents the premium paid by the bidding firm. T-statistics are computed using robust standard errors adjusted for heteroskedasticity. The symbols ***, **, and * denote statistical significance at 1%, 5%, and 10% level, respectively.

Table 3-18: Cross Sectional Regression Analysis of Wealth Transfer between Bidders' Market Value of Equity and Market Value of Debt for the "Complete Sample" (Daily Data)

Panel A: All M&A	I	II	III		IV	V		I	II	III		IV	V	
	[0;0]	[0;0]	[0;0]	[0;0]	[0;0]	[0;0]	[0;0]	[−1;1]	[−1;1]	[−1;1]	[−1;1]	[−1;1]	[−1;1]	[−1;1]
Intercept	283.21	259.80	211.55	–	346.93	195.68	–	373.00	433.67	321.93	–	299.61	190.57	–
ACMVD	−10.153	−8.603	−10.019	–	−7.087	−5.651	–	−4.736	−4.187	−5.415	–	−5.161	−4.578	–
Ln(Market Cap)	−33.079	−30.789	−30.411	–	−42.008	−34.046	–	−38.175	−40.054	−36.883	–	−44.791	−40.155	–
Ln(Deal Size)	−1.294	−4.712	0.456	–	2.161	6.307	–	−9.991	−12.283	−11.421	–	16.696	13.356	–
Current Ratio	–	−13.471	–	–	–	−16.694	–	–	−31.100	–	–	–	−44.788	–
ROA	–	0.545	–	–	–	−2.331	–	–	−0.574	–	–	–	−0.963	–
Bidder Leverage	–	6.423	–	–	–	18.953	–	–	−12.459	–	–	–	22.664	–
Market to Book	–	10.110*	–	–	–	10.559**	–	–	5.383	–	–	–	11.075	–
Policy Act 2005-Dummy	–	–	51.719	–	–	76.805	–	–	–	−70.856	–	–	−37.665	–
Policy Act 2007-Dummy	–	–	−35.113	–	–	−45.966	–	–	–	94.093	–	–	93.892	–
Industry-Dummy	–	–	−6.170	–	–	−6.880	–	–	–	−30.737	–	–	−8.689	–
SIC-49-Dummy	–	–	24.176	–	–	14.956	–	–	–	25.729	–	–	39.972	–
SIC-13-Dummy	–	–	61.708*	–	–	67.072*	–	–	–	131.43***	–	–	130.73**	–
SIC-29-Dummy	–	–	−84.572	–	–	−92.283	–	–	–	42.716	–	–	52.342	–
Percentage of Stock	–	–	–	–	8.070	−1.579	–	–	–	–	–	−114.55	−122.29	–
Industry Liquidity Index	–	–	–	–	−234.79	142.091	–	–	–	–	–	169.61	456.65	–
Shareholder Approval Dummy	–	–	–	–	−218.91**	−249.98***	–	–	–	–	–	−64.796	−68.104	–
Takeover Premium	–	–	–	–	0.356	0.327	–	–	–	–	–	−0.237	−0.255	–

Panel A: All M&A	I	II	III		IV	V		I	II	III		IV	V	
	[0;0]	[0;0]	[0;0]	[0;0]	[0;0]	[0;0]	[0;0]	[−1;1]	[−1;1]	[−1;1]	[−1;1]	[−1;1]	[−1;1]	[−1;1]
N	204	204	204	–	204	204	–	203	203	203	–	203	203	–
max. VIF	1.14	1.32	3.96	–	2.26	4.34	–	1.16	1.26	3.94	–	2.26	4.32	–
R^2	2.69%	4.56%	5.77%	–	7.08%	12.77%	–	1.92%	2.40%	3.96%	–	4.64%	7.52%	–
adj. R^2	1.23%	1.15%	1.40%	–	3.76%	4.80%	–	0.44%	−1.11%	−0.52%	–	1.22%	−0.98%	–
F-statistic	0.73	0.68	1.08	–	1.87*	1.60*	–	0.64	0.63	1.37	–	0.98	0.97	–
Panel B: Non-disclosing M&A	I	II	III		IV	V		I	II	III		IV	V	
	[0;0]	[0;0]	[0;0]	[0;0]	[0;0]	[0;0]	[0;0]	[−1;1]	[−1;1]	[−1;1]	[−1;1]	[−1;1]	[−1;1]	[−1;1]
Intercept	337.69	435.29	252.93	–	362.37	294.68	–	327.26	449.15	294.16	–	347.01	348.88	–
ACMVD	−1.791	−4.230	−1.467	–	−0.705	−4.830	–	−2.803	−3.483	−3.333	–	−2.595	−3.630	–
Ln(Market Cap)	−35.129	−39.681	−29.475	–	−43.954	−39.810	–	−34.509	−41.733	−31.176	–	−44.690	−43.191	–
Ln(Deal Size)	−7.984	−10.514	−6.471	–	1.927	5.181	–	−6.965	−9.761	−11.266	–	8.096	3.384	–
Current Ratio	–	−17.529	–	–	–	15.808	–	–	−2.462	–	–	–	3.285	–
ROA	–	−0.419	–	–	–	−3.232	–	–	−0.494	–	–	–	−1.734	–
Bidder Leverage	–	−42.396	–	–	–	−51.307	–	–	−65.095	–	–	–	−37.866	–
Market to Book	–	1.700	–	–	–	6.176	–	–	1.594	–	–	–	5.050	–
Policy Act 2005-Dummy	–	–	50.873	–	–	58.060	–	–	–	−57.196	–	–	−59.597	–
Policy Act 2007-Dummy	–	–	−49.060	–	–	−57.263	–	–	–	25.698	–	–	29.696	–
Industry-Dummy	–	–	−14.133	–	–	−2.229	–	–	–	−23.572	–	–	−14.876	–
SIC-49-Dummy	–	–	22.312	–	–	24.269	–	–	–	19.096	–	–	28.131	–
SIC-13-Dummy	–	–	69.291**	–	–	55.875	–	–	–	130.123**	–	–	115.08*	–
SIC-29-Dummy	–	–	−100.010	–	–	−125.663	–	–	–	67.65	–	–	41.615	–
Percentage of Stock	–	–	–	–	36.967	31.563	–	–	–	–	–	−100.377	−122.57	–
Industry Liquidity Index	–	–	–	–	57.605	454.38	–	–	–	–	–	−99.507	46.907	–
Shareholder Approval Dummy	–	–	–	–	−343.912	−394.303	–	–	–	–	–	−113.821	−132.33	–
Takeover Premium	–	–	–	–	0.741	0.830	–	–	–	–	–	−0.212	−0.033	–

Panel B: Non-disclosing M&A	I	II	III		IV	V		I	II	III		IV	V	
	[0;0]	[0;0]	[0;0]	[0;0]	[0;0]	[0;0]	[0;0]	[−1;1]	[−1;1]	[−1;1]	[−1;1]	[−1;1]	[−1;1]	[−1;1]
N	171	171	171	–	171	171	–	170	170	170	–	170	170	–
max. VIF	1.10	1.33	4.06	–	2.28	4.49	–	1.11	1.29	4.04	–	2.28	4.49	–
R^2	2.44%	3.16%	6.21%	–	6.09%	11.56%	–	1.42%	2.20%	3.32%	–	3.12%	5.28%	–
adj. R^2	0.69%	−1.00%	0.96%	–	2.06%	1.73%	–	−0.37%	−2.03%	−2.12%	–	−1.07%	−5.32%	–
F-statistic	0.27	0.95	0.88	–	1.04	1.06	–	0.34	0.86	1.24	–	1.72	1.19	–

Panel C: Disclosing M&A	I	II	III		IV	V		I	II	III		IV	V	
	[0;0]	[0;0]	[0;0]	[0;0]	[0;0]	[0;0]	[0;0]	[−1;1]	[−1;1]	[−1;1]	[−1;1]	[−1;1]	[−1;1]	[−1;1]
Intercept	164.53	−35.798	−32.67	−1.676	346.30	216.47	2.913	570.263	1,260.04	494.36	607.91	71.92	−592.64	1,650.4
ACMVD	−22.385	−4.807	−18.883	−18.940	−16.940	8.157	7.871	−18.196	−18.337	−4.905	−7.201	−22.474	26.883	19.779
Ln(Market Cap)	−30.881	−22.930	−17.516	−28.890	−51.435	−44.730	−49.796	−64.002	−112.122	−64.059	−101.802	−46.576	9.947	−203.13
Ln(Deal Size)	13.756	6.306	13.045	15.914	15.305	19.588	30.809	−13.137	−8.796	26.175	33.702	52.119	50.526	54.495
Current Ratio	–	−59.492	–	–	–	−198.72	−120.473	–	−295.06	–	–	–	−257.35	−631.53*
ROA	–	15.450	–	–	–	3.665	5.048	–	−0.691	–	–	–	−16.730	−10.811
Bidder Leverage	–	104.64***	–	–	–	149.862**	122.718*	–	78.63	–	–	–	184.958*	112.75
Market to Book	–	23.941***	–	–	–	24.499*	30.860***	–	0.291	–	–	–	48.786	20.438
Policy Act 2005-Dummy	–	–	100.40	96.71	–	131.77	–	–	–	−424.21	−437.66	–	−139.173	–
Policy Act 2007-Dummy	–	–	82.47	54.642	–	203.38	208.75	–	–	788.79	688.57	–	1,115.12*	705.56*
Industry-Dummy	–	–	61.618	38.084	–	32.014	5.181	–	–	−87.427	−164.35	–	286.40	−20.505
SIC-49-Dummy	–	–	−100.87	–	–	−239.04	–	–	–	−338.39	–	–	−723.24	–
SIC-13-Dummy	–	–	−83.16	8.688	–	−139.32	59.178	–	–	−224.65	82.692	–	−446.60	146.003
SIC-29-Dummy	–	–	5.446	68.04	–	−9.045	115.08	–	–	−227.07	−18.838	–	−102.384	190.13
Percentage of Stock	–	–	–	–	−29.683	134.337	248.15	–	–	–	–	−57.98	518.52	−171.170
Industry Liquidity Index	–	–	–	–	−1,720.163	−1,336.2	−880.27	–	–	–	–	2,507.39	4,260.8	525.13
Shareholder Approval Dummy	–	–	–	–	−161.03	−196.194	−238.21	–	–	–	–	−65.618	−35.653	67.38
Takeover Premium	–	–	–	–	0.327	0.184	–	–	–	–	–	−0.511	−0.906	–

Panel C: Disclosing M&A	I	II	III		IV	V		I	II	III		IV	V	
	[0;0]	[0;0]	[0;0]	[0;0]	[0;0]	[0;0]	[0;0]	[−1;1]	[−1;1]	[−1;1]	[−1;1]	[−1;1]	[−1;1]	[−1;1]
N	33	33	33	33	33	33	33	33	33	33	33	33	33	33
max. VIF	1.59	2.00	5.50	3.88	3.02	7.18	4.06	1.64	2.09	5.63	3.88	3.11	7.22	3.93
R^2	11.32%	36.78%	17.54%	16.84%	23.46%	59.58%	53.91%	5.81%	−12.82%	23.44%	21.46%	15.32%	55.18%	40.93%
adj. R^2	2.15%	19.08%	−14.73%	−10.88%	2.03%	13.78%	18.07%	−3.94%	11.86%	−6.52%	−4.72%	−8.40%	4.39%	−5.02%
F-statistic	0.64	29.51***	0.38	0.44	1.27	14.70***	18.96***	1.01	2.40*	0.79	0.90	0.26	2.14*	1.33

This table presents the results of a cross sectional regression analysis of abnormal change in the market value of equity (ACMVE) over the windows [0;+0] and [−1;+1] surrounding the M&A announcement date for the "Complete Sample", i.e. no adjustments for confounding events are performed. ACMVE on day t is calculated as the multiplication of a firm's market capitalization on day t-1 and the abnormal stock return on day t. Panel A displays the results for the full sample, Panel B for the non-disclosing deals, and Panel C for the disclosing deals. Due to missing data, one observation had to be removed from the sample. Moreover, due to missing price data, another observation had to be removed from the [−1;1] regression of Panel A and B. Regressions with a maximum VIF of five or higher are recalculated only containing variables with a maximum VIF under five. Variables are defined as follows (in table order): Abnormal change in the market value of debt (ACMVD) on day t is calculated by first multiplying each abnormal bond return on day t with the bond's respective market value on day t-1. Second, the equally weighted average is computed for every firm in the sample. Ln(Market Cap) presents the natural logarithm of market capitalization measured at fiscal year-end prior to the announcement. Ln(Deal Size) presents the natural logarithm of the amount paid for the target firm in the merger transaction. Current Ratio presents the ratio of current assets and current liabilities measured at fiscal year-end prior to the announcement. ROA is the return on assets measured at fiscal year-end prior to the announcement. Bidder leverage presents the ratio of total debt and the market value of equity measured at fiscal year-end prior to the announcement. Market to Book presents the ratio of the market price and the book value per share measured at fiscal year-end prior to the announcement. Due to outlier the variable Market to Book was winsorized at the 0.5% and 99.5% level. Policy Act 2005- (2007-) Dummy is a dummy variable equal to one for deals announced after the Energy Policy Act of 2005 (Energy Independence and Security Act of 2007) was signed into law. Industry-Dummy is a dummy variable equal to one, if the bidder's and target's two-digit SIC code are the same. SIC-49- (13-) (29-) Dummy is a dummy variable equal to one if the bidding firm's two-digit SIC code is 49 (13) (29). Percentage of Stock presents the percentage equity financing of the deal. The Industry Liquidity Index is computed following Schlingemann et al. (2002), which represents the ratio of the value of M&A transactions in the energy industry (excluding minority stake purchases, leveraged buyouts, spin-offs, recapitalizations, self-tenders, exchange offers, repurchases and the sample deals) in a year and the total book value of assets of firms in the same two-digit SIC code for that year. Shareholder Approval-Dummy is a dummy variable equal to one, if shareholders of the bidding firm have to approve the deal. Takeover Premium presents the premium paid by the bidding firm. T-statistics are computed using robust standard errors adjusted for heteroskedasticity. The symbols ***, **, and * denote statistical significance at 1%, 5%, and 10% level, respectively.

Table 3-19: Cross Sectional Regression Analysis of Wealth Transfer between Bidders' Market Value of Equity and Market Value of Debt for the "Control Sample" (Daily Data)

Panel A: All M&A	I	II	III		IV	V		I	II	III		IV	V	
	[0;0]	[0;0]	[0;0]	[0;0]	[0;0]	[0;0]	[0;0]	[−1;1]	[−1;1]	[−1;1]	[−1;1]	[−1;1]	[−1;1]	[−1;1]
Intercept	635.70*	775.60**	540.86*	–	699.56*	677.24*	685.50*	778.90**	934.07**	759.52**	–	683.86*	593.93	607.943
ACMVD	−19.554*	−15.287**	−18.819*	–	−15.823**	−11.263*	−11.940*	−5.008	−3.488	−5.862	–	−6.489	−3.913	−4.291
Ln(Market Cap)	−72.181*	−78.553**	−68.198**	–	−81.314**	−86.132**	−80.735**	−86.596**	−95.226**	−90.776**	–	−94.460**	−105.42*	−95.454*
Ln(Deal Size)	−8.880	−12.449	−7.193	–	−4.253	3.561	4.255	−11.978	−14.110	−10.541	–	22.068	25.410	26.838
Current Ratio	–	−77.392	–	–	–	−64.938	−65.826	–	−64.961	–	–	–	−54.897	−56.569
ROA	–	−4.231	–	–	–	−7.288**	−7.356***	–	−2.808	–	–	–	−4.448	−4.582
Bidder Leverage	–	5.003	–	–	–	−1.621	8.462	–	−19.165	–	–	–	17.815	37.141
Market to Book	–	15.358**	–	–	–	16.845***	15.409**	–	11.379**	–	–	–	28.224***	25.639**
Policy Act 2005-Dummy	–	–	18.117	–	–	73.326	72.276	–	–	−87.110	–	–	−20.421	−21.911
Policy Act 2007-Dummy	–	–	−44.501	–	–	−62.511	−62.456	–	–	83.855	–	–	57.921	58.465
Industry-Dummy	–	–	19.323	–	–	29.259	30.486	–	–	−59.322	–	–	−18.678	−16.113
SIC-49-Dummy	–	–	62.804	–	–	72.759	–	–	–	66.482	–	–	135.011	–
SIC-13-Dummy	–	–	78.019**	–	–	81.707*	26.507	–	–	177.31***	–	–	211.54***	109.270
SIC-29-Dummy	–	–	−96.182	–	–	−88.079	−148.795	–	–	94.101	–	–	151.875	39.193
Percentage of Stock	–	–	–	–	1.327	14.561	11.004	–	–	–	–	−118.07	−96.00	−102.218
Industry Liquidity Index	–	–	–	–	−535.76	−348.073	−398.534	–	–	–	–	24.23	203.11	107.545
Shareholder Approval Dummy	–	–	–	–	−210.66**	−260.26***	−272.38***	–	–	–	–	−53.898	−43.168	−66.964
Takeover Premium	–	–	–	–	0.347	0.223	0.244	–	–	–	–	−0.448	−0.665*	−0.624

Panel A: All M&A	I	II	III		IV	V		I	II	III		IV	V	
	[0;0]	[0;0]	[0;0]	[0;0]	[0;0]	[0;0]	[0;0]	[−1;1]	[−1;1]	[−1;1]	[−1;1]	[−1;1]	[−1;1]	[−1;1]
N	157	157	157	–	157	157	157	156	156	156	–	156	156	156
max. VIF	1.14	1.34	4.22	–	2.17	5.04	2.36	1.14	1.33	4.2	–	2.16	5	2.33
R^2	13.24%	19.14%	17.75%	–	17.97%	28.72%	28.38%	7.13%	8.83%	9.29%	–	12.24%	18.29%	17.76%
adj. R^2	11.54%	15.34%	12.72%	–	14.12%	20.00%	20.19%	5.30%	4.51%	3.69%	–	8.09%	8.23%	8.29%
F-statistic	2.42*	2.81***	1.38	–	2.76***	2.66***	2.66***	1.73	1.57	2.05**	–	1.83*	1.78**	1.77**
Panel B: Non-disclosing M&A	**I**	**II**	**III**		**IV**	**V**		**I**	**II**	**III**		**IV**	**V**	
	[0;0]	[0;0]	[0;0]	[0;0]	[0;0]	[0;0]	[0;0]	[−1;1]	[−1;1]	[−1;1]	[−1;1]	[−1;1]	[−1;1]	[−1;1]
Intercept	770.54*	911.17**	627.02*	–	794.92*	771.56**	788.00**	796.34**	877.85**	758.72**	–	822.96*	771.89*	794.07*
ACMVD	−7.978*	−9.240*	−6.053	–	−8.606**	−9.173	−9.455*	−2.267	−2.359	−2.441	–	−2.131	−2.358	−2.437
Ln(Market Cap)	−81.129*	−83.107*	−73.106*	–	−89.406**	−87.277**	−84.212**	−87.608*	−92.920*	−87.611*	–	−99.078*	−98.730*	−94.399*
Ln(Deal Size)	−19.477	−22.495	−15.182	–	−9.627	−3.556	−2.337	−13.157	−13.641	−13.018	–	3.221	2.679	4.554
Current Ratio	–	−90.316	–	–	–	−41.234	−40.439	–	−22.671	–	–	–	−6.733	−5.481
ROA	–	−4.478	–	–	–	−6.029*	−5.943*	–	−2.239	–	–	–	−3.269	−3.146
Bidder Leverage	–	2.709	–	–	–	−38.163	−34.089	–	−32.364	–	–	–	−7.113	−1.047
Market to Book	–	6.082	–	–	–	6.990	4.953	–	9.504	–	–	–	12.047	9.182
Policy Act 2005-Dummy	–	–	14.315	–	–	42.463	38.576	–	–	−65.223	–	–	−47.123	−52.803
Policy Act 2007-Dummy	–	–	−58.835	–	–	−72.244	−73.697	–	–	−3.544	–	–	−10.452	−12.452
Industry-Dummy	–	–	37.263	–	–	59.916	61.696	–	–	−36.019	–	–	−22.092	−19.407
SIC-49-Dummy	–	–	71.840	–	–	54.117	–	–	–	73.769	–	–	76.627	–
SIC-13-Dummy	–	–	63.808	–	–	34.914	−7.756	–	–	169.08***	–	–	157.05**	96.947
SIC-29-Dummy	–	–	−123.444	–	–	−129.570	−176.96*	–	–	100.21	–	–	82.399	15.199
Percentage of Stock	–	–	–	–	46.733	40.162	41.907	–	–	–	–	−45.740	−75.38	−73.175
Industry Liquidity Index	–	–	–	–	−280.058	−186.28	−231.681	–	–	–	–	−441.335	−411.837	−477.514
Shareholder Approval Dummy	–	–	–	–	−398.14*	−393.565	−410.97*	–	–	–	–	−192.386	−145.16	−169.824
Takeover Premium	–	–	–	–	0.906	0.745	0.761	–	–	–	–	−0.098	−0.086	−0.064

Panel B: Non-disclosing M&A	I	II	III		IV	V		I	II	III		IV	V	
	[0;0]	[0;0]	[0;0]	[0;0]	[0;0]	[0;0]	[0;0]	[−1;1]	[−1;1]	[−1;1]	[−1;1]	[−1;1]	[−1;1]	[−1;1]
N	131	131	131	–	131	131	131	130	130	130	–	130	130	130
max. VIF	1.11	1.30	4.60	–	2.45	5.97	2.62	1.11	1.29	4.56	–	2.45	5.94	2.62
R^2	14.16%	17.35%	20.46%	–	19.80%	27.93%	27.77%	7.80%	8.62%	9.91%	–	9.72%	12.09%	11.92%
adj. R^2	12.13%	12.65%	14.54%	–	15.24%	17.08%	17.63%	5.60%	3.38%	3.15%	–	4.54%	−1.25%	−0.55%
F-statistic	2.44*	1,82*	1.2	–	1.97*	1.43	1.57*	1.42	1.08	1.86*	–	1.94*	1.41	1.31

Panel C: Disclosing M&A	I	II	III		IV	V		I	II	III		IV	V	
	[0;0]	[0;0]	[0;0]	[0;0]	[0;0]	[0;0]	[0;0]	[−1;1]	[−1;1]	[−1;1]	[−1;1]	[−1;1]	[−1;1]	[−1;1]
Intercept	274.22	326.923	−56.03	88.250	247.00	76.45	569.453	760.920	1,886.66	479.37	765.93	−436.02	−860.91	2,443.1*
ACMVD	−42.242**	−25.416	−42.491*	−43.633*	−37.421*	−6.803	−16.160	−29.827**	−51.020	−20.338*	−22.901*	−70.488***	−6.015	−13.581
Ln(Market Cap)	−52.834	−60.760	−33.673	−63.297*	−68.803	−101.76*	−127.31**	−95.161	−162.782	−89.614	−147.700	−75.897	−89.790	−291.72*
Ln(Deal Size)	20.366	10.836	32.757	33.352	55.710	117.09**	83.097**	−7.427	−15.248	50.737	50.963	175.09*	216.969	105.666
Current Ratio	–	−196.23*	–	–	–	−31.46	−214.73*	–	−640.97*	–	–	–	60.07	−793.86**
ROA	–	28.326*	–	–	–	−15.712	8.776	–	23.025	–	–	–	−52.167	–
Bidder Leverage	–	83.995	–	–	–	−58.48	−20.646	–	199.20	–	–	–	−128.852	77.84
Market to Book	–	20.045**	–	–	–	35.868***	21.425***	–	−18.737	–	–	–	57.556*	–
Policy Act 2005-Dummy	–	–	157.73	137.34	–	305.88**	242.68**	–	–	−335.67	−376.42	–	186.387	21.640
Policy Act 2007-Dummy	–	–	120.77	34.374	–	−38.16	–	–	–	863.00	691.88	–	579.566	521.425
Industry-Dummy	–	–	49.418	−10.996	–	13.281	−37.299	–	–	−100.034	−219.64	–	246.09	−132.644
SIC-49-Dummy	–	–	−265.24	–	–	−83.00	–	–	–	−522.81	–	–	−382.78	–
SIC-13-Dummy	–	–	−23.99	207.20*	–	141.89	130.189	–	–	−183.19	273.614	–	125.94	291.397
SIC-29-Dummy	–	–	119.245	250.95*	–	234.043	304.57**	–	–	−0.44	261.210	–	434.254	336.79
Percentage of Stock	–	–	–	–	−133.613	−33.220	−303.54**	–	–	–	–	−188.23	240.36	−590.268
Industry Liquidity Index	–	–	–	–	−1,152.848	−1,383.3	−2,298.2*	–	–	–	–	5,289.1**	4,590.5	−819.29
Shareholder Approval Dummy	–	–	–	–	−121.34	−332.64*	–	–	–	–	–	−173.510	−326.333	124.36
Takeover Premium	–	–	–	–	0.082	−0.271	–	–	–	–	–	−1.467***	−1.779**	–

Panel C: Disclosing M&A	I	II	III		IV	V		I	II	III		IV	V	
	[0;0]	[0;0]	[0;0]	[0;0]	[0;0]	[0;0]	[0;0]	[−1;1]	[−1;1]	[−1;1]	[−1;1]	[−1;1]	[−1;1]	[−1;1]
N	26	26	26	26	26	26	26	26	26	26	26	26	26	26
max. VIF	1.26	2.26	5.05	3.20	2.71	7.06	3.13	1.42	4.55	5.08	3.20	2.70	10.25	4.79
R^2	32.50%	57.68%	55.60%	50.51%	15.72%	87.79%	79.83%	11.12%	23.39%	35.47%	30.90%	58.74%	83.71%	52.47%
adj. R^2	23.29%	41.22%	30.63%	27.23%	39.31%	61.85%	57.98%	−1.00%	−6.40%	−0.82%	−1.62%	42.70%	49.10%	0.97%
F-statistic	2.65*	52.64***	1.32	1.70	2.10*	113.98***	23.86***	2.09	2.06	1.80	1.66	4.92***	18.21***	1.74

This table presents the results of a cross sectional regression analysis of abnormal change in the market value of equity (ACMVE) over the windows [0;+0] and [−1;+1] surrounding the M&A announcement date for the "Control Sample", i.e. deals with confounding events at the three days surrounding the announcement day are excluded from the sample. ACMVE on day t is calculated as the multiplication of a firm's market capitalization on day t-1 and the abnormal stock return on day t. Panel A displays the results for the full sample, Panel B for the non-disclosing deals, and Panel C for the disclosing deals. Due to missing data, one observation had to be removed from the sample. Moreover, due to missing price data, another observation had to be removed from the [−1;1] regression of Panel A and B. Regressions with a maximum VIF of five or higher are recalculated only containing variables with a maximum VIF under five. Variables are defined as follows (in table order): Abnormal change in the market value of debt (ACMVD) on day t is calculated by first, multiplying each abnormal bond return on day t with the bond's respective market value on day t-1. Second, the equally weighted average is computed for every firm in the sample. Ln(Market Cap) presents the natural logarithm of market capitalization measured at fiscal year-end prior to the announcement. Ln(Deal Size) presents the natural logarithm of the amount paid for the target firm in the merger transaction. Current Ratio presents the ratio of current assets and current liabilities measured at fiscal year-end prior to the announcement. ROA is the return on assets measured at fiscal year-end prior to the announcement. Bidder leverage presents the ratio of total debt and the market value of equity measured at fiscal year-end prior to the announcement. Market to Book presents the ratio of the market price and the book value per share measured at fiscal year-end prior to the announcement. Due to outlier the variable Market to Book was winsorized at the 0.5% and 99.5% level. Policy Act 2005- (2007-) Dummy is a dummy variable equal to one for deals announced after the Energy Policy Act of 2005 (Energy Independence and Security Act of 2007) was signed into law. Industry-Dummy is a dummy variable equal to one if the bidder's and target's two-digit SIC code are the same. SIC-49- (13-) (29-) Dummy is a dummy variable equal to one if the bidding firm's two-digit SIC code is 49 (13) (29). Percentage of Stock presents the percentage equity financing of the deal. The Industry Liquidity Index is computed following Schlingemann et al. (2002), which represents the ratio of the value of M&A transactions in the energy industry (excluding minority stake purchases, leveraged buyouts, spin-offs, recapitalizations, self-tenders, exchange offers, repurchases and the sample deals) in a year and the total book value of assets of firms in the same two-digit SIC code for that year. Shareholder Approval-Dummy is a dummy variable equal to one if shareholders of the bidding firm have to approve the deal. Takeover Premium presents the premium paid by the bidding firm. T-statistics are computed using robust standard errors adjusted for heteroskedasticity. The symbols ***, **, and * denote statistical significance at 1%, 5%, and 10% level, respectively.

3.4 Summary and Conclusion

One of the upcoming topics in empirical M&A research is the investigation of management's decision to voluntarily disclose synergy estimates and how they affect stockholder returns. So far, researchers agree on a positive wealth effect for bidding firm shareholders indicating that synergies serve as a valid instrument to signal successful deals and to reduce prevalent information asymmetries. Still unclear, however, is the impact on merging firm's bondholders. On the one hand, bondholders might share the benefits of management forecasts of merger-related gains with shareholders, leading to a positive impact on bondholders' wealth. This would be in line with the synergy hypothesis. On the other hand, gains for shareholders might be expropriated from the firm's bondholders, causing negative bond returns (incentive hypothesis). The objective is to shed light on the bondholder wealth effect due to disclosing deals.

The impact of synergy forecast by merging firm's management on bidders' stock and bond returns is examined in the US energy industry. This industry is selected because it's one with the highest bond issuing and synergy disclosure rate. This thesis is the first of which the author is aware to provide insight into the difference between the impact of disclosing and non-disclosing deals on bondholder wealth.

Consistent with prior research the results show that management's decision to disclose synergy estimates has a positive impact on the abnormal stock returns of bidding companies. Cross sectional regression suggests that synergy estimates along with the merger announcement result in approximately 1.3% higher stock announcement returns. In contrast to the bidding firm's stock returns, bondholders on average experience a wealth loss of approximately –20 bps over the three day event window [–1;1]. This negative impact of synergy forecasts is confirmed by the regression analysis with a statistically significant negative coefficient, which also indicates the existence of a wealth transfer from bondholders to stockholders.

The Person correlation and a second regression analysis with the abnormal change in the market value of equity as a dependent and the abnormal change in the market value of debt as an independent variable is calculated to investigate if wealth is expropriated from bondholders to stockholders. Browsing the results of the Pearson correlation presents no significant impact for the full sample (disclosing and non-disclosing deals) and the non-disclosing M&A. Yet, disclosing deals present highly significant coefficients which, in line with the expectations, point to the existence of a redistribution of wealth. Cross sectional regression, however, provides inconsistent results which exhibit statistically significant and insignificant coefficients, depending on the applied model. The assumption, however, is that this discrepancy stems from a purely statistical requirement, i.e. the necessity of a large enough number of observations to conduct cross sectional regressions. To infer the non-existence of a transfer of wealth from the results would be at least as incorrect as the conclusion that a clear redistribution effect was detected. Altogether, the strong results of the Pearson correlation, the fact that most coefficients in the regression analysis turn out to be negative and that several of them exhibit statistical significance, lead to the conclusion that evidence was found, albeit weak, that synergy disclosing deals experience an expropriation of wealth from bondholders to stockholders.

Overall, the conclusion is that management's decision to voluntarily disclose synergy estimates leads to negative abnormal bond returns as well as a wealth transfer from bondholders to stockholders. Therefore synergy forecasts no longer can be seen as purely firm value enhancing strategy, proving the necessity for management and research to regard both stakeholder classes to fully assess the impact. Future research might analyze how merging companies associated with voluntary synergy disclosure fare after deal completion. It would be interesting to further examine if the credit risk really has increased.

4. Wealth Effects of Corporate Bond Reopenings

The cost of capital and its implication for corporate finance is one of the crucial challenges for a company's management. Thus, executives are frequently confronted with the question how to finance investments, through equity, debt, or a combination of both. Due to its importance, this subject has also found its way into the academic world and lead to outstanding papers like the seminal work by Modigliani and Miller (1958) about the irrelevance of a firm's capital structure. However, since the assumptions in a Modigliani and Miller world about capital markets are rather strict and do not apply to the real world in general, various researchers devoted themselves to empirically investigate the impact of financing decisions on firm value. Several hypotheses were developed and tested like the Pecking Order Theory (Myers & Majluf, 1984), the Free Cash Flow Theory (Jensen, 1986), or the Market Timing Hypothesis (Baker & Wurgler, 2002). However, the greater part of this research investigates changes in a company's equity, demonstrating a clear dominance of equity securities over debt securities.[46] In the past, the issuance of bonds did not possess the same appeal for researchers as SEO did, for instance. The result of this disregard is that empirical evidence on the impact of debt offerings on firm value is scarce and inconclusive. Present research however, begins to discover the potential of this subject and reveals new and interesting challenges that need to be investigated. This thesis is one of them and deals with a purely debt related subject, academics and practitioners should be interested in: reopenings of corporate bonds.

A new tendency is emerging for companies in Europe with regard to raising funds from the debt market: reopenings, also referred to as tap issues.[47] A reopening, usually known in context with government bonds (Bertocchi, 1993;

---

46 For instance, conducting a keyword search in the Wiley Online Library utilizing the keywords "Event Study" (chosen because Event Study methodology is frequently used to examine effects on firm value) and "Equity Offering" lead to 370 hits, while using the keywords "Event Study" and "Debt Offering" leads to just 89 hits (Date: December 10, 2014).

47 The "Tap Issue Flag" in Thomson One Banker identifies reopenings of corporate bonds. Therefore, the terms reopening (to reopen) and tap (to tap) are used interchangeably, only referring to announcements that lead to actual bond issues hereby excluding shelf offerings.

del Valle & Ugolini, 2001; Weil, 1973), describes the fact that an issuing entity (e.g. a government or corporation) decides to reopen an existing debt issue. This procedure includes two steps: First, a new issue is conducted with identical configurations (i.e. final maturity date, coupon rate, covenants, etc.) as the prior debt offering. The only modification concerns the price of the bond that adjusts to the present conditions of the debt market. Second, the new issue is consolidated with the prior offering forming a single series. Such an offering of debt has several advantages compared to regular issues, which makes them attractive not only for governments but also for corporations. First and foremost, the issuing company is not required to prepare a new prospectus as the terms are already finalized in the previous offering. Thus, reopenings represent an inexpensive way to raise extra money compared to regular issues. Second, the liquidity in the secondary market of the reopened bond is enhanced which leads to higher prices and lowers the yield. Third, the investor sentiment can be tested before choosing an offering size that is too large and hence not all bonds can be placed. Or managers can take advantage of the window of opportunity and issue fast new debt while the corporate bond is still overvalued.

To provide an impression about the development of reopenings in Europe Table 4-1 documents all straight corporate bond issues (except by "Financials"[48]) issued between January 01, 2000 and February 20, 2014 (Source: Thomson One Banker).

48 As indicated by the Thomson One Banker Macro Description.

Table 4-1: Number of Debt Offerings by Issue Year

Year	No. of bond issues	No. of reopenings	Percentage of reopened issues
2000	369	0	0.00%
2001	401	0	0.00%
2002	314	0	0.00%
2003	323	0	0.00%
2004	275	0	0.00%
2005	245	8	3.27%
2006	303	36	11.88%
2007	261	34	13.03%
2008	273	86	31.50%
2009	560	58	10.36%
2010	392	30	7.65%
2011	428	40	9.35%
2012	690	62	8.99%
2013	632	40	6.33%
2014	79	10	12.66%
Total	**5545**	**404**	**7.29%**

This table presents the number of debt offerings and the number of reopenings per year. The sample consists of straight corporate debt issues (including zeros and excluding convertibles, asset- and mortgage-backed securities, perpetuals, preferred shares as well as issues by financial firms) issued between January 01, 2000 and February 20, 2014. Only offerings with a "Tap Issue Flag" set Y for Yes or N for No are included.

Table 4-1 clearly shows that European companies refrained from reopening bonds till the year 2005. In 2008 the portion of reopened issues reached a maximum with 31.5% of all issues, while only a third of this value was reached in subsequent years. Nevertheless, considering only the years 2005 to 2014 shows that about 10% of all debt offerings are reopenings, further highlighting the significance of this bond issue type.

The main contribution to financial research is twofold: First, managers are provided with the first evaluation of how shareholders and bondholders respond to bond reopenings in comparison to regular debt offerings. As exemplified in Table 4-1, reopenings represent a rather new and innovative way to offer debt. This chapter provides first evidence to enhance chief financial management's understanding of reopenings and shows the impact of the offering type on short-term firm value. Second, prior research of debt offerings on stockholder and bondholder wealth is characterized by mixed evidence and various attempts to explain the diverging results. Nevertheless, no paper differentiates between regular offerings and offerings through reopening, thus providing no assessment about the impact of the offering type on bond and stock returns. The growing significance of taps in recent years, especially in Europe, as a convenient way to raise funds highlights the necessity for a separated examination of this offering type. Thereby, this chapter helps to further explain the discrepancy of event study results concerning debt offerings.

4.1 Related Research

So far research has neglected to address the issue of different debt offering types. This is the reason why, to this point, no paper examines how capital markets act in response to reopenings. Reviewing literature about debt offerings provides conflicting results about stockholder and bondholder wealth effects. Table 4-2 provides an overview of empirical results concerning shareholder and bondholder wealth effects due to bond issue announcements.

Table 4-2: Results of Papers examining Debt Offering Announcements

Paper	Security	Effect	Window	(C)AR	Test-statistic	
Dann & Mikkelson (1984)	Stock	–	[–1,0]	–0.37%	–1.76	t-statistic
Eckbo (1986)	Stock	0	[–1,0]	–0.06%	–0.44	z-statistic
Mikkelson & Partch (1986)	Stock	0	[–1,0]	–0.23%	–1.4	z-statistic
Kolodny & Suhler (1988)	Stock	0	[0]	–0.014%	–0.075	t-statistic
	Bond	+	[0] month	1.95%	2.33	t-statistic
Hansen & Crutchley (1990)	Stock	0	[–1,0]	0.11%	0.52	NA
Jensen & Pugh (1991)	Stock	–	[–1,0]	–0.51%	–1.38	z-statistic
Shyam-Sunder (1991)	Stock	0	[–1,0]	–0.11%	–0.76	t-statistic
Chaplinsky & Hansen (1993)	Stock	0	[–1,0]	0.05%	0.22	NA
Cook & Easterwood (1994)	Stock	0	[–1,+1]	–0.11%	–0.73	z-statistic
	Bond	+	[0] month	0.16%	1.97	z-statistic
Johnson (1995)	Stock	0	[–1,0]	0.32%	1.13	z-statistic
Akhigbe et al. (1997)	Stock	0	[–1,+1]	–0.17%	–1.28	z-statistic
	Bond	+	[0] week[a]	0.19%	1.70	t-statistic
Datta et al. (1997)	Bond	0	[1;1]	0.154%	0.67	z-statistic
Howton et al. (1998)	Stock	–	[0;0]	–0.387%	–5.53	t-statistic
Castillo (2001)	Stock	0	[–1,0]	–0.28%	–1.16	t-statistic
Chen (2013)	Bond	–	[–1,1]	–0.16	NA	t-statistic
	Stock	+	[–3;3]	0.45%	NA	t-statistic

This table presents abnormal stock and bond returns around the announcement day of prior research investigating debt offerings. The signs +, –, and 0 in the "Effect" column indicate significantly positive, significantly negative, or insignificant price responses, respectively. Windows are daily unless indicated otherwise. [a]indicates that the utilized period is not stated clearly in the paper.

Several papers find negative abnormal stock returns (Dann & Mikkelson, 1984; Howton, Howton, & Perfect, 1998; Jensen & Pugh, 1991) while most researchers present results which reveal that stockholders generally do not react at the announcement of bond issues (Akhigbe, Easterwood, & Pettit, 1997; Castillo, 2001; Chaplinsky & Hansen, 1993; Cook & Easterwood, 1994; Eckbo, 1986; Hansen & Crutchley, 1990; Johnson, 1995; Kolodny & Suhler, 1988; Mikkelson & Partch, 1986; Shyam-Sunder, 1991). With regard to abnormal bond returns most research presents positive effects. While Datta, Iskandar-Datta, and Patel (1997) find statistically insignificant price responses, Kolodny and Suhler (1988), Cook and Easterwood (1994), and Akhigbe et al. (1997) show that bondholders experience a wealth appreciation at bond issue announcements. The latest paper by Chen (2013) however, detects that stock prices increase while bond prices decline at the announcement, hereby contradicting all prior evidence and adding further to the inconclusiveness of results.

Various hypotheses have been developed to predict stockholder and bondholder wealth effects due to debt offering announcements, the most common being the positive signaling or free cash flow hypothesis by Ross (1977) and Jensen (1986), the negative signaling or cash flow shortfall hypothesis by Miller and Rock (1985) and the wealth transfer hypothesis by Merton (1974), Galai and Masulis (1976), and Smith Jr and Warner (1979). According to Ross (1977) higher leverage signals more productive firms, because they can sustain greater risk. Jensen (1986) argues that debt reduces the agency costs of free cash flows, by ensuring that cash is paid out to bondholders and not invested in unprofitable projects.[49] Therefore, both predict positive abnormal stock and bond returns. Negative price effects are predicted by Miller and Rock (1985) who expect financing announcements to be adverse events when a firm's expected net cash flow had been positive. Finally, if newly raised debt increases a firm's riskiness and the market value remains unchanged, then positive stock returns are a pure redistribution of wealth from the company's bondholders to equityholders (Galai & Masulis, 1976; Merton, 1974; Smith Jr & Warner, 1979). Nevertheless, no study so far has considered that capital markets respond differently with regard to the bond issue types. It is the objective of this chapter to fill this gap. Reopenings, unlike regular debt offerings, provide a different setting as management might exploit overvalued debt by reopening existing bonds. This would be consistent with the window of opportunity framework and should have a negative impact on the wealth effects associated with reopenings (Loughran & Ritter, 1995; Ritter, 1991)

49 Jensen (1986) calls this hypothesis "control hypothesis".

On the one hand, investors could react independently from the issue type, generating the same price responses for taps as for regular bond offerings. On the other hand, reopenings could also be interpreted by investors as an adverse signal that management and arranging banks have clearly miscalculated the capital needs of a company. This would be in line with the negative signaling hypothesis and ought to lead to negative bond and stock returns as unnecessary expenses arise that could have been avoided. Furthermore, the regular issue could have met such strong demand that management decided to exploit these favorable conditions and to quickly issue more debt. This would lead to a higher leverage and thus, increase the firm's default risk. The result would be a transfer of wealth from the bondholders to the stockholders. Lastly, taps can also be expected to generate weaker price reactions than regular issues. The rationale is that investors monitor companies and the performance of their outstanding debt, which leads to a stronger anticipation effect for reopenings.

Altogether, price effects consistent with a transfer of wealth are expected for both issue types, i.e. positive abnormal stock returns and negative abnormal bond returns. However, as prior research only provides theoretical verification for the wealth transfer, but fails to empirically confirm the interdependence of bond and stock prices (see Chen, 2013), this chapter also expects to detect no statistical relationship between stockholder and bondholder wealth effects for regular offerings. Reopenings, on the other hand, provide a setting were management takes advantage of favorable market conditions which ought to lead to increased default risk through a higher leverage. Thus, a negative impact on the wealth effects and a clearly pronounced redistribution of wealth is expected for the announcement of reopenings.

4.2 Data and Methodology

4.2.1 Data and Descriptive Statistics

Corporate bond offerings executed exclusively by issuers in Europe between January 01, 2000 and February 20, 2014 are collected from the Thomson One Banker database for bonds. In a first step, all financials are excluded as indicated by the macro industry description. Second, the sample is limited to offerings made in Euro. Next, all zero-coupon, convertible, preferred shares and perpetual bonds are removed since they are prone to cause different, more equity-like market reactions. Finally, the requirement for an offering to be included in the sample is that: (i) the debt offering must be reopened at least once (as indicated by the "Tap Issue Flag"), (ii) a bond's ISIN is available from Thomson One Banker, and (iii) issuing company's Sedol or ISIN is available from Thomson One Banker. These requirements lead to a preliminary sample of 174 bond issues including 94 announcements of reopenings and 80 regular offerings. Next, stock price data and credit ratings from S&P as well as bond price and term to maturity data had to be obtainable from Thomson Reuters Datastream. Thus, a final sample size of 138 straight bond offerings is utilized, of which 85 offerings are reopenings and the remaining 53 offerings represent regular issues.

Table 4-3 shows which industry (Panel A) and what country (Panel B) the issuing companies belong to. The four top issuing industries are Telecommunication (37 issues), Energy and Power (26 issues), as well as Industrials and Materials (each with 17 issues). All four represent industries with a high proportion of fixed assets on their balance sheets. Not surprisingly, the energy and

Table 4-3: Number of Regular Issues and Reopenings by Industry and Country

Panel A: Industry	**No. of Regular Issues**	**No. of Reopenings**
Consumer Products and Services	0	1
Consumer Staples	0	1
Energy and Power	10	16
Healthcare	1	1
High Technology	1	1
Industrials	6	11
Materials	7	10
Media and Entertainment	4	6
Real Estate	3	7
Retail	6	9
Telecommunications	15	22
Panel B: Country		
Belgium	0	1
Czech Republic	2	3
France	35	57
Germany	4	5
Italy	3	4
Netherlands	2	2
Portugal	0	2
Spain	0	1
Sweden	5	6
United Kingdom	2	4

This table presents the number of regular offerings and the number of reopenings separated by industry (TF Macro Description) in Panel A and country in Panel B. Only issues between January 01, 2005 and February 20, 2014 are included.

telecommunication sectors capture almost 50% of the sample, since both industries are frequent bond issuers due to their need to finance large projects (e.g. Blumental, 1998; Reviglio, 2012). Furthermore, 66.6% of all issues in the sample are executed by French companies as Panel B shows. Apparently, French firms reopen bonds much more frequently than other European companies.

Table 4-4 displays the number and average principal amount of sample regular offerings and reopenings by year. Not unexpectedly, reopenings turn out to be significantly smaller than regular issues.[50] On average, European companies tend to increase a €600 million bond issue by €200 million through a reopening. The number of reopened issues shows the same pattern as the universe of taps in Table 4-1 with 2008 and 2012 representing the years with the highest quantity. Finally, Table 4-5 presents information about the time gap between regular and reopenings. Most taps are issued between one month and two years after the regular issue. Even so, six reopenings are conducted in the first month after the regular issue while only four issues take more than three years.

Table 4-4: Number and Average Principal Amount of Regular Issues and Reopenings by year

		Regular Issues Principal Amount [€ mil.]			**Reopenings Principal Amount [€ mil.]**	
Year	**No.**	**Mean**	**Median**	**No.**	**Mean**	**Median**
2005	5	740.00	750.00	1	250.00	250.00
2006	3	633.33	600.00	2	225.00	225.00
2007	5	1,070.00	1,000.00	1	250.00	250.00
2008	5	630.00	650.00	22	211.59	200.00
2009	5	630.00	600.00	11	234.09	250.00
2010	8	506.25	500.00	11	205.45	200.00
2011	7	618.57	580.00	9	138.89	50.00
2012	8	391.25	415.00	19	176.21	100.00
2013	7	666.29	600.00	8	246.25	275.00
2014	0	0.00	0.00	1	150.00	150.00
Total	53	630.64	600.00	85	201.86	200.00

This table presents the number of regular offerings and the number of reopenings by year and the corresponding mean and median principal amount. Only issues between January 01, 2005 and February 20, 2014 are included.

50 Wilcoxon rank sum z-statistic (p-value): 8.022 (0.005) and t-test t-statistic (p-value): 11.754 (0.000).

Table 4-5: Calendar Days between Regular Bond Issue and Corresponding Reopening(s)

Period	No.
t ≤ 30 days	6
30 days < t ≤ 90 days	18
90 days < t ≤ 180 days	23
180 days < t ≤ 1 year	12
1 year < t ≤ 2 years	16
2 years < t ≤ 3 years	6
3 years < t ≤ 4 years	2
4 years < t ≤ 5 years	1
5 years < t ≤ 6 years	1

This table presents the number of reopenings issues by calendar days between regular issue and reopening. 360 calendar days correspond to one year.

4.2.2 Methodology

Abnormal bond returns are estimated with the matched portfolio model approach following Bessembinder et al. (2009).[51] First, it starts with all corporate bond offerings conducted in Europe included in the Thomson One Banker database. Next, all financial companies, as indicated by the Macro Industry description, zeros, convertibles and tap issues[52] are removed. Moreover historical ratings from S&P as well as price and term to maturity data to be available from Thomson Reuters Datastream is demanded. By utilizing six rating categories (AAA plus AA, A, BBB, BB, B, CCC and less) and three different maturity classes (long-term, intermediate, and short-term) 18 reference portfolios are created, which provide the expected bond return depending on the respective bond's term to maturity and risk classification. To split the portfolios by maturity, the 33 and 66 percentile calculated for every single trading day in the event window is utilized. Bond returns are value weighted to calculate the respective portfolio return. Table 4-6 presents the distribution of portfolio bonds for the announcement day. The assumption is that the portfolios are sufficient since applied portfolios consist at least of seven bonds and the median portfolio exhibits over 100 bonds. Again, the expected return is deducted from the observed bond return to retrieve the abnormal bond return. A parametric (standard t-test) and non-parametric test (Wilcoxon signed rank) are utilized to test abnormal bond returns for statistical significance. Additionally,

51 To obtain the used formulas see chapter 2.2.5 for a general description and chapter 3.2.2 for a detailed application of bond event study methodology.

52 Reopenings are dropped because they are consolidated with the reopened bond.

this analysis follows the reasoning by Ederington et al. (2012) and applies both test statistics on standardized abnormal returns to check the robustness of the results.

Since several companies choose to issue more than one bond, leading to multiple contemporaneously outstanding bonds, each bond is considered as an individual event (known as bond level approach (Bessembinder et al., 2009)). Additionally, a firm's outstanding abnormal bond returns are combined into a single abnormal firm return (known as firm level approach (Bessembinder et al., 2009)). Equally weighted abnormal firm returns are computed following Ederington et al. (2012).

Table 4-6: Distribution of the number of portfolio bonds for the event day [0;0]

Mean	1st Quartile	Median	3rd Quartile	Maximum	Minimum
80.23	36	102	110	155	7

The standard market model event study methodology following MacKinlay (1997) is applied to calculate abnormal stock returns.[53] Abnormal returns are computed by subtracting expected stock returns from actual returns. Expected returns are estimated over a 250 day period starting −253 trading days prior to the announcement and ending −4 trading days before the announcement date [0;0]. The S&P 350 Europe Total Return Index is used as the benchmark market index. Source for the stock data is Thomson Reuters Datastream, while the Total Return Index is applied to calculate stock returns. The standard t-test, the Boehmer-test (Boehmer et al., 1991), the Wilcoxon signed rank-test, and the Corrado-test (Corrado, 1989; Corrado & Zivney, 1992) are used to check for statistical significance.

To use the event study methodology it is vital to ensure that the examined event date represents the first time that investors received new information (Binder, 1998; McWilliams & Siegel, 1997). That is why, in a following process, press releases published by the issuing company as well as Nexis database are utilized to identify the first announcement date of the bond offering and compare it with the "Issue Date[54]" provided by Thomson One Banker. Following Chen (2013) one month before to one month after the "Issue Date" is searched. At the respective firm's homepage every press release headline in the selected time window is studied for a publicly available note that announces the offering. Subsequently, a Nexis search is conducted employing the company name plus the keyword "bond". The event day is changed to the earliest date clearly announcing the respective issue

53 Also see chapter 3.2.3 for a thorough description.

54 Thomson One Banker specifies the issue date as "the pricing date of the issue".

whenever an announcement preceding the "Issue Date" is found. In the end, three primary issue dates are changed by one trading day.[55]

Another important issue with the event study methodology is the coincidence of other firm specific news with the examined event, i.e. the debt offering announcement. Failing to control for such confounding events can cause unwanted changes in stock and bond returns and lead to erroneous conclusions about the impact of an announcement (Broughton & Smith, 1997; McWilliams & Siegel, 1997). Therefore, following Chen (2013), the company's news room and/or press release section as well as Nexis search engine is used to seek out firm specific announcements during the three-day window, starting one day before and ending one day after the actual event (−1;1). 15 sample events (12 reopenings plus 3 regular issues) coincide with confounding events, such as mergers and acquisitions, financial reports, and major contracts. Consequently, two different samples are used for this analysis: 1. "Complete Sample" without any adjustments for confounding events and 2. "Control Sample" where events that overlap with other critical announcements are excluded.

4.3 Empirical Results

4.3.1 Bond Event Study

Two different methodologies are used to infer the reaction of a respective firm's bondholders due to debt issue announcements: 1. the bond level approach and 2. the firm level approach. The interpretation of the results is focused on the firm level approach, since the bond level approach is inferior to the firm level approach due to high correlation across the sample returns from the same company leading to inflated test statistics (Bessembinder et al., 2009; Eberhart & Siddique, 2002). Even so, abnormal returns with bonds as single observations are computed as well, since firm returns can also lead to misinterpretations. The reason for that is that bond returns from the same company are not perfectly correlated leading to upward biased standard errors which causes deflated test statistics (Eberhart & Siddique, 2002). Therefore, the bond level approach is utilized as a robustness check for the firm results.[56] Again, the "Complete" and the "Control" sample are utilized to control for confounding events. Table 4-7 and Table 4-8 display the firm level results.

---

55 The rather small number of date changes is consistent with Chen (2013), who shows that most announcement dates from databases like Thomson Reuters SDC represent the actual first announcement of debt offerings.

56 Additionally, bond level data is necessary to compute the variable for the wealth transfer regression.

Table 4-7: Issuer's Abnormal Bond Returns and Univariate Comparison for the "Complete Sample" (Firm Level Approach)

Event Window	(C)AAR		t-test	signed rank-test	N	t-test	signed rank-test	N
Panel A: All Issues	**Mean**	**Median**	**Unstandardized ARs**			**Standardized ARs**		
[-1;0]	-0.098%	-0.073%	-2.614***	-2.430**	138	-4.232***	-3.944***	137
[0;0]	-0.107%	-0.066%	-3.714***	-3.308***	138	-4.662***	-4.378***	137
[0;1]	-0.117%	-0.098%	-3.163***	-2.925***	138	-4.694***	-4.333***	137
[-1;1]	-0.108%	-0.087%	-2.310**	-2.186**	138	-4.268***	-4.073***	137
[-2;2]	-0.042%	-0.069%	-0.618	-0.781	137	-2.370**	-2.418**	137
[-3;3]	0.003%	-0.085%	0.034	-0.401	137	-1.603	-1.806*	137
Panel B: Reopenings								
[-1;0]	-0.022%	-0.041%	-0.540	-0.892	85	-2.028**	-2.101**	84
[0;0]	-0.058%	-0.066%	-2.073**	-1.921*	85	-3.200***	-3.122***	84
[0;1]	-0.060%	-0.098%	-1.468	-1.786*	85	-3.137***	-3.193***	84
[-1;1]	-0.024%	-0.061%	-0.434	-0.633	85	-2.204**	-2.466**	84
[-2;2]	0.074%	-0.062%	0.833	-0.495	84	-0.790	-0.749	84
[-3;3]	0.165%	-0.021%	1.275	-1.017	84	-0.092	-0.120	84
Panel C: Regular Issues								
[-1;0]	-0.220%	-0.110%	-3.153***	-2.731***	53	-3.947***	-3.448***	53
[0;0]	-0.187%	-0.039%	-3.149***	-2.616***	53	-3.468***	-3.085***	53
[0;1]	-0.209%	-0.105%	-3.001***	-2.598***	53	-3.521***	-3.076***	53
[-1;1]	-0.243%	-0.106%	-2.982***	-2.678***	53	-3.894***	-3.315***	53
[-2;2]	-0.225%	-0.107%	-2.271**	-1.828*	53	-2.617**	-2.722***	53
[-3;3]	-0.254%	-0.141%	-2.156**	-2.023**	53	-2.432**	-2.651***	53
			t-test	**rank sum-test**		**t-test**	**rank sum-test**	
Panel D: Difference between Panel B and C			**Unstandardized ARs**			**Standardized ARs**		
[-1;0]	0.198%	0.068%	2.620***	-1.882*		2.808***	-2.468**	
[0;0]	0.129%	-0.027%	2.192**	-0.932		1.889*	-1.279	
[0;1]	0.150%	0.007%	1.986**	-1.033		1.544	-1.032	
[-1;1]	0.219%	0.045%	2.318**	-1.747*		2.320**	-2.062**	
[-2;2]	0.299%	0.045%	2.187**	-1.690*		1.845*	-2.031**	
[-3;3]	0.419%	0.119%	2.227**	-2.106**		1.892*	-2.124**	

This table presents (cumulative) abnormal bond returns of issuing firms over several event windows surrounding the issue announcement date. The calculations are carried out not including adjustment for confounding events. Abnormal bond returns are computed as the bond's return minus the return on a risk and maturity matched portfolio. Portfolio bonds are weighted by their relative market value. When a firm has multiple bonds, its abnormal bond return is computed as the equally weighted average of each bond's abnormal return. To check for statistical significance, one parametric and one non-parametric test are used: the one-sample standard t-test and the Wilcoxon signed rank-test. Both test statistics are calculated utilizing standardized bond returns following Ederington et al. (2012). Standardized abnormal bond returns are computed by dividing the abnormal return by the standard deviation of abnormal returns over the [-10;10] window, excluding returns across event day [0;0]. Panel A reports (cumulative) abnormal bond returns for all issues. Panel B reports (cumulative) abnormal bond returns for reopenings. Panel C reports (cumulative) abnormal bond returns for new bond issues. Panel D reports the difference in means and medians between Panel B and Panel C. To check for statistical significance, the parametric two-sample standard t-test and the non-parametric Wilcoxon rank sum-test are used. All tests are two-tailed. The symbols ***, **, and * denote statistical significance at 1%, 5%, and 10% level, respectively.

Table 4-8: Issuer's Abnormal Bond Returns and Univariate Comparison for the "Control Sample" (Firm Level Approach)

Event Window	(C)AAR		t-test	signed rank-test	N	t-test	signed rank-test	N
Panel A: All Issues	**Mean**	**Median**	**Unstandardized ARs**			**Standardized ARs**		
[-1;0]	-0.123%	-0.101%	-3.026***	-2.893***	123	-4.665***	-4.473***	122
[0;0]	-0.122%	-0.066%	-3.884***	-3.443***	123	-4.886***	-4.623***	122
[0;1]	-0.134%	-0.104%	-3.306***	-3.089***	123	-4.690***	-4.266***	122
[-1;1]	-0.134%	-0.100%	-2.662***	-2.663***	123	-4.485***	-4.281***	122
[-2;2]	-0.086%	-0.101%	-1.185	-1.483	122	-2.633***	-2.804***	122
[-3;3]	-0.065%	-0.097%	-0.650	-1.279	122	-2.058**	-2.431**	122
Panel B: Reopenings								
[-1;0]	-0.056%	-0.090%	-1.246	-1.691*	73	-2.916***	-3.014***	72
[0;0]	-0.077%	-0.086%	-2.549**	-2.345**	73	-3.757***	-3.597***	72
[0;1]	-0.085%	-0.109%	-1.870*	-2.273**	73	-3.437***	-3.429***	72
[-1;1]	-0.063%	-0.092%	-1.046	-1.509	73	-2.809***	-3.109***	72
[-2;2]	0.003%	-0.121%	0.034	-0.701	72	-1.464	-1.622	72
[-3;3]	0.055%	-0.097%	0.379	-0.297	72	-0.919	-1.223	72
Panel C: Regular Issues								
[-1;0]	-0.220%	-0.105%	-2.983***	-2.476**	50	-3.721***	-3.277***	50
[0;0]	-0.187%	-0.019%	-2.990***	-2.331**	50	-3.322***	-2.910***	50
[0;1]	-0.206%	-0.079%	-2.781***	-2.206**	50	-3.210***	-2.746***	50
[-1;1]	-0.239%	-0.102%	-2.765***	-2.331**	50	-3.542***	-2.988***	50
[-2;2]	-0.215%	-0.075%	-2.050**	-1.501	50	-2.252**	-2.351**	50
[-3;3]	-0.236%	-0.103%	-1.905*	-1.713*	50	-2.082**	-2.322**	50
			t-test	**rank sum-test**		**t-test**	**rank sum-test**	
Panel D: Difference between Panel B and C			**Unstandardized ARs**			**Standardized ARs**		
[-1;0]	0.165%	0.015%	2.025**	-1.141		2.099**	-1.731*	
[0;0]	0.110%	-0.067%	1.741*	-0.487		1.367	-0.711	
[0;1]	0.121%	-0.030%	1.476	-0.296		0.944	-0.367	
[-1;1]	0.176%	0.009%	1.721*	-0.883		1.584	-1.210	
[-2;2]	0.218%	-0.046%	1.484	-0.716		1.081	-1.117	
[-3;3]	0.291%	0.006%	1.445	-1.059		1.060	-1.106	

This table presents (cumulative) abnormal bond returns of issuing firms over several event windows surrounding the issue announcement date. To control for confounding events issues coinciding with other company relevant announcements over a three day window [-1;1] are excluded from the sample. Abnormal bond returns are computed as the bond's return minus the return on a risk and maturity matched portfolio. Portfolio bonds are weighted by their relative market value. When a firm has multiple bonds, its abnormal bond return is computed as the equally weighted average of each bond's abnormal return. To check for statistical significance, one parametric and one non-parametric test are used: the one-sample standard t-test and the Wilcoxon signed rank-test. Both test statistics are calculated utilizing standardized bond returns following Ederington et al. (2012). Standardized abnormal bond returns are computed by dividing the abnormal return by the standard deviation of abnormal returns over the [-10;10] window, excluding returns across event day [0;0]. Panel A reports (cumulative) abnormal bond returns for all issues. Panel B reports (cumulative) abnormal bond returns for reopenings. Panel C reports (cumulative) abnormal bond returns for new bond issues. Panel D reports the difference in means and medians between Panel B and Panel C. To check for statistical significance, the parametric two-sample standard t-test and the non-parametric Wilcoxon rank sum-test are used. All tests are two-tailed. The symbols ***, **, and * denote statistical significance at 1%, 5%, and 10% level, respectively.

Statistically significant and negative abnormal bond returns are found for all issues (Panel A) regardless of controlling for confounding events. After splitting all issues by their offering type (i.e. reopening or regular offering) reveals that bond prices decline for both subsamples at the announcement as shown in Panel B and Panel C. However, discrepancies can be found by the number of significant event windows around the announcement date. Regular issues seem to cause stronger bondholder responses in a way that these responses are more pronounced over a longer time window. The unstandardized returns in particular demonstrate this disparity between Panel B and Panel C. Furthermore, the mean abnormal returns for regular issues are considerably higher than for the reopenings, additionally indicating that both subsamples diverge. Therefore, in a next step, a univariate test between Panel B and Panel C is performed to assess whether both subsamples show statistically significant differences in abnormal bond returns. Consistent with the expectation, Table 4-7 shows that regular issues generate stronger bond price reactions than reopenings (Panel D). However, excluding events that overlap with other firm-relevant announcements in Table 4-8 reveals less clear results. Only the two-day window [−1;0] presents statistically significant values for the parametric and non-parametric test statistic.

As expected, repeating the bond event studies utilizing the bond level approach generally confirms the previous results.

Debt offering announcements produce bondholder wealth depreciation regardless of the offering type, and the magnitude of the wealth loss turns out to be higher for regular issues. Different results present the univariate tests in Panel D. Most test statistics remain significant even after controlling for confounding events (Table 4-10), contradicting the results of the firm level approach. In summary, this investigation identifies clear evidence that both classes of bond issue announcements cause negative debtholder wealth effects. Moreover, indications supporting the hypothesis that regular issues generate stronger abnormal bond returns are found. However, this result varies depending on the examined sample. Thus, the necessity to conduct further analyses is acknowledged by performing another cross sectional regression in the next section.

Table 4-9: Issuer's Abnormal Bond Returns and Univariate Comparison for the "Complete Sample" (Bond Level Approach)

Event Window	(C)AAR		t-test	signed rank-test	N	t-test	signed rank-test	N
Panel A: All Issues	**Mean**	**Median**	**Unstandardized ARs**			**Standardized ARs**		
[−1;0]	−0.084%	−0.039%	−3.748***	−4.989***	677	−6.276***	−5.819***	669
[0;0]	−0.084%	−0.034%	−5.677***	−6.752***	677	−7.685***	−7.385***	669
[0;1]	−0.071%	−0.046%	−3.301***	−5.643***	677	−6.708***	−6.674***	669
[−1;1]	−0.071%	−0.050%	−2.382**	−4.573***	677	−5.585***	−5.621***	669
[−2;2]	0.002%	−0.044%	0.051	−2.595***	676	−2.909***	−3.685***	669
[−3;3]	0.077%	−0.043%	1.316	−1.561	676	−1.298	−2.704***	669
Panel B: Reopenings								
[−1;0]	−0.003%	−0.012%	−0.108	−1.361	434	−1.787*	−1.853*	428
[0;0]	−0.033%	−0.028%	−2.124**	−3.827***	434	−3.962***	−4.067***	428
[0;1]	−0.005%	−0.034%	−0.203	−2.604***	434	−3.058***	−3.636***	428
[−1;1]	0.025%	−0.028%	0.658	−1.207	434	−1.574	−2.120**	428
[−2;2]	0.128%	−0.033%	2.282**	−0.139	433	0.250	−0.844	428
[−3;3]	0.274%	−0.026%	3.414***	−1.073	433	1.632	−0.207	428
Panel C: Regular Issues								
[−1;0]	−0.229%	−0.070%	−5.776***	−6.333***	243	−7.156***	−6.668***	241
[0;0]	−0.175%	−0.049%	−5.914***	−6.055***	243	−6.873***	−6.550***	241
[0;1]	−0.187%	−0.065%	−5.304***	−5.906***	243	−6.642***	−6.126***	241
[−1;1]	−0.242%	−0.090%	−5.214***	−6.001***	243	−6.827***	−6.293***	241
[−2;2]	−0.222%	−0.068%	−3.775***	−4.189***	243	−5.064***	−4.874***	241
[−3;3]	−0.275%	−0.076%	−3.831***	−4.243***	243	−4.762***	−4.778***	241
			t-test	**rank sum-test**		**t-test**	**rank sum-test**	
Panel D: Difference between Panel B and C			**Unstandardized ARs**			**Standardized ARs**		
[−1;0]	0.226%	0.057%	4.921***	−4.594***		6.033***	−5.379***	
[0;0]	0.142%	0.020%	4.668***	−3.025***		5.242***	−4.330***	
[0;1]	0.182%	0.032%	4.124***	−3.064***		4.462***	−3.455***	
[−1;1]	0.267%	0.062%	4.354***	−4.005***		5.119***	−4.508***	
[−2;2]	0.350%	0.035%	4.029***	−2.974***		4.336***	−3.644***	
[−3;3]	0.549%	0.050%	4.578***	−3.678***		4.571***	−4.120***	

This table presents (cumulative) abnormal bond returns of issuing firms over several event windows surrounding the issue announcement date. The calculations are carried out not including adjustment for confounding events. Abnormal bond returns are computed as the bond's return minus the return on a risk and maturity matched portfolio. Portfolio bonds are weighted by their relative market value. Each bond is treated as a separate observation. To check for statistical significance, one parametric and one non-parametric test are used: the one-sample standard t-test and the Wilcoxon signed rank-test. Both test statistics are calculated utilizing standardized bond returns following Ederington et al. (2012). Standardized abnormal bond returns are computed by dividing the abnormal return by the standard deviation of abnormal returns over the [−10;10] window, excluding returns across event day [0;0]. Panel A reports (cumulative) abnormal bond returns for all issues. Panel B reports (cumulative) abnormal bond returns for reopenings. Panel C reports (cumulative) abnormal bond returns for new bond issues. Panel D reports the difference in means and medians between Panel B and Panel C. To check for statistical significance, the parametric two-sample standard t-test and the non-parametric Wilcoxon rank sum-test are used. All tests are two-tailed. The symbols ***, **, and * denote statistical significance at 1%, 5%, and 10% level, respectively.

Table 4-10: Issuer's Abnormal Bond Returns and Univariate Comparison for the "Control Sample" (Bond Level Approach)

Event Window	(C)AAR		t-test	signed rank-test	N	t-test	signed rank-test	N
Panel A: All Issues	**Mean**	**Median**	**Unstandardized ARs**			**Standardized ARs**		
[-1;0]	-0.112%	-0.049%	-4.403***	-5.811***	574	-7.195***	-6.859***	567
[0;0]	-0.093%	-0.037%	-5.585***	-6.749***	574	-7.915***	-7.664***	567
[0;1]	-0.085%	-0.050%	-3.469***	-6.184***	574	-6.657***	-6.698***	567
[-1;1]	-0.104%	-0.065%	-3.099***	-5.429***	574	-6.154***	-6.285***	567
[-2;2]	-0.062%	-0.060%	-1.325	-3.667***	573	-3.892***	-4.607***	567
[-3;3]	-0.037%	-0.065%	-0.582	-3.210***	573	-3.076***	-4.338***	567
Panel B: Reopenings								
[-1;0]	-0.037%	-0.035%	-1.179	-2.689***	344	-3.410***	-3.563***	338
[0;0]	-0.042%	-0.031%	-2.312**	-4.149***	344	-4.708***	-4.806***	338
[0;1]	-0.021%	-0.050%	-0.648	-3.610***	344	-3.361***	-3.980***	338
[-1;1]	-0.016%	-0.056%	-0.359	-2.604***	344	-2.632***	-3.269***	338
[-2;2]	0.040%	-0.054%	0.604	-1.756*	343	-1.241	-2.310**	338
[-3;3]	0.111%	-0.062%	1.217	-1.258	343	-0.666	-2.106**	338
Panel C: Regular Issues								
[-1;0]	-0.224%	-0.065%	-5.394***	-5.827***	230	-6.710***	-6.232***	229
[0;0]	-0.169%	-0.048%	-5.487***	-5.536***	230	-6.488***	-6.110***	229
[0;1]	-0.181%	-0.051%	-4.872***	-5.314***	230	-6.144***	-5.619***	229
[-1;1]	-0.236%	-0.081%	-4.835***	-5.427***	230	-6.295***	-5.810***	229
[-2;2]	-0.214%	-0.062%	-3.462***	-3.659***	230	-4.557***	-4.365***	229
[-3;3]	-0.257%	-0.068%	-3.427***	-3.615***	230	-4.243***	-4.231***	229
			t-test	**rank sum-test**		**t-test**	**rank sum-test**	
Panel D: Difference between Panel B and C			**Unstandardized ARs**			**Standardized ARs**		
[-1;0]	0.187%	0.030%	3.637***	-2.924***		4.331***	-3.601***	
[0;0]	0.127%	0.016%	3.799***	-1.971**		3.962***	-3.046***	
[0;1]	0.160%	0.001%	3.233***	-1.506		3.297***	-2.145**	
[-1;1]	0.220%	0.025%	3.228***	-2.234**		3.636***	-2.863***	
[-2;2]	0.253%	0.009%	2.670***	-1.317		2.843***	-2.102**	
[-3;3]	0.368%	0.005%	2.890***	-1.656*		2.675***	-2.164**	

This table presents (cumulative) abnormal bond returns of issuing firms over several event windows surrounding the issue announcement date. To control for confounding events issues coinciding with other company relevant announcements over a three day window [-1;1] are excluded from the sample. Abnormal bond returns are computed as the bond's return minus the return on a risk and maturity matched portfolio. Portfolio bonds are weighted by their relative market value. Each bond is treated as a separate observation. To check for statistical significance, one parametric and one non-parametric test are used: the one-sample standard t-test and the Wilcoxon signed rank-test. Both test statistics are calculated utilizing standardized bond returns following Ederington et al. (2012). Standardized abnormal bond returns are computed by dividing the abnormal return by the standard deviation of abnormal returns over the [-10;10] window, excluding returns across event day [0;0]. Panel A reports (cumulative) abnormal bond returns for all issues. Panel B reports (cumulative) abnormal bond returns for reopenings. Panel C reports (cumulative) abnormal bond returns for new bond issues. Panel D reports the difference in means and medians between Panel B and Panel C. To check for statistical significance, the parametric two-sample standard t-test and the non-parametric Wilcoxon rank sum-test are used. All tests are two-tailed. The symbols ***, **, and * denote statistical significance at 1%, 5%, and 10% level, respectively.

In addition to the standard bondholder wealth effects due to debt offerings, an investigation of the impact of reopening announcements just on the reopened regular issued bond is conducted. What distinguishes this empirical investigation from the standard bond event study already conducted is that not all bonds from a debt offering company are considered but only bonds whose reopening is part of the examined sample. The event date is the announcement of the reopening. Table 4-11 presents the results.

Table 4-11: Issuer's Abnormal Bond Returns for the Regularly Issued Bond at the Announcement of the Reopening

Event Window	(C)AAR		t-test	signed rank-test	N	t-test	signed rank-test	N
Panel A: Complete Sample	**Mean**	**Median**	**Unstandardized ARs**			**Standardized ARs**		
[−1;0]	−0.098%	−0.043%	−1.212	−1.093	56	−1.493	−1.287	54
[0;0]	−0.129%	−0.126%	−2.622**	−2.716***	56	−2.772***	−2.682***	54
[0;1]	−0.108%	−0.153%	−1.303	−1.974**	56	−1.947*	−2.097**	54
[−1;1]	−0.077%	−0.142%	−0.660	−0.938	56	−1.125	−1.038	54
[−2;2]	−0.054%	−0.143%	−0.299	−0.644	56	−0.811	−0.908	54
[−3;3]	0.051%	−0.060%	0.198	−0.269	56	−0.180	−0.306	54
Panel B: Control Sample								
[−1;0]	−0.164%	−0.146%	−1.750*	−1.744*	45	−2.362**	−2.137**	43
[0;0]	−0.161%	−0.226%	−2.806***	−2.782***	45	−3.162***	−2.958***	43
[0;1]	−0.133%	−0.164%	−1.369	−2.150**	45	−2.003*	−2.246**	43
[−1;1]	−0.136%	−0.196%	−0.998	−1.405	45	−1.593	−1.618	43
[−2;2]	−0.195%	−0.199%	−0.968	−1.428	45	−1.444	−1.534	43
[−3;3]	−0.173%	−0.161%	−0.594	−1.191	45	−0.976	−1.147	43

This table presents (cumulative) abnormal bond returns exclusively for every regularly issued bond at the announcement of the reopening over several event windows surrounding the announcement date. Abnormal bond returns are computed as the bond's return minus the return on a risk and maturity matched portfolio. To check for statistical significance, one parametric and one non-parametric test are used: the one-sample standard t-test and the Wilcoxon signed rank-test. Both test statistics are calculated utilizing standardized bond returns following Ederington et al. (2012). Standardized abnormal bond returns are computed by dividing the abnormal return by the standard deviation of abnormal returns over the [−10;10] window, excluding returns across event day [0;0]. Panel A reports (cumulative) abnormal bond returns without adjustments for confounding events and utilizing value weighted portfolios. Panel B reports (cumulative) abnormal bond returns with adjustments for confounding events and utilizing value weighted portfolios. All tests are two-tailed. The symbols ***, **, and * denote statistical significance at 1%, 5%, and 10% level, respectively.

In line with the window of opportunity framework, clear evidence that reopened bonds experience a wealth loss of approximately 0.1–0.2% on the announcement date is found. This result is robust when controlled for confounding events. Apparently, prices decline when companies decide to reopen previously issued bonds leading to a wealth loss for existing holders of that particular bond. This is remarkable, as the increased liquidity should have a positive impact on the price of the bond. Apparently, bondholders consider the announcement of reopenings as a signal that bond prices are actually overvalued.

4.3.2 Stock Event Study

The following section presents stock price reactions to bond issue announcements in Europe.

Analyzing the full sample (Table 4-12) reveals no significant market reaction when both regular issues and reopenings are considered together (Panel A). Only dividing the full sample into reopening announcements (Panel B) and regular issue announcements (Panel C) presents statistically significant positive abnormal stock returns for the second subsample. Firms issuing new debt experience a wealth gain of 0.5% over the two-day window [0;1]. Taps, on the other hand, generate no stock price reaction. All four test statistics are insignificant for every event window. At a first glance, observers could be inclined to deduce that stockholders' reactions diverge depending on whether already issued bonds are tapped or completely new debt issues are carried out. However, conducting an univariate analysis between both subsamples in Panel D reveals only weak evidence for a significant difference between reopenings and new issues.

Results turn out to be similar with the adjusted "Control" sample in Table 4-13. Consistent with Table 4-12, no significant abnormal stock returns for reopenings can be found in Panel B of Table 4, while the two- [0;1] and three-day window [–1;1] for regular issues display positive price responses to the issue announcement. Furthermore, the tests for differences between Panel B and Panel C find no statistically significant results again in contrast to the prior expectations. However, this time significant price reactions are detected for the full sample as well, as Panel A shows. Apparently, confounding events are one reason for the insignificant results in Table 4-12.

Table 4-12: Issuer's Abnormal Stock Returns and Univariate Comparison for the "Complete Sample" (Regular Estimation Window)

Event Window	(C)AAR		t-test	Boehmer-test	signed rank-test	Corrado-test	N
Panel A: All Issues	**Mean**	**Median**					
[-1;0]	0.147%	0.084%	0.862	1.564	-1.144	0.839	138
[0;0]	0.074%	-0.027%	0.693	0.991	-0.411	0.404	138
[0;1]	0.202%	0.081%	1.218	1.416	-0.637	1.363	138
[-1;1]	0.275%	0.205%	1.226	1.798*	-1.240	1.565	138
[-2;2]	0.107%	0.111%	0.376	1.050	-0.549	0.568	138
[-3;3]	-0.053%	0.053%	-0.172	0.292	-0.473	-0.024	138
Panel B:Reopenings							
[-1;0]	0.036%	-0.018%	0.150	0.827	-0.497	0.368	85
[0;0]	0.038%	-0.162%	0.247	0.463	-0.156	-0.165	85
[0;1]	0.037%	-0.216%	0.160	0.372	-0.410	0.188	85
[-1;1]	0.035%	0.002%	0.115	0.677	-0.164	0.550	85
[-2;2]	-0.121%	-0.240%	-0.301	0.530	-0.103	0.116	85
[-3;3]	0.052%	0.481%	0.125	0.956	-0.848	0.600	85
Panel C: Regular Issues							
[-1;0]	0.326%	0.391%	1.431	1.493	-1.120	0.893	53
[0;0]	0.132%	0.071%	0.989	1.086	-1.102	0.885	53
[0;1]	0.466%	0.200%	2.189**	2.358**	-1.810*	1.998**	53
[-1;1]	0.659%	0.371%	2.102**	2.278**	-1.828*	1.849*	53
[-2;2]	0.472%	0.326%	1.302	1.142	-1.076	0.782	53
[-3;3]	-0.221%	-0.173%	-0.510	-0.839	-0.385	-0.836	53
Panel D: Difference between Panel B and C			**t-test**	**rank sum-test**			
[-1;0]	-0.290%	-0.410%	-0.827	0.482			
[0;0]	-0.095%	-0.233%	-0.430	0.827			
[0;1]	-0.429%	-0.416%	-1.260	1.668*			
[-1;1]	-0.624%	-0.369%	-1.357	1.283			
[-2;2]	-0.592%	-0.565%	-1.016	0.902			
[-3;3]	0.273%	0.654%	0.434	-0.827			

This table presents (cumulative) abnormal stock returns of issuing firms over several event windows surrounding the issue announcement date. The calculations are carried out not including adjustment for confounding events. Abnormal stock returns are computed using the market model based on the S&P Europe 350 index. The estimation window starts -253 days and ends -4 days prior to the announcement (regular estimation period). Panel A reports (cumulative) abnormal stock returns for all issues. Panel B reports (cumulative) abnormal stock returns for reopenings. Panel C reports (cumulative) abnormal stock returns for new bond issues. To check for statistical significance, two parametric and two non-parametric tests are used: the one-sample standard t-test, the Boehmer-test (Boehmer et al., 1991), the Wilcoxon signed rank-test, and the Corrado-test (Corrado, 1989; Corrado & Zivney, 1992). Panel D reports the difference in means and medians between Panel B and Panel C. To check for statistical significance, the parametric two-sample standard t-test and the non-parametric Wilcoxon rank sum test are used. All tests are two-tailed. The symbols ***, **, and * denote statistical significance at 1%, 5%, and 10% level, respectively.

Table 4-13: Issuer's Abnormal Stock Returns and Univariate Comparison for the "Control Sample" (Regular Estimation Window)

Event Window	(C)AAR		t-test	Boehmer-test	signed rank-test	Corrado-test	N
Panel A: All Issues	**Mean**	**Median**					
[-1;0]	0.215%	0.290%	1.220	1.801*	-1.737*	1.504	123
[0;0]	0.104%	0.035%	0.917	1.163	-0.790	0.842	123
[0;1]	0.293%	0.153%	1.676*	1.859*	-1.398	2.063**	123
[-1;1]	0.403%	0.371%	1.733*	2.244**	-1.969**	2.427**	123
[-2;2]	0.217%	0.191%	0.722	1.331	-1.100	1.163	123
[-3;3]	0.047%	0.184%	0.144	0.502	-0.858	0.515	123
Panel B: Reopenings							
[-1;0]	0.200%	0.130%	0.772	1.407	-1.366	1.305	73
[0;0]	0.077%	-0.032%	0.464	0.631	-0.201	0.309	73
[0;1]	0.122%	0.058%	0.486	0.654	-0.162	0.836	73
[-1;1]	0.245%	0.163%	0.748	1.280	-0.976	1.569	73
[-2;2]	0.073%	0.142%	0.167	0.991	-0.542	0.840	73
[-3;3]	0.270%	0.680%	0.587	1.375	-1.509	1.296	73
Panel C: Regular Issues							
[-1;0]	0.236%	0.391%	1.101	1.117	-0.941	0.795	50
[0;0]	0.144%	0.162%	1.017	1.109	-1.144	0.964	50
[0;1]	0.541%	0.447%	2.458**	2.661***	-2.138**	2.266**	50
[-1;1]	0.634%	0.532%	2.013**	2.147**	-1.868*	1.943*	50
[-2;2]	0.428%	0.385%	1.149	0.914	-1.028	0.823	50
[-3;3]	-0.277%	-0.135%	-0.611	-0.992	-0.468	-0.775	50
Panel D: Difference between Panel B and C			**t-test**	**rank sum-test**			
[-1;0]	-0.037%	-0.262%	-0.102	-0.281			
[0;0]	-0.067%	-0.194%	-0.289	0.492			
[0;1]	-0.419%	-0.390%	-1.179	1.383			
[-1;1]	-0.389%	-0.369%	-0.819	0.754			
[-2;2]	-0.354%	-0.243%	-0.576	0.368			
[-3;3]	0.547%	0.815%	0.816	-1.285			

This table presents (cumulative) abnormal stock returns of issuing firms over several event windows surrounding the issue announcement date. To control for confounding events issues coinciding with other company relevant announcements over a three day window [-1;1] are excluded from the sample. Abnormal stock returns are computed using the market model based on the S&P Europe 350 index. The estimation window starts -253 days and ends -4 days prior to the announcement (regular estimation period). Panel A reports (cumulative) abnormal stock returns for all issues. Panel B reports (cumulative) abnormal stock returns for reopenings. Panel C reports (cumulative) abnormal stock returns for new bond issues. To check for statistical significance, two parametric and two non-parametric tests are used: the one-sample standard t-test, the Boehmer-test (Boehmer et al., 1991), the Wilcoxon signed rank-test, and the Corrado-test (Corrado, 1989; Corrado & Zivney, 1992). Panel D reports the difference in means and medians between Panel B and Panel C. To check for statistical significance, the parametric two-sample standard t-test and the non-parametric Wilcoxon rank sum test are used. All tests are two-tailed. The symbols ***, **, and * denote statistical significance at 1%, 5%, and 10% level, respectively.

The first two stock event studies are replicated with an alternative estimation period since debt issues and concomitant changes in leverage can affect a firm's beta factor (DeJong & Collins, 1985; Drobetz & Seidel, 2011; Kapoor & Pope, 1997; Melicher, 1974). The new estimation window ("irregular estimation window") starts 4 trading days after and ends 253 trading days after the event day [4;253]. 12 (11) events had to be removed from the full (adjusted) sample to conduct the analysis due to missing price data after the announcement date. Table 4-14 presents the results for the "Complete" sample while Table 4-15 shows the results for the "Control Sample".

Table 4-14: Issuer's Abnormal Stock Returns and Univariate Comparison for the "Complete Sample" (Irregular Estimation Window)

Event Window	(C)AAR		t-test	Boehmer-test	signed rank-test	Corrado-test	N
Panel A: All Issues	**Mean**	**Median**					
[-1;0]	0.176%	0.251%	1.011	1.701*	-1.167	1.247	126
[0;0]	0.176%	0.080%	1.540	1.912*	-1.279	1.584	126
[0;1]	0.308%	0.029%	1.714*	2.181**	-1.036	2.118**	126
[-1;1]	0.308%	0.063%	1.352	2.039**	-1.153	1.833*	126
[-2;2]	0.195%	0.337%	0.661	1.162	-0.849	0.753	126
[-3;3]	0.184%	0.426%	0.631	1.282	-0.897	0.643	126
Panel B: Reopenings							
[-1;0]	0.028%	0.037%	0.115	0.926	-0.206	0.574	77
[0;0]	0.116%	-0.175%	0.688	1.286	-0.246	0.645	77
[0;1]	0.089%	-0.250%	0.356	0.897	-0.287	0.578	77
[-1;1]	0.001%	-0.235%	0.004	0.711	-0.277	0.567	77
[-2;2]	-0.029%	0.331%	-0.069	0.552	-0.170	0.161	77
[-3;3]	0.292%	0.482%	0.745	1.667*	-1.120	0.898	77
Panel C: Regular Issues							
[-1;0]	0.408%	0.488%	1.850*	1.626	-1.795*	1.232	49
[0;0]	0.270%	0.244%	2.108**	1.583	-2.034**	1.672*	49
[0;1]	0.653%	0.394%	2.723***	2.710***	-2.372**	2.602***	49
[-1;1]	0.791%	0.675%	2.631**	2.647***	-2.412**	2.165**	49
[-2;2]	0.547%	0.344%	1.441	1.271	-1.248	0.982	49
[-3;3]	0.015%	-0.269%	0.035	-0.047	-0.124	-0.140	49
Panel D: Difference between Panel B and C			**t-test**	**rank sum-test**			
[-1;0]	-0.380%	-0.451%	-1.063	1.116			
[0;0]	-0.154%	-0.419%	-0.656	1.176			
[0;1]	-0.564%	-0.643%	-1.537	2.207**			
[-1;1]	-0.790%	-0.910%	-1.701*	1.927*			
[-2;2]	-0.576%	-0.013%	-0.950	0.826			
[-3;3]	0.276%	0.751%	0.460	-0.666			

This table presents (cumulative) abnormal stock returns of issuing firms over several event windows surrounding the issue announcement date. The calculations are carried out not including adjustment for confounding events. Abnormal stock returns are computed using the market model based on the S&P Europe 350 index. The estimation window starts +4 days and ends +253 days after the announcement (irregular estimation period). Panel A reports (cumulative) abnormal stock returns for all issues. Panel B reports (cumulative) abnormal stock returns for reopenings. Panel C reports (cumulative) abnormal stock returns for new bond issues. To check for statistical significance, two parametric and two non-parametric tests are used: the one-sample standard t-test, the Boehmer-test (Boehmer et al., 1991), the Wilcoxon signed rank-test, and the Corrado-test (Corrado, 1989; Corrado & Zivney, 1992). Panel D reports the difference in means and medians between Panel B and Panel C. To check for statistical significance, the parametric two-sample standard t-test and the non-parametric Wilcoxon rank sum test are used. All tests are two-tailed. The symbols ***, **, and * denote statistical significance at 1%, 5%, and 10% level, respectively.

Table 4-15: Issuer's Abnormal Stock Returns and Univariate Comparison for the "Control Sample" (Irregular Estimation Window)

Event Window	(C)AAR		t-test	Boehmer-test	signed rank-test	Corrado-test	N
Panel A: All Issues	**Mean**	**Median**					
[−1;0]	0.222%	0.330%	1.228	1.883*	−1.605	1.727*	112
[0;0]	0.194%	0.153%	1.573	1.905*	−1.486	1.775*	112
[0;1]	0.387%	0.194%	2.026**	2.462**	−1.594	2.599***	112
[−1;1]	0.415%	0.297%	1.757*	2.420**	−1.690*	2.507**	112
[−2;2]	0.267%	0.361%	0.842	1.240	−1.190	1.191	112
[−3;3]	0.253%	0.455%	0.800	1.321	−1.097	1.076	112
Panel B: Reopenings							
[−1;0]	0.161%	0.261%	0.592	1.422	−0.853	1.270	66
[0;0]	0.132%	−0.002%	0.703	1.260	−0.406	0.832	66
[0;1]	0.146%	−0.161%	0.539	1.048	−0.105	0.969	66
[−1;1]	0.176%	−0.110%	0.517	1.239	−0.265	1.347	66
[−2;2]	0.116%	0.361%	0.250	0.832	−0.668	0.704	66
[−3;3]	0.472%	0.538%	1.087	1.951*	−1.581	1.469	66
Panel C: Regular Issues							
[−1;0]	0.309%	0.414%	1.513	1.276	−1.622	1.107	46
[0;0]	0.283%	0.264%	2.091**	1.590	−2.016**	1.698*	46
[0;1]	0.733%	0.477%	2.941***	2.948***	−2.649***	2.781***	46
[−1;1]	0.759%	0.703%	2.522**	2.575**	−2.409**	2.195**	46
[−2;2]	0.483%	0.367%	1.234	0.986	−1.098	0.967	46
[−3;3]	−0.061%	−0.330%	−0.134	−0.301	−0.082	−0.111	46
Panel D: Difference between Panel B and C			**t-test**	**rank sum-test**			
[−1;0]	−0.148%	−0.152%	−0.400	0.447			
[0;0]	−0.152%	−0.266%	−0.602	0.914			
[0;1]	−0.586%	−0.639%	−1.518	2.026**			
[−1;1]	−0.582%	−0.812%	−1.215	1.541			
[−2;2]	−0.367%	−0.006%	−0.568	0.269			
[−3;3]	0.533%	0.868%	0.827	−1.109			

This table presents (cumulative) abnormal stock returns of issuing firms over several event windows surrounding the issue announcement date. To control for confounding events issues coinciding with other company relevant announcements over a three day window [−1;1] are excluded from the sample. Abnormal stock returns are computed using the market model based on the S&P Europe 350 index. The estimation window starts +4 days and ends +253 days after the announcement (irregular estimation period). Panel A reports (cumulative) abnormal stock returns for all issues. Panel B reports (cumulative) abnormal stock returns for reopenings. Panel C reports (cumulative) abnormal stock returns for new bond issues. To check for statistical significance, two parametric and two non-parametric tests are used: the one-sample standard t-test, the Boehmer-test (Boehmer et al., 1991), the Wilcoxon signed rank-test, and the Corrado-test (Corrado, 1989; Corrado & Zivney, 1992). Panel D reports the difference in means and medians between Panel B and Panel C. To check for statistical significance, the parametric two-sample standard t-test and the non-parametric Wilcoxon rank sum test are used. All tests are two-tailed. The symbols ***, **, and * denote statistical significance at 1%, 5%, and 10% level, respectively.

This time both tables indicate a positive stock market reaction for all issues during the two- [0;1] and three-day event window [-1;1]. Splitting all issues in reopenings (Panel B) and regular issues (Panel C) shows the same stock market reactions as with the regular estimation period, i.e. no abnormal returns for bond reopenings and statistically significant positive price effects for new debt offerings. This confirms the previous results that taps cause no stockholder wealth effects while regular issues generate a stock price appreciation. Additionally, stronger indications for differences between both bond issue types is found as the non-parametric test for the two-day window [0;1] in Panel D turns out to be statistically significant with a p-value of less than 5%. While this is in line with the expectations, it contradicts the results obtained with the regular estimation period.

Altogether, the analysis detects evidence that the announcement of bond reopenings, unlike regular bond issues, produce no stock price reaction. In contrast, regular issues show robust positive abnormal stock returns implying that both events produce diverging reactions from stockholders. This is in line with the expectations. However, conducting univariate tests reveal rather weak support for the hypothesis that investors react differently regarding both issue types. Therefore, further analyses are required to offer a more in-depth analysis.

4.3.3 Cross Sectional Regression Analysis

Since event study methodologies are unable to retrieve consistent results about the diverging impact of reopenings and regular bond issues, carrying out univariate analysis, the following section follows the reasoning of Chen (2013) and performs cross sectional regression analyses in this section. The variable of interest is a bond reopening dummy (REOPEN) which equals one when the announced debt offering is a reopening, otherwise zero. The expectation is a statistically significant and negative coefficient, confirming the window of opportunity hypothesis.

Moreover, several control variables are included that may be related to the wealth effects of debt offerings. Ln(PROCEEDS) and Ln(TOTAL ASSETS) present the natural logarithm of proceeds of a bond issue and the natural logarithm of the total assets of the examined company measured at fiscal year-end prior to the announcement year (FY-1). Both variables control for a possible size effect, which is crucial for the analysis because reopenings tend to be smaller in terms of issue volume than regular issues.[57] Additionally, PROCEEDSRatio is included which measures the ratio of gained proceeds scaled by long-term debt. The variables MATURITY, YIELD, and RATING are added to further control for bond specific attributes. MATURITY presents the term to maturity (in years), YIELD the yield to maturity at offering date (in percent), and RATING a value corresponding to S&P's credit rating at offering. The variable is created by assigning 1 to a rating of AAA, 2 to a rating of AA+, 3 to a rating of AA, etc. and captures the impact of risk on price reactions. FRANCE is a dummy variable that equals one when the bond is issued in France. This variable is included because France covers 66% of all regular issues and 67% of all taps in the sample. ENERGY is also a dummy variable equal to one when the company belongs to the "Energy and Power" industry as indicated by the Thomson One Banker Macro Description. Research that investigates debt offerings frequently excludes utilities from their sample (Cook & Easterwood, 1994; Dann & Mikkelson, 1984; Kolodny & Suhler, 1988; Mikkelson & Partch, 1986) or analyze them separately (Chen, 2013; Eckbo, 1986) because the energy industry is more heavily regulated than other industries and therefore might behave differently. This dummy variable is utilized to control for any differences. Company specific variables are the natural logarithm of long-term debt (Ln(LTDEBT)), Return-on-Equity ratio (ROE), Market-to-Book ratio (MARKETtoBOOK), and Debt-to-Equity ratio (DEBTtoEQUITY), which control for the company's leverage, profitability and growth opportunities. All four variables are measured at fiscal year-end prior to the announcement year (FY-1)[58].

Investors might act differently depending on the intended use of proceeds. Announced expansions could cause more favorable price reactions than pure refinancing or general corporate purpose, underlining the necessity for an adjustment. Therefore, the issuing company's homepage and the homepage of the exchange were the bond is listed is screened, and google search for the prospectus of the respective bond issue is conducted. In the end 20 prospectuses are unavailable, leaving a final sample of 118 events (70 reopenings plus 48 regular issues). Two dummy variables REFINANCING and EXPANSIONS are created depending on the intended use. They equal one when the prospectus states the corresponding use (the third and omitted dummy is "general corporate purposes").

---

57 See section 4.2.1.

58 Twice the Market-to-Book ratio was not available and replaced by the subsequent year's value (FY0). Source for Pproceeds and rating at issuance is Thomson One Banker. Source for total assets, longterm debt, and debt-to-equity is Worldscope. Source for market-to-book is Datastream.

Additionally, following the reasoning by Cook and Easterwood (1994) this model controls for covenants including put options for investors by screening the prospectus and adding the variable INVESTORPUT to the regression. This variable equals one when the holder has the option to redeem the bond in case of certain "Put Events" (for instance in the case of a change of control). Finally, a possible tax effect is controlled for by including the variable TAX which presents the ratio of income taxes and pretax income measured at fiscal year-end prior to the announcement.[59] Tax rate was unavailable for 15 events, reducing the full sample to 123 observations. Furthermore, following Tang and Singer (1993) the tax rate is multiplied by the proceeds of the bond issue and the variable TAXAMOUNT added to the model. Additionally, VIF are calculated to control for multicollinearity and recompute regressions while eliminating independent variables with VIF of five or higher. They are removed successively starting with the highest value until only variables with VIFs of less than five are included into the regression.

While standard OLS-regression with heteroskedasticity adjusted standard errors represents a widespread method in finance research to examine the interdependency of firm and security related determinants with security returns, the author is aware that applying this regression model disregards clustering of data. Clusters occur in the setting due to two specifications: First, all sample firms announce regular debt offerings as well as reopenings. Thus, these firms might be found at least twice in the sample, depending on the number of reopenings. Second, companies that decided to issue debt once, usually tend to do so again further increasing the sample with identical firms. Such clustering can affect the standard errors, leading to inflated t-statistics and unjustified statistically significant determinants (Moulton, 1990). Therefore, this thesis controls for possible error term dependency within clusters to validate the robustness of the results and the significant impact of the REOPEN variable. However, with small group sizes (N << 50) the cure (i.e. utilization of cluster-robust estimation) can have worse effects than the illness (disregard of possible interdependences within groups) (Donald & Lang, 2007; Wooldridge, 2003). Thus, both methodologies are used to validate the results.

59 Source for this variable is Worldscope.

Table 4-16: Cross Sectional Regression Analysis of Reopening Announcements on Bond Returns

Dependent Variable: ABR [0;0] in bps									
Panel A: Complete Sample	**Model I**	**Model II**		**Model III**	**Model IV**		**Model V**	**Model VI**	
Intercept	−0.206	0.220	0.285	−0.074	0.623	0.458	−0.016	0.326	0.384
REOPEN	0.059	0.123	0.113	0.039	0.065	0.061	0.016	0.079	0.069
Ln(PROCEEDS)	−0.068***(°°)	−0.020	−0.017	−0.065*	−0.047	−0.038	−0.078***(°°)	−0.030	−0.035
Ln(TOTAL ASSETS)	0.041*(°)	−0.088*	−0.009	0.032	−0.130*	−0.007	0.030	−0.115*	−0.014
MATURITY	–	0.014	0.016*(°)	–	0.013	0.016	–	0.012	0.014*(°)
YIELD	–	−0.065**(°°)	−0.058*(°)	–	−0.054*(°)	−0.046(°)	–	−0.066**(°°)	−0.059*(°)
FRANCE	–	0.040	0.040	–	0.016	0.022	–	0.096	0.098
ENERGY	–	−0.028	−0.036	–	−0.088	−0.068	–	0.073	0.065
RATING	–	−0.015	−0.018	–	−0.022	−0.025	–	−0.008	−0.012
Ln(LTDEBT)	–	0.103*	–	–	0.138*	–	–	0.120**	−0.558(°°°)
PROCEEDSRatio	–	−0.126	−0.512(°°°)	–	0.034	−0.397(°°°)	–	−0.145	0.000
ROE	–	−0.001	−0.001	–	−0.002	−0.002	–	0.000	0.005*(°)
MARKETtoBOOK	–	0.010*	0.009*	–	0.014**(°)	0.011***(°°°)	–	0.004	–
DEBTtoEQUITY	–	0.000	0.000	–	0.000	–	–	0.000	–
REFINANCING	–	–	–	−0.011	−0.039	0.025	–	–	–
EXPANSIONS	–	–	–	0.059	−0.123	−0.039	–	–	–
INVESTORPUT	–	–	–	−0.059	−0.068	−0.037	–	–	–
TAXRATE	–	–	–	–	–	–	0.000	0.000	−0.001
TAXAMOUNT	–	–	–	–	–	–	0.000	0.000	0.000
N(Cluster)	138(40)	138(40)	138(40)	118(33)	118(33)	118(33)	123(36)	123(36)	123(36)
Max. VIF	1.619	7.765	4.542	1.985	11.601	2.525	3.683	9.865	3.906
R^2	0.071	0.199	0.183	0.070	0.187	0.164	0.058	0.228	0.204
adj. R^2	0.050	0.115	0.104	0.020	0.059	0.051	0.017	0.119	0.109
F-Statistic	4.792***(3.399°°)	2.330***(5.502°°°)	2.412***(5.492°°°)	2.037*(3.010°°°)	1.802**(6.829°°°)	1.807**(6.235°°°)	2.216*(1.810)	2.204**(5.022°°°)	1.963**(4.952°°°)
Panel B: Control Sample									
Intercept	−0.188	0.261	0.373	−0.104	0.631	0.486	0.000	0.431	0.533
REOPEN	0.035	0.097	0.088	0.007	0.030	0.026	0.000	0.062	0.052
Ln(PROCEEDS)	−0.083***(°°°)	−0.028	−0.016	−0.082**(°)	−0.059	−0.044	−0.096***(°°°)	−0.043	−0.040
Ln(TOTAL ASSETS)	0.048*(°)	−0.102**	−0.018	0.043(°)	−0.118	−0.009	0.039	−0.129**	−0.022

MATURITY	–	0.012	0.015	–	0.012	0.015	–	0.009	0.011
YIELD	–	–0.060*(°)	–0.055*	–	–0.046	–0.041	–	–0.063**(°°)	–0.059*(°)
FRANCE	–	0.063	0.058	–	0.064	0.069	–	0.106	0.104
ENERGY	–	–0.024	–0.036	–	–0.077	–0.063	–	0.073	0.063
RATING	–	–0.013	–0.014	–	–0.026	–0.026	–	–0.003	–0.008
Ln(LTDEBT)	–	0.117**(°°)	–	–	0.128*	–	–	0.134**(°°)	–
PROCEEDSRatio	–	–0.383	–0.898**(°)	–	–0.294	–0.753*	–	–0.470	–0.989**(°)
ROE	–	–0.001	–0.001	–	–0.002*	–0.002*(°)	–	0.000	0.000
MARKETtoBOOK	–	0.008	0.007	–	0.012	0.011***(°°)	–	0.004	0.004
DEBTtoEQUITY	–	0.000	0.000	–	0.000	–	–	0.000	–
REFINANCING	–	–	–	0.042	0.016	0.067	–	–	–
EXPANSIONS	–	–	–	0.086	–0.118	–0.036	–	–	–
INVESTORPUT	–	–	–	–0.037	–0.024	0.006	–	–	–
TAXRATE	–	–	–	–	–	–	0.000	–0.001	–0.001
TAXAMOUNT	–	–	–	–	–	–	0.000	0.000	0.000*(°)
N(Cluster)	123(39)	123(39)	123(39)	106(32)	106(32)	106(32)	109(35)	109(35)	109(35)
Max. VIF	1.566	7.921	4.630	1.970	11.170	2.738	3.693	10.122	3.922
R^2	0.074	0.214	0.195	0.075	0.201	0.181	0.067	0.255	0.228
adj. R^2	0.050	0.121	0.107	0.019	0.057	0.055	0.022	0.135	0.122
F-Statistic	5.498***(5.211°°°)	2.618***(1.951°°)	2.534***(2.495°°°)	2.093*(2.702°°)	2.002**(3.955°°°)	1.822**(3.530°°°)	2.894**(3.275°°°)	2.451***(2.605°°°)	2.155**(2.359°°°)

This table presents the results of a cross sectional regression analysis of abnormal bond returns (in basis points) on the bond issue announcement day [0;0]. Panel A displays results without adjustments for confounding events (Complete Sample), while Panel B shows results with adjustments (Control Sample). Regressions with a maximum VIF of five or higher are recalculated only containing variables with a maximum VIF under five. REOPEN is a dummy variable which equals one when the announced debt offering is a reopening. Ln(PROCEEDS) and Ln(TOTAL ASSETS) present the natural logarithm of proceeds of a bond issuance and the natural logarithm of the total assets of the examined company measured at fiscal year-end prior to the announcement year. MATURITY presents the term to maturity in years. YIELD presents the yield to maturity at offering date in percent. FRANCE is a dummy variable that equals one when the bond is issued in France. ENERGY is a dummy variable equal to 1 when the company belongs to the "Energy and Power" industry as indicated by the Thomson One Banker Macro Description. RATING presents the bond's S&P rating at offering in the following form: 1 to a rating of AAA, 2 to a rating of AA+, 3 to a rating of AA, etc. Ln(LTDEB) is the natural logarithm of a firm's long-term debt measured at fiscal year-end prior to the announcement year. PROCEEDSRatio measures the ratio of gained proceeds scaled by long-term debt. ROE presents the Return on Equity measured at fiscal year-end prior to the announcement year. MARKETtoBOOK presents the ratio of the market price and the book value per share measured at fiscal year-end prior to the announcement. DEBTtoEQUITY presents the ratio of total debt and common equity measured at fiscal year-end prior to the announcement. REFINANCING and EXPANSIONS are dummy variables indicating the intended usage of the funds as stated in the prospectus. INVESTORPUT is a dummy variable which equals one when the holder has the option to redeem the bond in case of certain "Put Events". TAXRATE represents the ratio of income taxes and pretax income measured at fiscal year-end prior to the announcement. TAXAMOUNT represents the product of TAXRATE and the proceeds of the bond issue. The symbols ***, **, and * denote statistical significance at 1%, 5%, and 10% level with robust standard errors adjusted for heteroskedasticity following White (1980), respectively. The symbols °°°, °°, and ° denote statistical significance at 1%, 5%, and 10% level with robust standard errors adjusted for clustering, respectively.

Table 4-17: Cross Sectional Regression Analysis of Reopening Announcements on Stock Returns

Dependent Variable: CASR [−1;1] in %									
Panel A: Complete Sample	**Model I**	**Model II**		**Model III**	**Model IV**		**Model V**	**Model VI**	
Intercept	0.082***(°°)	0.067**(°)	0.067**	0.045	0.052	0.052	0.073***(°)	0.070*(°)	0.067*
REOPEN	−0.016***(°°)	−0.013**(°)	−0.013**(°)	−0.011*(°)	−0.012*	−0.012*	−0.016***(°°)	−0.010	−0.011*
Ln(PROCEEDS)	−0.008***(°)	−0.007**	−0.007**	−0.005	−0.004	−0.005	−0.008***(°)	−0.006*	−0.006*
Ln(TOTAL ASSETS)	−0.002	−0.003	−0.002	−0.001	−0.002	−0.002	−0.002	−0.007	−0.002
MATURITY	–	0.000	0.000	–	0.000	0.000	–	0.000	0.001
YIELD	–	−0.002	−0.001	–	0.002	0.002	–	−0.002	−0.001
FRANCE	–	−0.010**	−0.010**	–	0.000	0.001	–	−0.013**(°)	−0.011*
ENERGY	–	−0.001	−0.001	–	0.004	0.004	–	−0.008	−0.008
RATING	–	0.002*	0.002*	–	−0.001	−0.001	–	0.002*	0.001
Ln(LTDEBT)	–	0.001	–	–	−0.001	–	–	0.004	–
PROCEEDSRatio	–	0.026	0.023	–	−0.002	0.008	–	0.025	0.025
ROE	–	0.000	0.000	–	0.000	0.000	–	0.000	0.000
MARKETtoBOOK	–	0.000	0.000	–	0.001	0.000	–	0.001	0.000
DEBTtoEQUITY	–	0.000**	0.000**	–	0.000	–	–	0.000**(°)	–
REFINANCING	–	–	–	−0.001	0.000	−0.001	–	–	–
EXPANSIONS	–	–	–	−0.002	0.000	−0.002	–	–	–
INVESTORPUT	–	–	–	0.016***(°°)	0.018***(°°)	0.018***(°°)	–	–	–
TAXRATE	–	–	–	–	–	–	0.000	0.001	0.000
TAXAMOUNT	–	–	–	–	–	–	0.000	0.000**(°)	0.000
N(Cluster)	138(40)	138(40)	138(40)	118(33)	118(33)	118(33)	123(36)	123(36)	123(36)
Max. VIF	1.619	7.765	4.542	1.985	11.601	2.525	3.683	9.865	3.906
R^2	0.072	0.123	0.123	0.143	0.173	0.166	0.081	0.166	0.142
adj. R^2	0.051	0.032	0.039	0.097	0.042	0.052	0.042	0.049	0.039
F-Statistic	4.171***(2.026)	2.955***(3.040°°°)	3.283***(3.286°°°)	3.789***(3.215°°°)	3.148***(3.577°°°)	2.835***(2.705°°°)	2.524**(2.705°°°)	2.475***2.455°°°)	1.460(1.871°°)
Panel B: Control Sample									
Intercept	0.069***(°)	0.035	0.040	0.046	0.031	0.029	0.062**	0.030	0.033
REOPEN	−0.014**(°°)	−0.013**(°)	−0.014**(°)	−0.011*(°)	−0.014**(°)	−0.014**(°)	−0.012**(°)	−0.011*	−0.012*(°)
Ln(PROCEEDS)	−0.009***(°°)	−0.012***(°°)	−0.011***(°°)	−0.007**(°)	−0.011**(°°)	−0.011***(°°)	−0.010***(°°)	−0.011***(°°)	−0.012***(°°)
Ln(TOTAL ASSETS)	−0.001	−0.001	0.003	0.000	0.002	0.004	0.000	−0.004	0.003

MATURITY	–	0.000	0.000	–	–0.001	–0.001	–	0.000	0.000
YIELD	–	0.000	0.000	–	0.003	0.003	–	0.000	0.001
FRANCE	–	–0.006	–0.007	–	0.003	0.004	–	–0.008	–0.007
ENERGY	–	–0.001	–0.002	–	0.003	0.004	–	–0.009	–0.009
RATING	–	0.001	0.001	–	–0.002	–0.002	–	0.001	0.000
Ln(LTDEBT)	–	0.006	–	–	0.001	–	–	0.009	–
PROCEEDSRatio	–	0.098**(°)	0.074**(°)	–	0.063	0.063*	–	0.101**(°)	0.078**
ROE	–	0.000	0.000	–	0.000	0.000	–	0.000	0.000
MARKETtoBOOK	–	0.000	0.000	–	0.000	0.000	–	0.000	0.000
DEBTtoEQUITY	–	0.000*	0.000	–	0.000	–	–	0.000*	–
REFINANCING	–	–	–	0.003	0.003	0.003	–	–	–
EXPANSIONS	–	–	–	–0.005	–0.003	–0.004	–	–	–
INVESTORPUT	–	–	–	0.013**(°°)	0.015**(°°)	0.015***(°°)	–	–	–
TAXRATE	–	–	–	–	–	–	0.000	0.000	0.000
TAXAMOUNT	–	–	–	–	–	–	0.000	0.000	0.000
N(Cluster)	123(39)	123(39)	123(39)	106(32)	106(32)	106(32)	109(35)	109(35)	109(35)
Max. VIF	1.566	7.921	4.630	1.970	11.170	2.738	3.693	10.122	3.922
R^2	0.072	0.152	0.144	0.123	0.194	0.193	0.085	0.202	0.174
adj. R^2	0.048	0.051	0.051	0.070	0.049	0.068	0.040	0.074	0.061
F-Statistic	4.019***(1.857)	2.987***(3.273°°°)	3.495***(3.114°°°)	3.434***(4.642°°°)	2.993***(3.129°°°)	2.780***(3.317°°°)	2.474**(1.236)	2.808***(3.251°°°)	1.904**(1.555)

This table presents the results of a cross sectional regression analysis of cumulative abnormal stock returns (in basis points) on the bond issue announcement day [–1;1]. Panel A displays results without adjustments for confounding events (Complete Sample), while Panel B shows results with adjustments (Control Sample). Regressions with a maximum VIF of five or higher are recalculated only containing variables with a maximum VIF under five. REOPEN is a dummy variable which equals one when the announced debt offering is a reopening. Ln(PROCEEDS) and Ln(TOTAL ASSETS) present the natural logarithm of proceeds of a bond issuance and the natural logarithm of the total assets of the examined company measured at fiscal year-end prior to the announcement year. MATURITY presents the term to maturity in years. YIELD presents the yield to maturity at offering date in percent. FRANCE is a dummy variable that equals one when the bond is issued in France. ENERGY is a dummy variable equal to 1 when the company belongs to the "Energy and Power" industry as indicated by the Thomson One Banker Macro Description. RATING presents the bond's S&P rating at offering in the following form: 1 to a rating of AAA, 2 to a rating of AA+, 3 to a rating of AA, etc. Ln(LTDEB) is the natural logarithm of a firm's long-term debt measured at fiscal year-end prior to the announcement year. PROCEEDSRatio measures the ratio of gained proceeds scaled by long-term debt. ROE presents the Return on Equity measured at fiscal year-end prior to the announcement year. MARKETtoBOOK presents the ratio of the market price and the book value per share measured at fiscal year-end prior to the announcement. DEBTtoEQUITY presents the ratio of total debt and common equity measured at fiscal year-end prior to the announcement. REFINANCING and EXPANSIONS are dummy variables indicating the intended usage of the funds as stated in the prospectus. INVESTORPUT is a dummy variable which equals one when the holder has the option to redeem the bond in case of certain "Put Events". TAXRATE represents the ratio of income taxes and pretax income measured at fiscal year-end prior to the announcement. TAXAMOUNT represents the product of TAXRATE and the proceeds of the bond issue. The symbols ***, **, and * denote statistical significance at 1%, 5%, and 10% level with robust standard errors adjusted for heteroskedasticity following White (1980), respectively. The symbols °°°, °°, and ° denote statistical significance at 1%, 5%, and 10% level with robust standard errors adjusted for clustering, respectively.

The results of the impact of differences in issue types on abnormal bond returns are reported in Table 4-16. Panel A displays the results for the "Complete Sample" and Panel B for the "Control Sample". Six different regression-models are computed: Model I simply controls for a potential size effect, Model II adds all variables available for the full sample, Model III accounts for size and information from the prospectus (i.e. intended use and put option), Model IV adds the variables from Model II, Model V controls for size and tax effects, and Model VI finally adds the variables from Model II. Almost all regressions (except Model V of Panel B) present a positive but insignificant coefficient for REOPEN, failing to show any differences in wealth effects for the two issue types. Obviously, bondholders do not react any differently whether new debt is offered through a regular issue or a reopening. Furthermore, only the variables YIELD and Ln(LTDEBT) show a robust impact on abnormal bond returns. A higher yield offered at issuance leads to lower bond returns. Not surprisingly, investors sell their bond investment when new issues offer increased yields. In addition, a higher level of long-term debt apparently affects announcement bond returns positively. However, almost all regressions containing Ln(LTDEB) reveal multicollinearity to some extent. Only the second regression of Model VI for the complete sample exhibits a max. VIF under five, and presents a significantly negative coefficient contradicting the other regressions. Thus, the final relationship between bond prices and amount of long-term debt remains unclear.

Table 4-17 presents similar regression models to investigate the connection between bond issue type and stockholder wealth effect. This time a completely different outcome is achieved compared to the bond price reactions. The results for the complete sample in Panel A present a negative and statistically significant coefficient for eight (five) regressions for the heteroskedasticity adjusted (cluster adjusted) t-statistics. The results are even stronger for the "Control Sample" in Panel B. All coefficients of the REOPEN-dummy are negative and statistically significant, regardless of the used test statistic adjustment. Thus, the analysis detects in line with the expectation that reopenings generate weaker abnormal stock returns than regular issues by 0.8–1.6%. Another significant and negative impact exhibits Ln(PROCEEDS). Model I through V of Panel B show that larger issues cause stronger stock depreciation at issue announcement. Consistent with Chen (2013) results detect no impact of the dummies for intended use refinancing and expansion. Both variables are statistically insignificant. INVESTORPUT, on the other hand, turns out to be significant for all regressions where the variable is included. Surprisingly, however, the coefficient is positive thereby contradicting the findings by Cook and Easterwood (1994) and confirming the entrenchment hypothesis[60] instead of the mutual interest hypothesis[61].

Altogether, robust results for the different impact of reopenings in contrast to regular bond issues on shareholder wealth are found compared to the univariate analysis. Several regressions for the full sample and all after accounting for confounding events confirm the expectation that abnormal returns decline for reopenings and that this effect is not merely driven by issue size.

The final cross sectional regression investigates the determinants of wealth effects for bonds that are reopened at the announcement of the reopening. Utilizing the bond event study methodology offers negative price responses in Table 4-11. Now, it is relevant which parameters affect the size of the abnormal bond returns. Seven variables from the previous analysis are included (Ln(PROCEEDS), Ln(TOTAL ASSETS), MATURITY, YIELD, FRANCE, ENERGY, and RATING)[62] plus the variable REOPENRatio. REOPENRatio presents the principal amount of the reopening scaled by the principal amount of the regular issue which is reopened. This variable is applied to check if taps that are large (small) compared to the original issue cause stronger (weaker) bondholder wealth effects. Panel A (Panel B) of Table 4-18 displays the result for the "Complete" ("Control") sample.

---

60 Cook and Easterwood explain the entrenchment hypothesis and its impact on stock and bond returns as follows: "... poison puts, as the name suggests, could be designed to make firms less attractive as takeover targets and thus provide additional mechanism for strengthening managerial resistance to hostile bids. This view will be termed the "entrenchment hypothesis". ... The entrenchment hypothesis predicts a negative stock price reaction at the issue announcement of protected bonds. The entrenchment hypothesis has no predicted impact on the value of an issuing firm's outstanding debt." (Cook & Easterwood, 1994 p. 1906)

61 Cook and Easterwood explain the mutual interest hypothesis and its impact on stock and bond returns as follows: "However, the interests of managers and bondholders may be complementary under some circumstances. Managers undertake actions that protect their positions. By coincidence, these actions could also offer benefits to bondholders. In this case, the interests of managers and bondholders would be aligned in that both wish to guard against hostile, debt-financed takeovers. Consequently, the interests of managers and bondholders would conflict with those of shareholders. This view is termed the "mutual interest hypothesis" and it suggests that stock price reactions could be negative while the price reaction of existing bonds could be positive." (Cook & Easterwood, 1994 p. 1908)

62 All bond related parameters belong to the reopening, not the preceding regular issue.

Table 4-18: Cross Sectional Regression Analysis of Bond Reopenings Announcements on Regularly Issued Bond Returns

Dependent Variable: ABR [0;0] in bp	
Panel A: Complete Sample	
Intercept	1.111
REOPENRatio	0.022
Ln(PROCEEDS)	-0.189**
Ln(TOTAL ASSETS)	-0.017
MATURITY	0.012
YIELD	0.025
FRANCE	0.047
ENERGY	-0.324**(°°)
RATING	-0.037*(°)
N(Cluster)	56(26)
Max. VIF	2.352
R^2	0.286
adj. R^2	0.164
F-Statistic	4.294***(10.879°°°)
Panel B: Control Sample	
Intercept	1.162
REOPENRatio	0.124
Ln(PROCEEDS)	-0.232**(°)
Ln(TOTAL ASSETS)	0.002
MATURITY	0.002
YIELD	0.040
FRANCE	0.066
ENERGY	-0.289**(°)
RATING	-0.048**(°)
N(Cluster)	45(26)
Max. VIF	2.252
R^2	0.285
adj. R^2	0.126
F-Statistic	3.487***(4.895°°°)

This table presents the results of a cross sectional regression analysis of abnormal bond returns (in basis points) on the announcement day of the reopening [0;0]. Panel A displays results without adjustments for confounding events (Complete Sample), while Panel B shows results with adjustments (Control Sample). REOPENRatio presents the principal amount of the reopening scaled by the principal amount of the regular issue that is reopened. Ln(PROCEEDS) and Ln(TOTAL ASSETS) present the natural logarithm of proceeds of a bond issuance and the natural logarithm of the total assets of the examined company measured at fiscal year-end prior to the announcement year. MATURITY presents the term to maturity in years. YIELD presents the yield to maturity at offering date in percent. FRANCE is a dummy variable that equals one when the bond is issued in France. ENERGY is a dummy variable equal to 1 when the company belongs to the "Energy and Power" industry as indicated by the Thomson One Banker Macro Description. RATING presents the bond's S&P rating at offering in the following form: 1 to a rating of AAA, 2 to a rating of AA+, 3 to a rating of AA, etc. The symbols ***, **, and * denote statistical significance at 1%, 5%, and 10% level with robust standard errors adjusted for heteroskedasticity following White (1980), respectively. The symbols °°°, °°, and ° denote statistical significance at 1%, 5%, and 10% level with robust standard errors adjusted for clustering, respectively.

Both, Panel A and Panel B show similar results. Comparing the insignificant variable REOPENRatio with the negative and significant coefficient for Ln(PROCEEDS) implies that the size of an offering affects the bond price reaction, but independently from the preceding regular issue. Investors apparently only consider the absolute size of an offering. Interestingly, results reveal that reopened bonds coming from energy sector firms react considerably stronger at the reopening announcement than bonds from other industries. Bondholders from this particular industry seem to suffer more from a management's decision to reopen an already issued bond instead of conducting a new debt offering. The reason for this effect could be that energy sector companies are frequent bond issuer, thus familiar with the whole process. Consequently, a reopening might be interpreted by investors as a clear signal that the bond is overvalued. Finally, the negative and significant coefficient of RATING indicates that better ratings generate less negative abnormal bond returns. Repeating the analysis with firm cluster adjusted standard errors leads to considerably lower test statistics for the determinants. Nevertheless, interpretation of the results are considered as valid since the p-value of Ln(PROCEEDS) in Panel A is close to statistical significance (untabulated p-value of 10.1%) and remains statistically significant in Panel B.

4.3.4 Potential Endogeneity

So far, the variable of interest REOPEN was considered to be uncorrelated with the error term in the regression models which is essential to obtain unbiased results when utilizing OLS regressions. Nevertheless, the complexity of the observed data might introduce unwanted biases which, in turn, can result in endogeneity. Examples are the simultaneous-equation and the omitted variable bias. The first bias occurs whenever the dependant and the explanatory variable are determined simultaneously, while the second affects regression results when a variable that correlates with the dependant and the independent variable is omitted from the regression model (Larcker & Rusticus, 2010).

A popular standard procedure to account for potential endogeneity is the utilization of instrumental variables or instruments. The key assumption for these variables to qualify as solution to the endogeneity issue is as follows: they have to be correlated with the endogenous regressor and, at the same time, be uncorrelated with the error term in the structural equation. While at first this sounds like an straightforward way to resolve the problem with endogenous variables, finding an adequate instrumental variable is difficult and can become a big challenge for researchers facing this problem. Moreover, applying a weak instrument can lead in estimates that are even more biased than standard OLS regressions

(Larcker & Rusticus, 2010). Thus, researchers need to be careful not to think that the utilization of any instrument can easily solve the endogeneity issue.

A strand of empirical literature that, as a result of their research objectives, often has to handle regressor variables that are endogenous stems from accounting research (e.g. Agarwal, Taffler, & Brown, 2011; Fu, Kraft, & Zhang, 2012; Wang & Hussainey, 2013). Furthermore, accounting studies provide alternative procedures to test the research setting for the potential to be affected by endogenous variables without the difficulty to choose the right instrument. Within this chapter an approach recommended by Larcker and Rusticus (2010) is applied which, in turn, stems from the paper by Frank (2000). The idea is to assess how large the endogeneity problem has to be to make the regressor variable statistically insignificant by examining the potential impact of unobserved confounding variables. For an unobserved variable to have an impact on the results it needs to be correlated with the regressor and the outcome variable, while controlling for other factors.

In a first step, the Impact Threshold for a Confounding Variable (ITCV) is computed following Frank (2000) as follows:

$$\mathrm{ITCV} = \left(\sqrt{(I - R^2_{x \cdot z}) \cdot (1 - R^2_{y \cdot z})}\right) \cdot \left(\frac{t^2 + t \cdot \sqrt{d}}{-(n - q - 1)} + \left(\frac{-d - t - \sqrt{d}}{-(n - q - 1)}\right) \cdot r_{y \cdot x|z}\right) \quad (31)$$

n equals the number of observations, q equals the number of model parameters (ex. intercept), t is the critical t-value, and d is calculated as $d = t^2 + (n - q - 1)$. $R^2_{x \cdot z}$ is the R^2 value from a regression predicting the regressor variable by the control variables in vector z, and $R^2_{y \cdot z}$ is the R^2 value from a regression predicting the outcome variable by the control variables in vector z. Lastly, $r_{y \cdot x|z}$ is the partial correlation between the outcome and the regressor variable, with the effect of the control variables. This figure represents the minimum correlation necessary to turn a statistically significant result into a borderline insignificant result. A high (low) ITCV concludes robust (not robust) results.

Second, the threshold value is compared with the impact of the control variables. Following Larcker and Rusticus (2010) the impact of a control variable is computed as the product of the partial correlation between the regressor variable and the control variables and the partial correlation between the outcome variable and the control variables. Table 4-19 presents the results.

Table 4-19: Analysis of the Impact of Unobservable Confounding Variables

Panel A: Abnormal Bond Return	Model I		Model II		Model III	
	ITCV	Impact	ITCV	Impact	ITCV	Impact
REOPEN	-0.073		-0.137		-0.105	
Ln(PROCEEDS)		0.078		0.089		0.072
Ln(TOTAL ASSETS)		-0.001		-0.001		-0.005
MATURITY		-0.045		-0.042		-0.046
YIELD		-0.011		-0.014		-0.035
FRANCE		0.001		0.010		0.012
ENERGY		-0.003		0.004		0.000
RATING		0.003		-0.001		0.000
Ln(LTDEBT)		0.006		0.000		0.004
PROCEEDSRatio		0.001		0.001		-0.013
ROE		-0.001		0.018		0.000
MARKETtoBOOK		0.006		0.004		-0.001
DEBTtoEQUITY		0.000		0.001		-0.001
REFINANCING		–		0.000		–
EXPANSIONS		–		0.008		–
INVESTORPUT		–		0.000		–
TAXRATE		–		–		-0.010
TAXAMOUNT		–		–		-0.021
Panel B: Abnormal Stock Return	**ITCV**	**Impact**	**ITCV**	**Impact**	**ITCV**	**Impact**
REOPEN	-0.305		-0.316		-0.285	
Ln(PROCEEDS)		0.116		0.090		0.105
Ln(TOTAL ASSETS)		0.004		0.006		0.006
MATURITY		-0.025		-0.002		-0.029
YIELD		-0.001		0.010		-0.002
FRANCE		-0.001		0.003		-0.012
ENERGY		-0.002		-0.003		0.000
RATING		-0.001		-0.001		0.000
Ln(LTDEBT)		-0.003		-0.002		-0.002
PROCEEDSRatio		-0.001		-0.001		0.010
ROE		0.001		0.000		-0.002
MARKETtoBOOK		0.002		0.001		-0.001
DEBTtoEQUITY		-0.001		-0.002		-0.010
REFINANCING		–		0.000		–
EXPANSIONS		–		-0.003		–
INVESTORPUT		–		0.004		–
TAXRATE		–		–		0.012
TAXAMOUNT		–		–		-0.008

This table shows the assessment of the impact of unobservable confounding variables following the approach illustrated by Larcker and Rusticus (2010). Panel A presents the results for abnormal bond returns and Panel B for abnormal stock returns. For the dummy variable REOPEN the Impact Threshold for a Confounding Variable (ITCV) is calculated following Frank (2000) indicating the minimum impact of a confounding variable that would be needed to render the coefficient statistically significant. Impact represents the impact of the inclusion of each control variable on the coefficient on REOPEN. It is defined as the product of the partial correlation between the regressor and the control variable and the partial correlation between the outcome and the control variable. The t refers to the critical t-value at the 5% level.

The results in Panel A are of less importance as the REOPEN dummy already turned out to be a statistically insignificant determinant for the bondholder wealth (see Table 4-16). Nevertheless, it should be mentioned that Model I of Panel A renders some concerns about omitted variables, because the amount of the threshold variable ITCV is smaller than the first impact. However, only one variable (i.e. Ln(PROCEEDS)) and one out of three models (Model I) raise doubts about the robustness of the regression results. More critical are the figures in Panel B as the REOPEN dummy is statistically significant in regard to the stockholder returns. Therefore, the analysis focuses on the data in Panel B.

The threshold value lies between –0.285 in Model III and –0.316 in Model II which suggests that the correlation between this variable and the outcome variable and between the outcome variable and the unobserved confounding variable need to be approximately between 0.534 ($=\sqrt{0.285}$) and 0.562 ($=\sqrt{0.316}$) for the OLS regression results to be overturned. More specifically, using equation (16) of Frank (2000) renders the minimum values 0.476, 0.483, and 0.455 for Model I, II, and III for which the t-statistic is not statistically significant. The variable with the largest impact on the coefficient for offering type is the natural logarithm of the proceeds for all three models, with a value between 0.116 and 0.090. An unmodeled confounding variable would have to be much more highly correlated than the variable for issue size with the dependent variable and issue type. Since, however, the regressions exhibit a comprehensive set of control variables, which are taken from prior research or included due to reasonable considerations about the determinants of the wealth effects of debt offerings, the suspected endogeneity problem related to the independent variable of offering type can confidently be ruled out.

4.3.5 Wealth Transfer of Different Debt Offering Types

Recent research by Chen (2013) on price responses due to debt offerings provides theoretical verification for the redistribution of wealth from bondholders to stockholders, but fails to confirm this result with an empirical analysis. Correlation between stockholder and bondholder abnormal returns turns out to be negative but not statistically significant. Since the results already presented evidence that stockholders react differently whether debt is offered through a regular issue or a reopening, the next logic step is to investigate the impact of issue type on the existence of a wealth transfer as well.

Following prior research about redistribution of wealth between shareholders and bondholders (Baran & King, 2010; Kitsabunnarat-Chatjuthamard et al., 2010; Maxwell & Rao, 2003; Maxwell & Stephens, 2003) this chapter utilizes Pearson correlation and cross sectional regression analysis with the abnormal change in the market value of equity (ACMVE) as the dependent variable and abnormal change in the market value of debt (ACMVD) as the independent variable. Both variables are computed over the three-day window surrounding the announcement [−1;1]. A negative and statistically significant coefficient signals that wealth is expropriated from one stakeholder class to another. As before, two different computations for the variables are used ("Daily Data" and "Yearly Data").[63] With the "Daily Data Approach" ACMVE is computed by multiplying a firm's market value on day t-1 with the abnormal stock return on day t over the event window [−3;3]. To calculate ACMVD, in a first step, each abnormal bond return on day t is multiplied with the bond's respective market value on day t-1 during the [−3;3] event window. Second, the equally weighted average for every firm in the sample is computed. The "Yearly Data Procedure" uses a firm's market capitalization and total debt at fiscal year-end prior to the event. Both are multiplied with the respective abnormal return on firm level to compute a second set of ACMVE and ACMVD variables.

Table 4-20 and Table 4-21 show the correlation coefficient between ACMVE and ACMVD for the "Yearly Data" and the "Daily Data". Both tables present statistically significant negative correlations for the full sample (i.e. all issues) which seem to be driven by the subsample of reopenings. For most event windows, reopenings show higher correlation coefficients and lower p-values than the full sample. Regular issues, on the other hand, show only insignificant (Table 4-21) or some positive (Table 4-20) correlations. Altogether, Pearson correlation provides evidence that wealth is redistributed from bondholders to stockholders and this effect is strongest for the announcement of the reopening of regular issues.

63 See chapter 3.3.4 for the rationale to use both approaches.

Table 4-20: Pearson Correlation between Abnormal Change in the Market Value of Equity and Debt (Yearly Data)

	All Issues		Reopenings		Regular Issues	
	Correlation	**p-value**	**Correlation**	**p-value**	**Correlation**	**p-value**
Panel A: Complete Sample						
[−1;0]	−0.201	0.018	−0.202	0.064	−0.212	0.127
[0;0]	−0.066	0.440	−0.066	0.547	−0.058	0.681
[0;1]	0.001	0.990	−0.406***	0.000	0.324**	0.018
[−1;1]	−0.100	0.244	−0.189*	0.084	0.160	0.253
[−2;2]	−0.096	0.264	−0.005	0.965	−0.226	0.104
[−3;3]	−0.212**	0.013	−0.315***	0.003	−0.198	0.156
Panel B: Control Sample						
[−1;0]	−0.226**	0.012	−0.248**	0.034	−0.211	0.141
[0;0]	−0.102	0.261	−0.153	0.197	−0.054	0.711
[0;1]	−0.038	0.677	−0.562***	0.000	0.329**	0.020
[−1;1]	−0.265***	0.003	−0.455***	0.000	0.166	0.249
[−2;2]	−0.246***	0.006	−0.280*	0.017	−0.226	0.115
[−3;3]	−0.147	0.106	−0.161	0.177	−0.198	0.167

This table presents the Pearson Correlation Coefficient and p-value between the abnormal change in the market value of equity (ACMVE) and the abnormal change in the market value of debt (ACMVD) for various event windows surrounding the event day. ACMVE on day t is calculated as the multiplication of a firm's market capitalization at fiscal year-end prior to the announcement and the abnormal stock return on day t. ACMVD on day t is calculated by multiplying each abnormal bond return (firm level) on day t with Total Debt at fiscal year-end prior to the announcement. Panel A reports the results for the "Complete Sample", while Panel B reports the result for the "Control Sample". The symbols ***, **, and * denote statistical significance at 1%, 5%, and 10% level, respectively.

The following four tables (Table 4-23, Table 4-24, Table 4-25 and Table 4-26) present cross sectional regression analyses to further examine the existence of a wealth transfer for reopening announcements. The first two tables utilize "Yearly Data" while the second set of tables uses the "Daily Data Set". Every table consists of three Panels: Panel A for all issues (i.e. regular issues plus reopenings), Panel B for reopenings and Panel C for regular issues. Adjustments for confounding events are performed with Table 4-24 and Table 4-26. Since the confirmation or refutation of the wealth transfer proposition is the objective of these computations other variables than ACMVD are not explored. Browsing Table 4-23 presents no sign for a redistribution of wealth between bondholders and stockholders. Neither Panel A, nor Panel B present significant values and only two coefficients in Panel C are statistically significant for both tests (i.e. heteroskedasticity adjusted and cluster robust). These, however, are positive further indicating the non-existence of a wealth transfer. Yet, controlling for confounding events (Table 4-24) considerably alters the results. Several regressions confirm the transfer effect for reopenings with highly significant and negative coefficients in Panel B. Both Panel A and Panel C, on the other hand, exhibit no statistically significant effect. Thus, as expected, redistribution of wealth is limited to reopenings. However, including variables for intended use (i.e. REFINANCING and EXPANSIONS) and put option for investors (INVESTORPUT) in Model III and Model IV leads to insignificant results for ACMVD. Hence, analysis of the wealth transfer regression with yearly data yields support for the existence of wealth redistribution from bondholders to stockholders. The effect, however, depends on the applied model.

Table 4-21: Pearson Correlation between Abnormal Change in the Market Value of Equity and Debt (Daily Data)

	All Issues		**Reopenings**		**Regular Issues**	
	Correlation	**p-value**	**Correlation**	**p-value**	**Correlation**	**p-value**
Panel A: Complete Sample						
[-1;0]	-0.056	0.514	-0.088	0.422	-0.020	0.888
[0;0]	0.021	0.807	0.013	0.909	0.067	0.635
[0;1]	0.014	0.875	-0.086	0.433	0.154	0.271
[-1;1]	-0.044	0.610	-0.098	0.374	0.103	0.461
[-2;2]	-0.169**	0.048	-0.255**	0.019	-0.071	0.611
[-3;3]	-0.116	0.179	-0.307***	0.005	-0.038	0.790
Panel B: Control Sample						
[-1;0]	-0.039	0.666	-0.072	0.545	-0.022	0.881
[0;0]	0.022	0.812	0.012	0.923	0.065	0.653
[0;1]	0.020	0.830	-0.100	0.398	0.149	0.300
[-1;1]	-0.028	0.759	-0.101	0.394	0.096	0.506
[-2;2]	-0.179**	0.048	-0.298**	0.011	-0.071	0.622
[-3;3]	-0.107	0.240	-0.311***	0.008	-0.035	0.809

This table presents the Pearson Correlation Coefficient and p-value between the abnormal change in the market value of equity (ACMVE) and the abnormal change in the market value of debt (ACMVD) for various event windows surrounding the event day. ACMVE on day t is calculated as the multiplication of a firm's market capitalization on day t-1 and the abnormal stock return on day t. ACMVD on day t is calculated by first, multiplying each abnormal bond return on day t with the bond's respective market value on day t-1. Second, the equally weighted average is computed for every firm in the sample. Panel A reports the results for the "Complete Sample", while Panel B reports the result for the "Adjustment Sample". The symbols ***, **, and * denote statistical significance at 1%, 5%, and 10% level, respectively.

Recalculating the regressions from Table 4-23 with daily data in Table 4-25 leads to similar results. Again, most coefficients are insignificant implying that a wealth transfer between debtholders and equityholders does not exist. Table 4-26 on the other hand, presents strong evidence for the redistribution effect. All regressions computed for the reopening sample (Panel B) show a statistically significant and negative coefficient up to the 1% level. In summary, the results show a clear negative correlation between the Euro gains of a firm's stockholders and the Euro losses of the same firm's bondholders for the subsample of reopenings, but only after accounting for confounding events. Apparently, increasing the level of debt by reopening outstanding bonds is considered to be a risk increasing event. A possible explanation could be that debt and equity investors expect reopening management just to exploit favorable market conditions, hereby causing higher cost of financial distress and leading to an increased overall firm risk. At first glance this is surprising, as results detect no significant abnormal stock return for this debt offering type and statistically significant price responses with diverging signs usually are interpreted as a sign for a wealth transfer. At second glance, however, these results can be interpreted in a way that evidence is found that wealth effects of regular bond issues for stockholders are not only driven by a transfer of wealth between stakeholder classes, but also by the positive signaling hypothesis. Reopenings, on the other hand, present a adverse signal for overvalued corporate bonds. Thus, the negative impact of the overvaluation signal nullifies the positive signaling effect and hereby reveals the existence of a wealth transfer.

4.3.6 Window of Opportunity Framework

This section is devoted to test whether increased bond prices/decreased yields are one of the main driver for the decision to reopen an existing corporate bond, before it reaches its final maturity. As already mentioned reopenings might present a convenient way to time the market and exploit the presence of overvalued corporate bonds. It is a known fact that managers decide to issue securities when they consider them to be overvalued (Carlson, Fisher, & Giammarino, 2006; Daniel, Hirshleifer, & Subrahmanyam, 1998; Loughran & Ritter, 1995). There is no reason to believe that managers only exploit a window of opportunity when it applies to a firm's shares. Thus, the development of the reopened bond price between the issuance day and the day of the reopening announcement is examined. A statistically significant increase in the bond price would imply that the firm's management did take advantage of overvalued bonds. And this, on the other hand, would explain the insignificant stock price reaction for reopenings and negative impact on the reopened bond, as investors would anticipate the actual reason for the reopening.

First the preliminary sample of debt offerings, which contains 174 announcements (94 reopenings and 80 regular offerings), is checked for bond price availability. To calculate the return between issuance and reopening, two prices for the regular issued bonds are necessary: the first price at issuance and the price at the reopening. Moreover, the price at the reopening announcement is replaced by the figure of the previous trading day. This is done to mitigate the impact of the announcement on the bond price. In the end, both figures are available for 86 announcements. Table 4-22 presents the results.

Table 4-22: Average Bond Return of the Reopened Corporate Bonds

Mean	0.92%
t-statistic	*1.956**
Median	0.70%
z-statistic	*–2.535***
N	86

This table presents the mean and median bond returns of the reopened issue computed for the time window starting at issuance and ending one trading day prior to the reopening announcement. Applied test statistics are the one-sample t-test for the mean and the Wilcoxon signed rank test for the median. The symbols ***, **, and * denote statistical significance at 1%, 5%, and 10% level

Both, the mean and median value are statistically significant and positive indicating that the price of the corporate bond did, in fact, increase till the reopening announcement. Thus, managers seem to exploit mispricing when reopening an existing corporate bond, hereby taking advantage of the window of opportunity framework. However, the return turns out to be rather small compared to stock price run-ups prior to stock offerings (see Asquith & Mullins Jr, 1986; Loughran & Ritter, 1997). The decisive factor for this difference could be that the period between the regular issue and the reopening announcement varies (see Table 4-5). Prior stock returns usually are computed for one or more years prior the offering, while most of the time windows between bond issuance and reopening are much shorter. Additionally, most bond investors are investors that hold until maturity further weakening the liquidity. Altogether, this analysis provides some indication for the existence of a window of opportunity effect for reopenings.

Table 4-23: Cross Sectional Regression Analysis of Wealth Transfer between Stockholders and Bondholders of Debt Offering Companies (Complete Sample/Yearly Data)

Dependent Variable: ACMVE yearly										
Panel A: All Issues	**Model I**	**Model II**		**Model III**	**Model IV**		**Model V**		**Model VI**	
Intercept	−3,504.120*	−3,743.070	−3,661.120	−7,174.270***(°°°)	−6,390.080*(°°)	−6,563.640*(°°)	−4,445.210*	–	−3,523.010	−3,757.140
ACMVD	−0.777	−0.074	−0.135	0.544	0.721	0.755	−0.558	–	0.424	0.422
Ln(PROCEEDS)	−115.192	−45.560	−32.766	80.381	111.267	92.156	−73.602	–	30.480	27.140
Ln(TOTAL ASSETS)	405.605*	200.357	337.224	588.517**(°°)	422.809	516.021(°°)	465.545*	–	218.986	375.126
MATURITY	–	49.302	54.419	–	5.847	6.407	–	–	44.087	52.661
YIELD	–	−98.926	−87.243	–	72.350	89.036	–	–	−95.593	−62.135
FRANCE	–	−1,011.900***(°°)	−1,009.810***(°°)	–	−385.577	−357.642	–	–	−1,388.260***(°°)	−1,307.620***(°°)
ENERGY	–	−294.722	−313.082	–	84.179	110.959	–	–	−410.745	−382.789
RATING	–	130.294**(°°)	126.010**(°°)	–	2.620	−16.901	–	–	149.922**(°°)	97.723*(°)
Ln(LTDEBT)	–	179.817	–	–	74.449	–	–	–	126.681	–
PROCEEDSRatio	–	1,550.210	874.123	–	186.616	222.878	–	–	1,222.580	1,395.540(°°)
ROE	–	6.955**(°)	7.013**(°)	–	4.353	2.554	–	–	6.620	−1.597
MARKETtoBOOK	–	34.370**	33.755**	–	26.756	−2.357	–	–	61.992**(°°)	20.902
DEBTtoEQUITY	–	−0.911***(°°)	−0.850**(°)	–	−0.701	–	–	–	−1.196**(°)	–
REFINANCING	–	–	–	−259.466	−277.186	−269.007	–	–	–	–
EXPANSIONS	–	–	–	631.956*(°)	751.509(°°)	750.945(°°)	–	–	–	–
INVESTORPUT	–	–	–	1,332.220***(°°°)	1,258.370***(°°°)	1,279.800***(°°°)	–	–	–	–
TAXRATE	–	–	–	–	–	–	5.493	–	−3.828	−5.918
TAXAMOUNT	–	–	–	–	–	–	−0.623	–	−0.292	−0.635
N(Cluster)	138(40)	138(40)	138(40)	118(33)	118(33)	118(33)	123(36)	–	123(36)	123(36)
Max. VIF	1.090	7.752	4.542	1.292	11.621	2.231	3.519	–	9.831	3.734
R^2	0.060	0.144	0.142	0.170	0.184	0.182	0.066	–	0.167	0.160
adj. R^2	0.039	0.054	0.060	0.125	0.055	0.071	0.026	–	0.050	0.060
F-Statistic	1.141(13.606°°°)	1.536(8.946°°°)	1.574(7.019°°°)	2.658**(22.492°°°)	1.365(10.410°°°)	1.530(11.113°°°)	1.070(9.328°°°)	–	1.441(8.940°°°)	1.434(8.227°°°)

Panel B: Reopenings										
Intercept	−2,815.480	−5,207.700	−4,487.660	−12,278.500**(°°)	−14,668.000*(°°)	−15,262.500**(°°)	−6,619.290	−3,609.520	−6,818.020	−4,110.060
ACMVD	−2.921	−1.976	−2.163	0.974	1.755	2.028	−2.473	−2.616	−2.035	−1.853
Ln(PROCEEDS)	−58.439	104.402	46.415	521.619	769.637	730.158	419.559	−50.836	660.080	127.874
Ln(TOTAL ASSETS)	298.574	30.528	350.915	810.036*(°°)	421.365	829.961(°°)	409.142	366.569	86.439	337.572
MATURITY	–	59.184	65.102	–	48.477	51.959	–	–	57.636	63.105
YIELD	–	−47.042	3.719	–	219.791	247.617	–	–	−15.531	−13.177
FRANCE	–	−980.944**	−985.038**(°)	–	−445.693	−413.984	–	–	−1,381.020**(°)	−1,390.060**(°)
ENERGY	–	−505.552	−486.294	–	171.744	329.342	–	–	−698.234	−574.488
RATING	–	131.291(°)	87.201	–	62.158	33.976	–	–	79.037	105.933
Ln(LTDEBT)	–	403.828	–	–	392.751	–	–	–	299.325	–
PROCEEDSRatio	–	3,695.860	2,209.600	–	1,570.390	615.101	–	–	3,010.760	2,003.890
ROE	–	6.077*	0.803	–	8.755*	5.282	–	–	−3.286	−2.600
MARKETtoBOOK	–	31.058*	6.970	–	37.416	−4.531	–	–	26.327	20.081
DEBTtoEQUITY	–	−0.851**	–	–	−1.169	–	–	–	−0.238	–
REFINANCING	–	–	–	−183.413	−431.915	−292.909	–	–	–	–
EXPANSIONS	–	–	–	1,755.970***(°°)	2,225.820**(°°)	2,394.830**(°°)	–	–	–	–
INVESTORPUT	–	–	–	2,068.240***(°°°)	2,108.520***(°°)	2,180.360***(°°)	–	–	–	–
TAXRATE	–	–	–	–	–	–	34.901**(°)	1.537	25.064*	−12.268
TAXAMOUNT	–	–	–	–	–	–	−12.594**(°)	–	−13.399**	–
N(Cluster)	85(40)	85(40)	85(40)	70(33)	70(33)	70(33)	77(36)	77(36)	77(36)	77(36)
Max. VIF	1.188	8.712	2.022	1.715	12.492	2.714	6.876	1.218	11.439	2.163
R^2	0.057	0.138	0.127	0.214	0.253	0.247	0.080	0.062	0.172	0.150
adj. R^2	0.022	−0.020	−0.004	0.139	0.028	0.056	0.015	0.010	−0.031	−0.009
F-Statistic	0.443(38.539°°°)	1.439(22.250°°°)	1.538(26.366°°°)	2.579**(175.162°°°)	2.194**18.453°°°)	2.130**(18.101°°°)	1.594(38.331°°°)	0.707(34.944°°°)	1.602*(15.322°°°)	1.506(16.009°°°)
Panel C: Regular Issues										
Intercept	−1,545.150	−995.632	−1,026.740	−3,501.370	−918.439	−1,032.770	−1,802.140	−1,893.160	372.636	1,153.930
ACMVD	2.800	4.123*(°)	4.110*(°)	2.747	4.501	4.347	2.971	2.972	4.678(°)	4.580(°)
Ln(PROCEEDS)	−588.868**(°°)	−508.887*(°)	−494.522*(°)	−227.270*	−257.805	−240.037	−619.694**(°)	−609.179**(°°)	−201.229	−266.813
Ln(TOTAL ASSETS)	524.435**(°°)	272.666	408.477*(°)	468.471*(°°)	240.208	324.447	565.103**(°°)	566.306**(°°)	142.845	–
MATURITY	–	−10.477	−5.605	–	−41.008	−37.503	–	–	−30.843	80.134

YIELD	–	25.943	37.224	–	101.334	103.477	–	–	15.299	–35.220
FRANCE	–	–764.722*(°)	–753.283	–	–522.069	–507.920	–	–	–1,371.090**(°°)	–19.910
ENERGY	–	–316.744	–350.791	–	–299.801	–286.018	–	–	–690.905	–1,418.760**(°°)
RATING	–	93.260	85.631	–	–12.738	–15.455	–	–	181.912*	–664.408
Ln(LTDEBT)	–	169.179	–	–	107.118	–	–	–	–54.604	190.884*
PROCEEDSRatio	–	496.819	57.540	–	–190.285	–491.652	–	–	–2,482.340	–2,297.140
ROE	–	3.691	3.805	–	2.106	2.188	–	–	3.145	5.920
MARKETtoBOOK	–	28.405	18.854	–	–56.250	–53.924	–	–	537.876	526.590
DEBTtoEQUITY	–	–1.492	–1.035	–	–0.807	–0.602	–	–	–3.659	–3.884
REFINANCING	–	–	–	–118.665	–353.905	–286.087	–	–	–	–
EXPANSIONS	–	–	–	–195.163	–368.394	–295.760	–	–	–	–
INVESTORPUT	–	–	–	604.730	296.298	343.099	–	–	–	–
TAXRATE	–	–	–	–	–	–	–0.367	0.853	1.759	–5.869
TAXAMOUNT	–	–	–	–	–	–	0.113	–	–0.820	–
N(Cluster)	53(28)	53(28)	53(28)	48(27)	48(27)	48(27)	46(24)	46(24)	46(24)	46(24)
Max. VIF	1.030	11.617	2.701	1.177	23.295	4.359	10.287	1.146	20.707	3.515
R^2	0.225	0.303	0.301	0.201	0.245	0.244	0.223	0.223	0.380	0.379
adj. R^2	0.178	0.071	0.092	0.084	–0.145	–0.110	0.126	0.147	0.070	0.126
F-Statistic	3.881**(5.998°°°)	1.477(6.286°°°)	1.440(4.245°°°)	1.531(4.307°°°)	0.998(15.086°°°)	0.977(5.951°°°)	2.322*(3.582°°°)	2.803**(4.385°°°)	1.542(10.941°°°)	1.671(5.819°°°)

This table presents the results of cross sectional regression analyses of abnormal change in the market value of equity (ACMVE) over the window [–1;1] without adjustments for confounding events (Complete Sample). Panel A displays results for all issues, Panel B only for reopenings, and Panel C for regular issues. ACMVE on day t is calculated as the multiplication of a firm's market capitalization at fiscal year-end prior to the announcement and the abnormal stock return on day t. Abnormal change in the market value of debt (ACMVD) on day t is calculated by first, multiplying each abnormal bond return on day t with Total Debt at fiscal year-end prior to the announcement. Second, the equally weighted average is computed for every firm in the sample. Ln(PROCEEDS) and Ln(TOTAL ASSETS) present the natural logarithm of proceeds of a bond issuance and the natural logarithm of the total assets of the examined company measured at fiscal year-end prior to the announcement year. MATURITY presents the term to maturity in years. YIELD presents the yield to maturity at offering date in percent. FRANCE is a dummy variable that equals one when the bond is issued in France. ENERGY is a dummy variable equal to 1 when the company belongs to the "Energy and Power" industry as indicated by the Thomson One Banker Macro Description. RATING presents the bond's S&P rating at offering in the following form: 1 to a rating of AAA, 2 to a rating of AA+, 3 to a rating of AA, etc. Ln(LTDEB) is the natural logarithm of a firm's long-term debt measured at fiscal year-end prior to the announcement year. PROCEEDSRatio measures the ratio of gained proceeds scaled by long-term debt. ROE presents the Return on Equity measured at fiscal year-end prior to the announcement year. MARKETtoBOOK presents the ratio of the market price and the book value per share measured at fiscal year-end prior to the announcement. DEBTtoEQUITY presents the ratio of total debt and common equity measured at fiscal year-end prior to the announcement. REFINANCING and EXPANSIONS are dummy variables indicating the intended usage of the funds as stated in the prospectus. INVESTORPUT is a dummy variable which equals one when the holder has the option to redeem the bond in case of certain "Put Events". TAXRATE represents the ratio of income taxes and pretax income measured at fiscal year-end prior to the announcement. TAXAMOUNT represents the product of TAXRATE and the proceeds of the bond issue. The symbols ***, **, and * denote statistical significance at 1%, 5%, and 10% level with robust standard errors adjusted for heteroskedasticity following White (1980), respectively. The symbols °°°, °°, and ° denote statistical significance at 1%, 5%, and 10% level with robust standard errors adjusted for clustering, respectively.

Table 4-24: Cross Sectional Regression Analysis of Wealth Transfer between Stockholders and Bondholders of Debt Offering Companies (Control Sample/Yearly Data)

Dependent Variable: ACMVE yearly										
Panel A: All Issues	**Model I**	**Model II**		**Model III**	**Model IV**		**Model V**		**Model VI**	
Intercept	-4,030.390**(°)	-6,373.300**(°°°)	-5,755.140**(°°)	-7,539.010***(°°°)	-9,581.410***(°°°)	-9,970.840***(°°°)	-4,494.650*	-	-6,517.250**(°°°)	-6,231.230**(°°)
ACMVD	-3.839(°°)	-2.718(°)	-2.930(°)	-2.923(°)	-2.338	-2.401	-3.753(°°)	-	-2.411	-2.503
Ln(PROCEEDS)	-422.737***(°°°)	-594.861**(°°°)	-491.231**(°°°)	-237.476	-416.830(°)	-380.782(°)	-477.062**(°°)	-	-574.524**(°°)	-546.704**(°°)
Ln(TOTAL ASSETS)	627.800***(°°)	235.403	759.440***(°°°)	789.202***(°°°)	714.338**(°)	997.640***(°°°)	697.894***(°°°)	-	309.501	862.149***(°°°)
MATURITY	-	-3.108	19.676	-	1.118	8.494	-	-	-2.709	15.101
YIELD	-	-38.472	-9.831	-	113.200	129.874	-	-	-20.620	12.661
FRANCE	-	-789.950***(°°)	-817.704***(°°)	-	-120.047	-99.995	-	-	-1,028.080**(°°)	-996.422**(°°)
ENERGY	-	10.440	-71.859	-	487.638(°)	524.845(°)	-	-	-39.536	-80.065
RATING	-	113.295**(°°)	100.522*	-	-4.778	-10.636	-	-	135.327**(°°)	88.365
Ln(LTDEBT)	-	746.562**(°°)	-	-	327.042	-	-	-	662.927*	-
PROCEEDSRatio	-	7,153.720***(°°°)	3,861.080***(°°°)	-	4,765.220**(°°)	3,655.530**(°°°)	-	-	6,999.470***(°°°)	4,736.590***(°°°)
ROE	-	5.148	5.435*	-	1.191	1.123	-	-	6.433	1.148
MARKETtoBOOK	-	27.849*	26.233	-	24.630	17.178*	-	-	46.713*(°)	26.296*(°)
DEBTtoEQUITY	-	-0.656*	-0.456	-	-0.277	-	-	-	-0.890	-
REFINANCING	-	-	-	123.770	124.339	252.056	-	-	-	-
EXPANSIONS	-	-	-	522.415	830.840(°)	1,025.280*(°°)	-	-	-	-
INVESTORPUT	-	-	-	1,380.770***(°°°)	1,354.700***(°°°)	1,432.210***(°°°)	-	-	-	-
TAXRATE	-	-	-	-	-	-	-0.474	-	-3.113	-8.014
TAXAMOUNT	-	-	-	-	-	-	0.284	-	0.038	0.285
N(Cluster)	123(39)	123(39)	123(39)	106(32)	106(32)	106(32)	109(35)	-	109(35)	109(35)
Max. VIF	1.075	7.915	4.630	1.329	11.179	2.692	3.534	-	10.096	3.763
R^2	0.235	0.347	0.317	0.355	0.405	0.400	0.249	-	0.364	0.343
adj. R^2	0.216	0.269	0.242	0.316	0.298	0.308	0.212	-	0.262	0.253
F-Statistic	4.914***(5.460°°°)	2.315***(4.951°°°)	2.331**(3.320°°°)	3.650***(7.461°°°)	2.187**(28.305°°°)	2.436***(13.374°°°)	3.117**(3.692°°°)	-	2.035**(5.927°°°)	2.063**(3.566°°°)

Panel B: Reopenings										
Intercept	-3,301.360	-7,735.460**(°)	-5,702.650*	-11,806.900**(°°)	-18,127.100***(°°)	-18,823.300***(°°)	-6,762.140*	-4,207.430	-9,317.900**(°)	-6,046.290*
ACMVD	-7.697***(°°°)	-6.085***(°°°)	-6.469***(°°°)	-4.366(°°)	-2.082	-1.818	-7.234***(°°°)	-7.375***(°°°)	-6.179***(°°°)	-6.024***(°°°)
Ln(PROCEEDS)	-486.996**(°)	-692.529*(°)	-677.367*(°)	-36.161	6.944	43.268	-94.633	-497.450**	-232.154	-649.803*
Ln(TOTAL ASSETS)	573.838*(°)	-7.331	819.100**(°°)	1,044.750***(°°°)	858.139	1,384.650***(°°°)	704.823**(°°)	670.373**(°)	35.464	877.699**(°°)
MATURITY	-	-44.161	-22.294	-	13.512	21.281	-	-	-37.905	-20.161
YIELD	-	55.616	103.289	-	280.801	311.410	-	-	89.921	94.111
FRANCE	-	-768.222*(°)	-968.686**(°°)	-	-213.707	-237.861	-	-	-987.411*(°)	-1,258.330**(°°)
ENERGY	-	94.625	-9.614	-	1,102.320*	1,200.190**(°)	-	-	-47.973	-4.794
RATING	-	136.940**(°)	104.542*	-	105.407	96.507	-	-	80.712	121.492*
Ln(LTDEBT)	-	1,175.330***(°°)	-	-	583.316	-	-	-	1,100.500**(°)	-
PROCEEDSRatio	-	10,418.400***(°°°)	4,525.450**(°°°)	-	6,050.340**(°)	3,581.060**(°)	-	-	9,951.480***(°°°)	4,765.360**(°°°)
ROE	-	1.993	1.590	-	4.065	4.521	-	-	-4.584	-0.844
MARKETtoBOOK	-	14.933	13.550	-	17.929	10.837	-	-	4.845	29.725*(°)
DEBTtoEQUITY	-	-0.397	-	-	-0.358	-	-	-	0.144	-
REFINANCING	-	-	-	302.093	65.971	226.294	-	-	-	-
EXPANSIONS	-	-	-	1,348.030**(°)	2,397.340**(°)	2,746.150***(°°)	-	-	-	-
INVESTORPUT	-	-	-	2,029.100***(°°°)	2,301.000***(°°)	2,464.230***(°°°)	-	-	-	-
TAXRATE	-	-	-	-	-	-	26.194**(°)	-2.295	25.125*	-12.067
TAXAMOUNT	-	-	-	-	-	-	-10.683**	-	-11.908*	-
N(Cluster)	73(39)	73(39)	73(39)	61(32)	61(32)	61(32)	66(34)	66(34)	66(34)	66(34)
Max. VIF	1.127	8.744	2.040	1.824	11.850	2.753	6.773	1.141	11.592	2.228
R^2	0.332	0.479	0.421	0.513	0.612	0.602	0.367	0.350	0.506	0.456
adj. R^2	0.303	0.364	0.316	0.459	0.471	0.481	0.314	0.307	0.358	0.333
F-Statistic	10.458***(14.552°°°)	6.283***(29.647°°°)	9.080***(18.349°°°)	11.274***(12.211°°°)	13.551***(75.161°°°)	18.460***(37.344°°°)	7.687***(15.676°°°)	8.469***(12.168°°°)	5.422***(29.650°°°)	9.014***(16.146°°°)

Panel C: Regular Issues										
Intercept	−1,648.960	−1,923.540	−1,923.810	−3,451.910	−494.923	−1,511.540	−1,875.330	−1,999.120	−1,289.150	991.148
ACMVD	2.867	3.973(°)	3.973(°)	2.892	4.342	4.606	3.077	3.078	4.607(°)	4.521
Ln(PROCEEDS)	-582.178**(°°)	-687.271**(°°)	-687.269**(°°)	−210.267	−416.203	−257.126	−609.866**(°)	−595.413**(°°)	−501.392	−363.296
Ln(TOTAL ASSETS)	531.955**(°°°)	626.412	627.851**(°°)	459.819*(°°)	619.922	399.009	571.045**(°°)	572.588**(°°)	653.669	-
MATURITY	-	−24.334	−24.313	-	−69.361	−48.591	-	-	−50.216	−48.184
YIELD	-	43.630	43.721	-	137.381	65.532	-	-	42.492	−30.294
FRANCE	-	−627.878	−627.686	-	−271.174	−531.335	-	-	−1,274.170**(°°)	−1,528.520**(°°)
ENERGY	-	−515.765	−516.233	-	−532.789	−363.559	-	-	−997.835	−799.043
RATING	-	21.964	21.816	-	−167.360	-	-	-	120.227	183.594
Ln(LTDEBT)	-	1.613	-	-	−166.182	-	-	-	−275.558	172.409
PROCEEDSRatio	-	2,625.060	2,622.390	-	544.937	259.506	-	-	1,114.380	359.363
ROE	-	4.541	4.542	-	0.268	3.701	-	-	7.087	8.561
MARKETtoBOOK	-	6.337	6.202	-	−138.540	−60.502	-	-	548.169*	614.314*
DEBTtoEQUITY	-	−0.060	−0.055	-	1.417	−0.849	-	-	−1.846	−3.866
REFINANCING	-	-	-	−177.668	−387.018	−337.706	-	-	-	-
EXPANSIONS	-	-	-	−257.081	−580.031	−311.560	-	-	-	-
INVESTORPUT	-	-	-	578.554	467.545	222.121	-	-	-	-
TAXRATE	-	-	-	-	-	-	−1.652	0.023	−1.138	−7.538
TAXAMOUNT	-	-	-	-	-	-	0.156	-	−0.434	-
N(Cluster)	50(26)	50(26)	50(26)	45(25)	45(25)	45(25)	43(22)	43(22)	43(22)	43(22)
Max. VIF	1.031	11.873	4.095	1.171	23.093	4.762	10.226	1.160	21.107	4.897
R^2	0.229	0.310	0.310	0.202	0.259	0.249	0.225	0.225	0.402	0.388
adj. R^2	0.178	0.061	0.087	0.077	−0.165	−0.101	0.120	0.143	0.070	0.114
F-Statistic	3.929**(6.386°°°)	1.697(6.504°°°)	1.838*(6.065°°°)	1.616(4.568°°°)	0.949(22.973°°°)	1.073(6.986°°°)	2.318*(3.865°°°)	2.803**(4.752°°°)	2.753**(48.524°°°)	2.459**(8.005°°°)

This table presents the results of cross sectional regression analyses of abnormal change in the market value of equity (ACMVE) over the window [−1;1] with adjustments for confounding events (Control Sample). Panel A displays results for all issues, Panel B only for reopenings, and Panel C for regular issues. ACMVE on day t is calculated as the multiplication of a firm's market capitalization at fiscal year-end prior to the announcement and the abnormal stock return on day t. Abnormal change in the market value of debt (ACMVD) on day t is calculated by first, multiplying each abnormal bond return on day t with Total Debt at fiscal year-end prior to the announcement. Second, the equally weighted average is computed for every firm in the sample. Ln(PROCEEDS) and Ln(TOTAL ASSETS) present the natural logarithm of proceeds of a bond issuance and the natural logarithm of the total assets of the examined company measured at fiscal year-end prior to the announcement year. MATURITY presents the term to maturity in years. YIELD presents the yield to maturity at offering date in percent. FRANCE is a dummy variable that equals one when the bond is issued in France. ENERGY is a dummy variable equal to 1 when the company belongs to the "Energy and Power" industry as indicated by the Thomson One Banker Macro Description. RATING presents the bond's S&P rating at offering in the following form: 1 to a rating of AAA, 2 to a rating of AA+, 3 to a rating of AA, etc. Ln(LTDEB) is the natural logarithm of a firm's long-term debt measured at fiscal year-end prior to the announcement year. PROCEEDSRatio measures the ratio of gained proceeds scaled by long-term debt. ROE presents the Return on Equity measured at fiscal year-end prior to the announcement year. MARKETtoBOOK presents the ratio of the market price and the book value per share measured at fiscal year-end prior to the announcement. DEBTtoEQUITY presents the ratio of total debt and common equity measured at fiscal year-end prior to the announcement. REFINANCING and EXPANSIONS are dummy variables indicating the intended usage of the funds as stated in the prospectus. INVESTORPUT is a dummy variable which equals one when the holder has the option to redeem the bond in case of certain "Put Events". TAXRATE represents the ratio of income taxes and pretax income measured at fiscal year-end prior to the announcement. TAXAMOUNT represents the product of TAXRATE and the proceeds of the bond issue. The symbols ***, **, and * denote statistical significance at 1%, 5%, and 10% level with robust standard errors adjusted for heteroskedasticity following White (1980), respectively. The symbols °°°, °°, and ° denote statistical significance at 1%, 5%, and 10% level with robust standard errors adjusted for clustering, respectively.

Table 4-25: Cross Sectional Regression Analysis of Wealth Transfer between Stockholders and Bondholders of Debt Offering Companies (Complete Sample/Daily Data)

Dependent Variable: ACMVE daily										
Panel A: All Issues	**Model I**	**Model II**		**Model III**	**Model IV**		**Model V**		**Model VI**	
Intercept	–3,375.620	–3,216.230	–3,117.230	–6,788.750**(°°°)	–5,247.380(°°)	–5,599.380(°°°)	–3,974.780	–	–2,323.560	–2,629.590
ACMVD	–42.555(°°°)	–46.615(°)	–41.455(°°)	–22.131(°)	–24.239	–20.791	–41.756(°°)	–	–41.255(°)	–30.301
Ln(PROCEEDS)	–203.645	–125.568	–92.623	52.970	79.284	69.324	–202.437	–	–67.278	–57.100
Ln(TOTAL ASSETS)	434.221(°)	43.372	332.358(°)	560.948(°°°)	255.927	463.576(°°)	485.209(°)	–	–10.585	338.806(°)
MATURITY	–	44.695	55.545	–	–0.387	2.792	–	–	40.861	56.421
YIELD	–	–175.070	–148.037	–	6.428	34.678	–	–	–180.699	–125.262
FRANCE	–	–1,092.040***(°°)	–1,090.240***(°°)	–	–473.952	–432.715	–	–	–1,499.440***(°°°)	–1,403.330***(°°)
ENERGY	–	–505.678	–536.376	–	–67.145	–18.295	–	–	–645.141	–631.041
RATING	–	151.778**(°°)	144.062**(°°)	–	15.942	–10.542	–	–	177.770*(°°)	109.259(°)
Ln(LTDEBT)	–	376.945	–	–	199.617	–	–	–	349.095	–
PROCEEDSRatio	–	1,960.550	572.009	–	336.898	46.230	–	–	1,539.270	1,102.920(°)
ROE	–	7.440**(°)	7.576**(°)	–	4.730	2.510	–	–	8.384	–1.705
MARKETtoBOOK	–	43.243**(°)	41.327**	–	35.987	–2.177	–	–	70.307***(°°)	21.141
DEBTtoEQUITY	–	–1.145***(°°)	–1.005***(°°)	–	–0.956	–	–	–	–1.537**(°°)	–
REFINANCING	–	–	–	–180.642	–231.931	–173.970	–	–	–	–
EXPANSIONS	–	–	–	649.615*	630.903(°)	696.341(°)	–	–	–	–
INVESTORPUT	–	–	–	1,303.880***(°°°)	1,134.620**(°°)	1,187.610**(°°°)	–	–	–	–
TAXRATE	–	–	–	–	–	–	2.126	–	–6.856	–10.205
TAXAMOUNT	–	–	–	–	–	–	–0.139	–	0.161	–0.145
N(Cluster)	138(40)	138(40)	138(40)	118(33)	118(33)	118(33)	123(36)	–	123(36)	123(36)
Max. VIF	1.106	7.872	4.582	1.292	11.748	2.124	3.535	–	9.980	3.778
R^2	0.058	0.154	0.147	0.152	0.164	0.161	0.062	–	0.176	0.164
adj. R^2	0.037	0.065	0.066	0.106	0.032	0.047	0.022	–	0.061	0.064
F-Statistic	1.066(4.702°°°)	1.588*(4.335°°°)	1.726**(3.932°°°)	2.805**(3.494°°°)	1.585*(8.760°°°)	1.701*(5.984°°°)	0.686(3.430°°°)	–	1.512(6.182°°°)	1.430(5.925°°°)

Panel B: Reopenings										
Intercept	−3,022.200	−4,704.430	−3,585.440	−11,085.800**(°°)	−10,667.800(°°)	−11,399.000(°°)	−7,218.800	−3,685.730	−6,226.250	−2,332.890
ACMVD	−81.921(°°°)	−103.258*(°°)	−78.736*(°°)	−38.343	−55.561	−37.088	−85.376(°°)	−83.359(°°)	−115.103**(°°)	−90.565*(°°)
Ln(PROCEEDS)	−250.720	−54.680	−138.654	409.343	602.067	555.066	314.044	−245.930	664.875	−23.839
Ln(TOTAL ASSETS)	408.426	−213.249	415.360	749.558(°°°)	−60.105	653.536(°°°)	516.619	470.888	−314.115	349.263
MATURITY	–	20.870	35.505	–	15.217	24.361	–	–	15.537	30.256
YIELD	–	−169.957	−83.005	–	106.927	167.058	–	–	−169.078	−136.372
FRANCE	–	−1,148.190**(°)	−1,177.210**(°°)	–	−608.521	−545.805	–	–	−1,638.240**(°°)	−1,711.020**(°°)
ENERGY	–	−808.166	−738.891	–	−375.890	−152.016	–	–	−955.172	−828.503
RATING	–	174.976(°)	109.211	–	66.748	12.036	–	–	121.089	139.087
Ln(LTDEBT)	–	792.490	–	–	735.659	–	–	–	819.077	–
PROCEEDSRatio	–	3,812.560	1,040.500	–	1,512.760	−437.878	–	–	3,414.830	397.964
ROE	–	7.501*	0.007	–	8.824	3.421	–	–	−6.535	−5.561
MARKETtoBOOK	–	47.684**	10.736	–	61.816	−1.185	–	–	30.894	27.617
DEBTtoEQUITY	–	−1.346**(°)	–	–	−1.830	–	–	–	−0.423	–
REFINANCING	–	–	–	−22.372	−400.370	−170.673	–	–	–	–
EXPANSIONS	–	–	–	1,674.230***(°°)	1,624.820(°°)	1,917.440*(°°°)	–	–	–	–
INVESTORPUT	–	–	–	1,924.560***(°°°)	1,714.830**(°°)	1,856.870**(°°°)	–	–	–	–
TAXRATE	–	–	–	–	–	–	38.146***(°°)	−1.643	27.643*	−21.784*
TAXAMOUNT	–	–	–	–	–	–	−15.057**(°)	–	−17.355**(°)	–
N(Cluster)	85(40)	85(40)	85(40)	70(33)	70(33)	70(33)	77(36)	77(36)	77(36)	77(36)
Max. VIF	1.062	8.927	1.675	1.679	12.929	2.258	6.867	1.066	11.895	1.882
R^2	0.056	0.166	0.137	0.191	0.224	0.208	0.085	0.062	0.210	0.168
adj. R^2	0.021	0.014	0.007	0.114	−0.010	0.006	0.021	0.010	0.015	0.012
F-Statistic	0.814(2.880°°)	1.592(3.277°°°)	1.497(2.682°°°)	3.092**(4.363°°°)	2.403***(9.297°°°)	2.241**(9.013°°°)	1.897(1.819)	0.593(2.222°)	1.664*(3.029°°°)	1.651*(3.232°°°)
Panel C: Regular Issues										
Intercept	−1,012.820	−1,057.200	−1,075.010	−3,234.930	−2,053.820	−1,628.510	−1,176.640	−1,418.940	850.918	1,174.000
ACMVD	−2.438	0.699	1.539	2.604	6.316	5.352	7.574	7.682	11.530	10.616
Ln(PROCEEDS)	−671.773**(°°)	−501.367	−489.872	−229.702(°)	−58.548	−129.248	−729.305*(°)	−701.134**(°°)	−239.667	–
Ln(TOTAL ASSETS)	517.203**(°°°)	248.985	353.529	436.405(°°)	598.728	246.018	559.209*(°°°)	–	154.435	−267.167
MATURITY	–	28.544	32.040	–	8.212	−1.243	–	–	4.222	7.881

YIELD	–	19.436	29.186	–	83.017	63.503	–	–	–11.779	–0.430
FRANCE	–	–558.000	–550.100	–	–189.121	–213.270	–	–	–1,168.810*(°)	–36.632
ENERGY	–	–154.336	–181.128	–	80.733	47.572	–	–	–597.653	–1,193.890*(°)
RATING	–	90.596	84.584	–	–23.627	–15.071	–	–	195.318*(°)	–552.114
Ln(LTDEBT)	–	131.073	–	–	–444.226		–	–	–174.790	199.609*(°)
PROCEEDSRatio	–	171.055	–171.381	–	–2,228.280	–996.816	–	–	–3,423.380	–2,889.210
ROE	–	1.473	1.570	–	0.476	–0.223	–	–	5.304	5.426
MARKETtoBOOK	–	111.310	103.784	–	63.875	68.086	–	–	673.699*	665.869*
DEBTtoEQUITY	–	–2.052	–1.690	–	–0.820	–1.743	–	–	–4.491*	–4.868
REFINANCING	–	–	–	–47.290	223.878	–17.482	–	–	–	–
EXPANSIONS	–	–	–	–162.173	144.051	–139.552	–	–	–	–
INVESTORPUT	–	–	–	637.646(°)	746.079	587.759	–	–	–	–
TAXRATE	–	–	–	–	–	–	0.327	562.325**(°°°)	0.282	–3.026
TAXAMOUNT	–	–	–	–	–	–	0.302	3.574	–0.248	0.000(°°°)
N(Cluster)	53(28)	53(28)	53(28)	48(27)	48(27)	48(27)	46(24)	46(24)	46(24)	46(24)
Max. VIF	1.090	11.707	2.717	1.217	20.225	4.366	10.289	1.244	22.719	3.489
R^2	0.197	0.250	0.249	0.152	0.185	0.177	0.200	0.200	0.334	0.332
adj. R^2	0.148	0.000	0.024	0.028	–0.236	–0.208	0.100	0.122	0.001	0.061
F-Statistic	3.235**(3.901°°)	1.044(1.630)	1.048(1.489)	1.244(2.781°°)	0.720(1.587)	0.886(2.716°°°)	1.787(2.195°)	2.191*(2.679°°)	1.434(6.310°°°)	1.336(5.977°°°)

This table presents the results of cross sectional regression analyses of abnormal change in the market value of equity (ACMVE) over the window [-1;1] without adjustments for confounding events (Complete Sample). Panel A displays results for all issues, Panel B only for reopenings, and Panel C for regular issues. ACMVE on day t is calculated as the multiplication of a firm's market capitalization on day t-1 and the abnormal stock return on day t. Abnormal change in the market value of debt (ACMVD) on day t is calculated by first, multiplying each abnormal bond return on day t with the bond's respective market value on day t-1. Second, the equally weighted average is computed for every firm in the sample. Ln(PROCEEDS) and Ln(TOTAL ASSETS) present the natural logarithm of proceeds of a bond issuance and the natural logarithm of the total assets of the examined company measured at fiscal year-end prior to the announcement year. MATURITY presents the term to maturity in years. YIELD presents the yield to maturity at offering date in percent. FRANCE is a dummy variable that equals one when the bond is issued in France. ENERGY is a dummy variable equal to 1 when the company belongs to the "Energy and Power" industry as indicated by the Thomson One Banker Macro Description. RATING presents the bond's S&P rating at offering in the following form: 1 to a rating of AAA, 2 to a rating of AA+, 3 to a rating of AA, etc. Ln(LTDEBT) is the natural logarithm of a firm's long-term debt measured at fiscal year-end prior to the announcement year. PROCEEDSRatio measures the ratio of gained proceeds scaled by long-term debt. ROE presents the Return on Equity measured at fiscal year-end prior to the announcement year. MARKETtoBOOK presents the ratio of the market price and the book value per share measured at fiscal year-end prior to the announcement. DEBTtoEQUITY presents the ratio of total debt and common equity measured at fiscal year-end prior to the announcement. REFINANCING and EXPANSIONS are dummy variables indicating the intended usage of the funds as stated in the prospectus. INVESTORPUT is a dummy variable which equals one when the holder has the option to redeem the bond in case of certain "Put Events". TAXRATE represents the ratio of income taxes and pretax income measured at fiscal year-end prior to the announcement. TAXAMOUNT represents the product of TAXRATE and the proceeds of the bond issue. The symbols ***, **, and * denote statistical significance at 1%, 5%, and 10% level with robust standard errors adjusted for heteroskedasticity following White (1980), respectively. The symbols °°°, °°, and ° denote statistical significance at 1%, 5%, and 10% level with robust standard errors adjusted for clustering, respectively.

Table 4-26: Cross Sectional Regression Analysis of Wealth Transfer between Stockholders and Bondholders of Debt Offering Companies (Control Sample/Daily Data)

Dependent Variable: ACMVE daily										
Panel A: All Issues	**Model I**	**Model II**		**Model III**	**Model IV**		**Model V**		**Model VI**	
Intercept	–4,658.760**(°)	–6,928.170***(°°°)	–6,249.050**(°°)	–8,334.680***(°°°)	–10,004.900***(°°°)	–10,654.000***(°°°)	–5,032.540**(°)	–	–6,423.020**(°°)	–6,184.970**(°°)
ACMVD	–56.092*(°)	–62.667*(°)	–51.994*(°)	–54.384*(°)	–53.017	–49.052	–59.670(°)	–	–63.980	–49.955
Ln(PROCEEDS)	–504.653***(°°°)	–683.466**(°°°)	–538.514**(°°)	–279.191	–475.419	–420.570	–588.415**(°°)	–	–679.757**(°°)	–624.230**(°°)
Ln(TOTAL ASSETS)	728.063***(°°°)	148.066	831.264***(°°°)	879.393***(°°°)	644.504	1,083.390***(°°°)	807.947***(°°°)	–	162.529	918.695***(°°°)
MATURITY	–	–11.388	17.853	–	–13.398	–2.946	–	–	–10.183	14.859
YIELD	–	–126.874	–84.092	–	33.728	63.839	–	–	–126.477	–70.542
FRANCE	–	–938.724***(°°)	–979.903***(°°)	–	–285.932	–250.128	–	–	–1,263.180***(°°°)	–1,212.430***(°°)
ENERGY	–	–102.113	–195.760	–	475.735	541.751	–	–	–135.564	–193.252
RATING	–	170.949***(°°)	155.847**(°)	–	57.248	44.470	–	–	212.293**(°°)	140.410**
Ln(LTDEBT)	–	967.752**(°)	–	–	499.157	–	–	–	898.756**	–
PROCEEDSRatio	–	7,853.150***(°°°)	3,659.960**(°°)	–	5,344.050**(°)	3,725.520**(°°)	–	–	7,486.060***(°°°)	4,585.350***(°°°)
ROE	–	6.901*(°)	7.277**(°)	–	3.491	3.069	–	–	9.197	0.827
MARKETtoBOOK	–	37.218**	33.907*	–	29.179	11.232	–	–	62.481**(°°)	28.332*(°)
DEBTtoEQUITY	–	–0.989**(°)	–0.704	–	–0.569	–	–	–	–1.390**(°)	–
REFINANCING	–	–	–	84.751	84.987	269.829	–	–	–	–
EXPANSIONS	–	–	–	593.393	876.135(°)	1,165.710*(°°)	–	–	–	–
INVESTORPUT	–	–	–	1,462.360***(°°°)	1,264.440***(°°°)	1,386.710***(°°°)	–	–	–	–
TAXRATE	–	–	–	–	–	–	–3.509	–	–8.320	–14.563
TAXAMOUNT	–	–	–	–	–	–	0.598	–	0.543	0.733
N(Cluster)	123(39)	123(39)	123(39)	106(32)	106(32)	106(32)	109(35)	–	109(35)	109(35)
Max. VIF	1.087	7.996	4.683	1.329	11.256	2.574	3.549	–	10.172	3.806
R^2	0.192	0.330	0.286	0.324	0.371	0.362	0.207	–	0.351	0.316
adj. R^2	0.171	0.250	0.208	0.283	0.257	0.263	0.169	–	0.247	0.223
F-Statistic	4.363***(3.685°°)	2.291**(6.349°°°)	2.067**(3.026°°°)	3.374***(5.664°°°)	2.126**(41.692°°°)	2.339***(256.792°°°)	2.669**(2.788°°)	–	1.997**(8.471°°°)	1.882**(5.287°°°)

Panel B: Reopenings										
Intercept	-5,164.040*	-9,508.340***(°°)	-6,844.830**	-14,756.500***(°°°)	-18,228.800***(°°°)	-19,073.900***(°°°)	-9,593.930**(°)	-6,252.790*	-10,844.200***(°°)	-6,431.050*
ACMVD	-116.702***(°°)	-148.567***(°°)	-105.056**(°)	-122.883***(°°)	-123.824**(°°)	-101.579**(°)	-126.987***(°°)	-124.450**(°°)	-162.484***(°°)	-125.788**(°)
Ln(PROCEEDS)	-652.648**(°)	-851.211**(°)	-854.930**(°)	-82.108	-130.847	-92.507	-125.659	-658.200**	-215.552	-750.397*
Ln(TOTAL ASSETS)	830.965**(°°)	-144.689	1,043.500***(°°)	1,321.090***(°°°)	630.626	1,513.670***(°°°)	991.077***(°°)	949.259***(°°)	-220.622	1,047.710***(°°)
MATURITY	–	-83.226	-48.279	–	-24.502	-10.104	–	–	-77.550	-47.260
YIELD	–	-103.848	-20.611	–	109.193	174.325	–	–	-115.214	-85.599
FRANCE	–	-1,011.890**(°°)	-1,252.290***(°°)	–	-395.614	-400.000	–	–	-1,396.860**(°°)	-1,738.990***(°°)
ENERGY	–	-1.734	-8.055	–	960.830	1,138.870*	–	–	-20.144	68.325
RATING	–	245.694***(°°)	185.266**	–	195.459	163.212	–	–	205.855*	232.439**(°)
Ln(LTDEBT)	–	1,651.720***(°°)	–	–	994.794*	–	–	–	1,648.400***(°°)	–
PROCEEDSRatio	–	11,090.100***(°°°)	3,772.570*	–	6,436.590**(°)	2,673.380	–	–	10,549.600***(°°)	3,475.140
ROE	–	6.013	1.987	–	7.335	6.187	–	–	-6.387	-4.245
MARKETtoBOOK	–	36.015	14.505	–	35.784	7.375	–	–	22.675	42.517**(°°)
DEBTtoEQUITY	–	-1.128*	–	–	-1.026	–	–	–	-0.284	–
REFINANCING	–	–	–	586.017	375.310	589.670	–	–	–	–
EXPANSIONS	–	–	–	1,725.910***(°°)	2,324.050***(°°)	2,836.060***(°°°)	–	–	–	–
INVESTORPUT	–	–	–	2,286.840***(°°°)	2,087.980***(°°°)	2,340.630***(°°°)	–	–	–	–
TAXRATE	–	–	–	–	–	–	31.496**(°°)	-6.263	20.843	-26.784**
TAXAMOUNT	–	–	–	–	–	–	-14.206**(°)	–	-15.001**	–
N(Cluster)	73(39)	73(39)	73(39)	61(32)	61(32)	61(32)	66(34)	66(34)	66(34)	66(34)
Max. VIF	1.059	8.991	1.817	1.772	12.274	2.491	6.763	1.097	11.991	1.981
R^2	0.235	0.452	0.349	0.495	0.586	0.559	0.289	0.263	0.490	0.403
adj. R^2	0.202	0.331	0.231	0.439	0.435	0.425	0.230	0.215	0.337	0.268
F-Statistic	3.668**(2.450°)	2.192**(2.232°°)	1.652(1.604)	3.899***(4.077°°°)	3.464***(6.095°°°)	3.532***(6.158°°°)	2.592**(1.727)	2.901**(2.096°)	2.024**(3.085°°°)	1.881*(29.223°°°)

Panel C: Regular Issues										
Intercept	−1,126.070	−2,238.620	−2,233.870	−3,175.210	−2,103.260	−2,409.680	−1,253.210	−1,534.550	−1,039.240	771.526
ACMVD	-4.490	-4.535	-4.621	0.884	0.779	0.454	4.935	5.080	0.777	7.529
Ln(PROCEEDS)	-668.236**(°°)	-709.572**(°)	-709.690**(°)	-217.758	-281.547	-184.687	-727.818*(°)	-694.738**(°°)	-590.890	-365.184
Ln(TOTAL ASSETS)	526.893**(°°°)	638.954	607.440*(°°)	428.794(°°°)	1,058.640	352.347	568.685**(°°°)	572.076**(°°°)	691.613	-
MATURITY	-	14.038	13.615	-	-20.158	-6.598	-	-	-14.400	-9.319
YIELD	-	36.440	34.288	-	120.872	27.059	-	-	8.256	-32.111
FRANCE	-	-406.186	-410.171	-	89.345	-203.790	-	-	-1,081.710*(°)	-1,316.620*(°)
ENERGY	-	-372.745	-362.454	-	-192.136	-24.117	-	-	-895.103	-706.100
RATING	-	17.311	20.542	-	-180.429	-	-	-	153.264	206.211
Ln(LTDEBT)	-	-35.468	-	-	-729.496	-	-	-	-394.503	81.643
PROCEEDSRatio	-	2,700.420	2,760.480	-	-772.175	112.837	-	-	543.542	-414.485
ROE	-	2.574	2.550	-	-0.834	1.265	-	-	11.883	9.740
MARKETtoBOOK	-	90.069	93.072	-	-14.051	76.074	-	-	704.693**	777.614**
DEBTtoEQUITY	-	-0.545	-0.659	-	1.625	-1.907	-	-	-2.852	-4.774
REFINANCING	-	-	-	-102.454	186.680	-39.934	-	-	-	-
EXPANSIONS	-	-	-	-218.593	-19.306	-99.601	-	-	-	-
INVESTORPUT	-	-	-	615.508(°)	928.613	506.462	-	-	-	-
TAXRATE	-	-	-	-	-	-	-0.816	2.991	-3.819	-3.332
TAXAMOUNT	-	-	-	-	-	-	0.354	-	0.401	-
N(Cluster)	50(26)	50(26)	50(26)	45(25)	45(25)	45(25)	43(22)	43(22)	43(22)	43(22)
Max. VIF	1.089	11.882	4.226	1.222	19.609	4.960	10.230	1.251	23.586	4.849
R^2	0.198	0.258	0.258	0.151	0.198	0.175	0.200	0.200	0.358	0.343
adj. R^2	0.146	-0.010	0.017	0.016	-0.260	-0.210	0.092	0.115	0.001	0.049
F-Statistic	3.334**(4.046°°)	1.290(1.663)	1.399(1.746°)	1.275(2.939°°)	0.744(1.455)	0.900(2.296°°)	1.819(2.248°)	2.233*(2.768°°)	2.532**(11.878°°°)	1.967*(4.098°°°)

This table presents the results of cross sectional regression analyses of abnormal change in the market value of equity (ACMVE) over the window [−1;1] with adjustments for confounding events (Control Sample). Panel A displays results for all issues, Panel B only for reopenings, and Panel C for regular issues. ACMVE on day t is calculated as the multiplication of a firm's market capitalization on day t-1 and the abnormal stock return on day t. Abnormal change in the market value of debt (ACMVD) on day t is calculated by first, multiplying each abnormal bond return on day t with the bond's respective market value on day t-1. Second, the equally weighted average is computed for every firm in the sample. Ln(PROCEEDS) and Ln(TOTAL ASSETS) present the natural logarithm of proceeds of a bond issuance and the natural logarithm of the total assets of the examined company measured at fiscal year-end prior to the announcement year. MATURITY presents the term to maturity in years. YIELD presents the yield to maturity at offering date in percent. FRANCE is a dummy variable that equals one when the bond is issued in France. ENERGY is a dummy variable equal to 1 when the company belongs to the "Energy and Power" industry as indicated by the Thomson One Banker Macro Description. RATING presents the bond's S&P rating at offering in the following form: 1 to a rating of AAA, 2 to a rating of AA+, 3 to a rating of AA, etc. Ln(LTDEB) is the natural logarithm of a firm's long-term debt measured at fiscal year-end prior to the announcement year. PROCEEDSRatio measures the ratio of gained proceeds scaled by long-term debt. ROE presents the Return on Equity measured at fiscal year-end prior to the announcement year. MARKETtoBOOK presents the ratio of the market price and the book value per share measured at fiscal year-end prior to the announcement. DEBTtoEQUITY presents the ratio of total debt and common equity measured at fiscal year-end prior to the announcement. REFINANCING and EXPANSIONS are dummy variables indicating the intended usage of the funds as stated in the prospectus. INVESTORPUT is a dummy variable which equals one when the holder has the option to redeem the bond in case of certain "Put Events". TAXRATE represents the ratio of income taxes and pretax income measured at fiscal year-end prior to the announcement. TAXAMOUNT represents the product of TAXRATE and the proceeds of the bond issue. The symbols ***, **, and * denote statistical significance at 1%, 5%, and 10% level with robust standard errors adjusted for heteroskedasticity following White (1980), respectively. The symbols °°°, °°, and ° denote statistical significance at 1%, 5%, and 10% level with robust standard errors adjusted for clustering, respectively.

4.4 Summary and Conclusion

Since the year 2005 a new technique to acquire debt capital is emerging for European companies: reopenings. Also known by the term tap issue, a reopening describes the execution of a new bond issue with identical configurations with regard to the maturity date, coupon and conditions as a previous offering, but with a market adjusted price, that is later consolidated with the previous bond issue. Despite the fact that this issue type gains in importance for the corporate world, capital market research paid no attention to reopenings when assessing the wealth effects of debt offerings. The objective of this chapter is to fill this research gap and to provide insight into how markets react to announcements of reopenings in comparison to regular debt offerings.

Stock and bond event studies are conducted and results detected that indicate that investors respond differently depending on the bond issue type. Stockholders experience a stronger price appreciation for regular issues compared to reopenings. Utilization of cross sectional regression analysis confirms this result and verifies that the differences between the two offering types are not driven by issue size. Regarding the abnormal bond returns event study analysis provides an indication for diverging investor behavior. Standard regression analysis, however, cannot confirm this result. However, when only the actually reopened bond is examined then results reveal that these bonds experience a negative price response at the announcement of the reopening. Thus, reopenings affect both bondholders and stockholders negatively. Subsequent analysis show that price responses due to regular issues demonstrate no significant inverse relationship between a firm's stockholders and bondholders, indicating that signaling effects alter the results. For bond taps, however, a statistically significant transfer of wealth from bondholders to shareholders can be found, providing further verification for the necessity to differentiate between both debt offering types. Finally, examining the bond price change between issuance and reopening presents evidence for a price runup, albeit only to a small degree.

Comparing the figures with the potential hypotheses predicting the price responses due to debt offerings leads to the following inference: Once more, empirical evidence for a transfer of wealth from bondholders to stockholders is detected for regular debt offerings, as the statistically significant negative abnormal bond returns and the positive stock returns imply. However, cross sectional regression is unable to confirm the redistribution. Apparently, wealth transfer plays a significant role in determining the price effect of regular bond issues, but it constitutes not the central effect. At least one of the two stakeholder classes exhibits price reactions driven by other effects. Comparing the results of the announcement of reopenings with the regular offerings presents evidence that a firm's stockholders conducting a regular offering are strongly affected by a positive signaling. Abnormal stock returns turn out to be stronger for regular issues in comparison to reopenings. For reopenings, however, cross sectional regressions detect strong support for the expected redistribution of wealth from bondholders to stockholders. Thus, the more positive stock price responses for regular bond issues constitute the source for the non-detectability of the wealth transfer. Yet, reopenings are not influenced by a positive signaling and present empirical evidence for an expropriation of wealth in line with the theoretical considerations. The reason for the revelation of the wealth transfer effect for reopenings stems from management's decision to take advantage of the window of opportunity. By announcing the reopening, management signals investors the presence of an overvaluation of the respective bond. This, in turn, prompts bondholders to reevaluate their investment, leading to negative price effects. Thus, the positive signaling effect, which drives the wealth effects of regular offerings, is nullified by a negative signaling associated with the reopening announcement, leaving only the wealth transfer from bondholders to stockholder as the sole wealth effect for reopenings.

Altogether, this chapter provides the first insights on bond reopenings and holds implications for theory and practice. First, research investigating debt offerings ought to control for bond issue type, as a considerably large portion of reopenings could potentially lead to insignificant stock returns and create inconsistent results. This reasoning also applies to bond returns as announcements are driven more by a redistribution of wealth than regular issues, confirming different hypotheses. Second, managers considering debt offerings gain more insight on how investors respond to different issue types, hereby providing support to select the proper debt offering type. As illustrated, it depends strongly on the stakeholder classes considered and the weighting scheme in the decision making process.

5. Concluding Remarks

5.1 Summary and Discussion of the Main Results

The importance and relevance of funds through debt for companies has grown dramatically over the last 15–20 years.[64] Financial and non-financial firms increasingly rely on bonds to finance their investments not only in the US and Europe, but also in many emerging markets. However, corporate debt and debt securities still play only a negligible role when it comes to empirical research on capital markets. Several reasons exist which explain this development, the main one being the poor availability of necessary data. Yet, 15 years after the beginning of the new millennium the provision of data on corporate bonds is much more improved and continues to do so. Moreover, specific empirical tools for debt securities are developed and tested by researchers widening the focus of capital market research from just stocks on to the companies' debt. Despite this pleasant development, most papers that investigate the incorporation of new information in firm value insist on limiting their analysis on equity securities. Thus, it is the strong belief of the author that research on capital markets needs to be steered to a more integrated approach including a firm's debt together with equity to assess firm value changes. This thesis is one of many first steps towards this goal.

Chapter 2 provides an overview of event study methodologies applied to detect bondholders' wealth effects, as well as discussion of bond specific characteristics which affect the utilization of event study methodology. Thus, this section provides the methodical foundation for the following chapters and helps the reader of this thesis to better understand some of the choices that were made in the following chapters.

An important factor that distinguishes bond price data from stock price data is the liquidity. In general, corporate bonds are less liquid than stocks, while government bonds possess the highest liquidity. This stems from the high percentage of institutional investors in the corporate bond market with long term investment horizons (a.k.a buy and hold investors). Another aspect is the number of securities outstanding per firm. Generally, listed companies have only one share making it easy to study the impact of certain events on a firm's stock price, while they often tend to issue more than one bond. Event study methodology must account for both factors.

64 See chapter 1.1 for a discussion of this topic.

Browsing 108 papers published between 1974 and 2014 reveals five outstanding methodologies applied to compute abnormal bond returns: (i) the market model, (ii) several multi-factor models, (iii) the valuation prediction error procedure, (iv) the mean adjusted model, and (v) the matching portfolio approach. While most procedures suffer from potential non-stationarity of coefficients, prior research reveals that the portfolio approach statistically outperforms most other methodologies. With regard to the test statistics utilized to detect significant abnormal bond returns, standardization seems to resolve the inherent heteroskedasticity in bond returns.

Not only the methodology applied to compute abnormal bond returns, but also the databases used vary since the first published bond event study in 1974. First, exchange-based price data from sources like the Wall Street Journal, Moody's Bond Record, or S&P's Bond Guide were used, only accounting for a negligible portion of the total trading. Later, after the 1990s the bond database provided by Lehman Brothers was the leading source for bond data. The advantage was a higher data-availability leading to larger sample sizes. However, the Lehman Brother Bond Database as well as the exchange based databases relied heavily on matrix prices potentially leading to weaker price responses. Finally, in 2002 the NASD introduced TRACE in an effort to increase the transparency of the US corporate debt market. Relying on real OTC secondary market transactions and providing intraday data, TRACE is the leading source for US corporate bond data to this date. For other markets and time frames starting before 2002, Thomson Financial Datastream offers a nearly equivalent service.

Lastly, the interdependency of bondholder and stockholder returns presented in prior research is reviewed. Two dominating hypotheses were detected: (i) the wealth transfer and (ii) the signaling hypothesis. The first predicts a negative correlation between bond and stock returns. Thus the price of one security class rises at the expense of the other class. Alternatively, the signaling hypothesis argues that bond and stock prices will move in the same direction. However, both theories are not necessarily mutually exclusive and can balance each other, leading to insignificant returns. To detect the predominating effect Pearson correlation and/or various cross sectional regression models are computed.

Altogether, the purpose of this chapter is to fill a gap in the existing literature and to provide future research with a thorough overview of utilized bond event study procedures. So far, researchers have created strong methodologies and discussed the necessary adjustments to obtain reliable results. This chapter offers guidance in choice of the proper setting to assess how certain events affect a firm's bondholders and how the price response is linked to the firm's stocks.

Chapter 3 analyzes the wealth effects of synergy disclosing and non-disclosing M&A announcements in the US energy sector between January 2000 and October 2012. So far, research provides only examinations of abnormal stock returns associated with forecasting deals, neglecting debt securities. In this framework, the communication of synergies are considered a purely wealth increasing event as bidders experience less negative announcement returns. However, this positive effect could be a mere transfer of wealth from bondholders to stockholders. Furthermore, papers dealing with the wealth effect of takeover deals on bondholders provide mixed and inconclusive results. Synergy communication might shed some light on the diverging conclusions.

A matching portfolio approach detects negative abnormal bond returns associated with disclosing deals, while non-disclosing deals experience zero price effects for bonds. Stock event study, on the other hand, provides evidence, albeit weak for a positive impact of synergy forecasts on equity returns. This negative impact on bondholders and positive impact on stockholders is confirmed by cross sectional regressions. Thus, adding a bidder's bondholders to the assessment of the wealth implications of synergy communication proves that this tactic can no longer be seen as a purely wealth enhancing procedure. Moreover, wealth transfer regression analysis reveals that the wealth effects of disclosing deals are the result of a redistribution of wealth from the bondholders to the stockholders.

In chapter 4 the bond and stock market reaction to different debt offering types of European companies between January 2005 and February 2014 is examined. To this point, researchers did not differentiate between offering types when assessing related wealth effects. Besides, papers present conflicting conclusions about the implications on firm value due to straight bond issues.

While stock event study only provides weak evidence for diverging abnormal returns, cross sectional regression presents a statistically significant and negative coefficient for the reopening dummy, indicating that reopenings experience less positive abnormal returns in comparison to regular issues. Bondholders, on the other hand exhibit similar wealth effects for both issue types when all outstanding bonds are considered. However, examining the impact of the announcement of a reopening on the regular issued bond presents a highly significant and negative coefficient. Apparently, bondholders perceive the announcement of management's decision to reopen an outstanding bond as risk increasing. Moreover, indications for a window of opportunity effect are detected as the price of the reopened bond increases between first issuance and reopening. Investigating the possibility of an expropriation of wealth through several methodologies, a strong indication for such a transfer is found for the subsample of reopenings. Obviously, the negative signaling of the reopening does nullify the positive signaling of the offering, resulting in a redistribution of wealth from the bondholders to the stockholders. This further verifies the need to treat regular issues and reopenings differently when investigating how debt offerings affect firm value.

Altogether, this thesis offers a comprehensive analysis of bondholders' response to key corporate events and the interconnection with the same firm's shareholders. Investigating corporate takeovers in the US energy sector and debt offerings of European companies, the results indisputably prove that the inclusion of debt capital is essential to thoroughly assess the impact of such events on firm value. Clean inference about the real consequences of new information emerging can only be drawn when debt securities are considered together with equity capital. Thus, it is the author's hope that this thesis encourages researchers to integrate the "debt perspective" when assessing corporate events.

5.2 Limitations and Avenues for Future Research

The empirical investigation of bondholder wealth effects together with the same firm's stockholder reactions possesses several drawbacks. First, listed companies have to have outstanding bonds. Otherwise, a comparison between these two classes is impracticable. Second, unlike most stock data, bond data, to some extent, exhibits worse data quality through higher illiquidity as most investors stem from the group of buy-and-hold investors. Thus, companies that lack sufficient bond price movements in the event window need to be excluded from the sample. These facts lead to smaller sample sizes, compared to stand-alone stock event studies. However, an easy technique to deal with this issue is to compare the results of the stockholder responses to prior studies only computing abnormal stock returns, and check whether they present the same patterns. If so, then the validity of the sample can be considered to have a sufficient level.

Another shortcoming is the rather small synergy communicating sample. Nevertheless, the sample size is in line with prior investigations. As a consequence, the results of the disclosing deals need to be interpreted carefully. Future research might repeat this analysis with a larger sample, checking the validity of the results. Moreover, the self selection problem of management's decision to forecast synergies needs to be addressed properly. The inclusion of the inverse Mill's ratio into the cross sectional regression presents one alternative. Future research might apply other methodologies (e.g. regression discontinuity design) to study the impact of the endogeneity issue in more detail. Moreover, the detected relation between risk and wealth effects associated with synergy disclosure provides additional attractive research. For instance, future research may analyze if the probability to disclose merger synergies presents a positive correlation with a higher risk of default. Additionally, as the disclosure of synergy forecasts actually constitutes a risk increasing event, researcher could be interested in investigating this risk shift and examine the impact on event study results.

Finally, this thesis only examines the short-term effects of two types of corporate events: M&A announcements and debt offerings. While every chapter of this thesis enriches past and current research, it disregards the long-term stockholder and bondholder wealth effects. In order to obtain a more thorough picture of the overall effects, future research could augment the short-term analyses with a long-term perspective.

6. Reference List

Acharya, V. V., Amihud, Y., & Bharath, S. T. (2013). Liquidity risk of corporate bond returns: conditional approach. *Journal of Financial Economics, 110*(2), 358–386.

Adams, J. C., & Mansi, S. A. (2009). CEO turnover and bondholder wealth. *Journal of Banking & Finance, 33*(3), 522–533.

Agarwal, V., Taffler, R., & Brown, M. (2011). Is Management Quality Value Relevant? *Journal of Business Finance & Accounting, 38*(9–10), 1184–1208.

Akhigbe, A., Easterwood, J. C., & Pettit, R. R. (1997). Wealth Effects of Corporate Debt Issues: The Impact of Issuer Motivations. *Financial Management, 26*(1), 32–47.

Alexander, G. J. (1980). Applying the Market Model to Long-Term Corporate Bonds. *The Journal of Financial and Quantitative Analysis, 15*(5), 1063–1080.

Amromin, G., Harrison, P., & Sharpe, S. (2008). How Did the 2003 Dividend Tax Cut Affect Stock Prices? *Financial Management, 37*(4), 625–646.

Andrade, G., Mitchell, M., & Stafford, E. (2001). New Evidence and Perspectives on Mergers. *The Journal of Economic Perspectives, 15*(2), 103–120.

Aslan, H., Kumar, P., & Maraachlian, H. (2010). *Managerial Agency and Shareholder-Bondholder Conflicts: Evidence from Effects of Hedge Fund Activism.* Working Paper.

Asquith, P., & Kim, E. H. (1982). The impact of merger bids on the participating firms' security holders. *The Journal of Finance, 37*(5), 1209–1228.

Asquith, P., & Mullins Jr, D. W. (1986). Equity issues and offering dilution. *Journal of Financial Economics, 15*(1–2), 61–89.

Asquith, P., & Wizman, T. A. (1990). Event risk, covenants, and bondholder returns in leveraged buyouts. *Journal of Financial Economics, 27*(1), 195–213.

Autore, D. M., Billingsley, R. S., & Kovacs, T. (2011). The 2008 short sale ban: Liquidity, dispersion of opinion, and the cross-section of returns of US financial stocks. *Journal of Banking & Finance, 35*(9), 2252–2266.

Baginski, S., Hassell, J., & Waymire, G. (1994). Some evidence on the news content of preliminary earnings estimates. *Accounting Review, 69*(1), 265–273.

Baginski, S. P., & Hassell, J. M. (1997). Determinants of management forecast precision. *Accounting Review, 72*(2), 303–312.

Baker, M., & Wurgler, J. (2002). Market Timing and Capital Structure. *The Journal of Finance, 57*(1), 1–32.

Bao, J., Pan, J., & Wang, J. (2011). The Illiquidity of Corporate Bonds. *The Journal of Finance, 66*(3), 911–946.

Baran, L. C., & King, T.-H. D. (2010). Going private transactions, bondholder returns, and wealth transfer effects. *Journal of Banking & Finance, 34*(8), 1856–1872.

Becher, D. A., Mulherin, J. H., & Walkling, R. A. (2008). *Industry Shocks and Merger Activity: An Analysis of US Public Utilities*. Working Paper.

Bernile, G., & Bauguess, S. (2011). *Do merger-related operating synergies exist?* Working Paper. University of Miami.

Bernile, G., & Lyandres, E. (2013). *The Effects of Horizontal Merger Synergies on Competitors, Customers, and Suppliers*. Working Paper.

Bertocchi, G. (1993). A Theory of Public Debt Management with Unobservable Demand. *The Economic Journal, 103*(419), 960–974.

Bessembinder, H., Kahle, K. M., Maxwell, W. F., & Xu, D. (2009). Measuring Abnormal Bond Performance. *The Review of Financial Studies, 22*(10), 4219–4258.

Bessembinder, H., & Maxwell, W. (2008). Markets: Transparency and the Corporate Bond Market. *The Journal of Economic Perspectives, 22*(2), 217–234.

Bessembinder, H., Maxwell, W., & Venkataraman, K. (2006). Market transparency, liquidity externalities, and institutional trading costs in corporate bonds. *Journal of Financial Economics, 82*, 251–288.

Bethel, J. E., Hu, G., & Wang, Q. (2009). The market for shareholder voting rights around mergers and acquisitions: Evidence from institutional daily trading and voting. *Journal of Corporate Finance, 15*(1), 129–145.

Bhat, G., Frankel, R., & Martin, X. (2011). Panacea, Pandora's box, or placebo: Feedback in bank mortgage-backed security holdings and fair value accounting. *Journal of Accounting and Economics, 52*(2–3), 153–173.

Biais, B., Declerck, F., Dow, J., Portes, R., & von Thadden, E.-L. (2006). European Corporate Bond Markets: transparency, liquidity, efficiency. *Centre for Economic Policy Research.*

Billett, M. T., Jiang, Z., & Lie, E. (2010). The effect of change-in-control covenants on takeovers: Evidence from leveraged buyouts. *Journal of Corporate Finance, 16*(1), 1–15.

Billett, M. T., King, T.-H. D., & Mauer, D. C. (2004). Bondholder Wealth Effects in Mergers and Acquisitions: New Evidence from the 1980s and 1990s. *The Journal of Finance, 59*(1), 107–135.

Billings, M. B., Klein, A., & Zur, E. (2011). *Shareholder Class Action Suits and the Bond Market*. Working Paper.

Binder, J. (1998). The Event Study Methodology Since 1969. *Review of Quantitative Finance and Accounting, 11*(2), 111–137.

Blaylock, B., Edwards, A., & Stanfield, J. (2011). *The Market-Wide Consequences of Government Intervention*. Working Paper. University of New South Wales.

Blumental, D. (1998). Sources of Funds and Risk Management for International Energy Projects. *Berkeley Journal of International Law, 16*(2), 267–296.

Boehmer, E., Musumeci, J., & Poulsen, A. B. (1991). Event-Study Methodology under Conditions of Event-Induced Variance. *Journal of Financial Economics, 30*(2), 253–272.

Bowen, R. M., Davis, A. K., & Matsumoto, D. A. (2002). Do Conference Calls Affect Analysts' Forecasts? *The Accounting Review, 77*(2), 285–316.

Brennan, M. J., & Schwartz, E. S. (1980). Analyzing Convertible Bonds. *The Journal of Financial and Quantitative Analysis, 15*(4), 907–929.

Brewer, E., III, & Jagtiani, J. (2013). How Much Did Banks Pay to Become Too-Big-To-Fail and to Become Systemically Important? *Journal of Financial Services Research, 43*(1), 1–35.

Brewer, E., & Jackson, W. (2000). Requiem for a Market Maker: The Case of Drexel Burnham Lambert and Junk Bonds. *Journal of Financial Services Research, 17*(3), 209–235.

Broughton, J. B., & Smith, D. M. (1997). Option Listing Effects and the Role of Confounding Events. *Quarterly Journal of Business & Economics, 36*(4), 15–23.

Brown, D. T., James, C. M., & Mooradian, R. M. (1994). Asset sales by financially distressed firms. *Journal of Corporate Finance, 1*(2), 233–257.

Brown, S. J., & Warner, J. B. (1980). Measuring Security Price Performance. *Jounal of Financial Economics, 8*(3), 205–258.

Brown, S. J., & Warner, J. B. (1985). Using Daily Stock Returns. The Case of Event Studies. *Journal of Financial Economics, 14*(1), 3–31.

Bruner, R. (2004). Where M&A Pays and Where It Strays: A Survey of the Research. *Journal of Applied Corporate Finance, 16*(4), 63–76.

Bushee, B. J., Matsumoto, D. A., & Miller, G. S. (2004). Managerial and Investor Responses to Disclosure Regulation: The Case of Reg FD and Conference Calls. *The Accounting Review, 79*(3), 617–643.

Campbell, J. Y., & Taksler, G. B. (2003). Equity Volatility and Corporate Bond Yields. *The Journal of Finance, 58*(6), 2321–2349.

Carhart, M. M. (1997). On Persistence in Mutual Fund Performance. *The Journal of Finance, 52*(1), 57–82.

Carlson, M., Fisher, A., & Giammarino, R. O. N. (2006). Corporate Investment and Asset Price Dynamics: Implications for SEO Event Studies and Long-Run Performance. *The Journal of Finance, 61*(3), 1009–1034.

Castillo, A. (2001). The Announcement Effect of Junk Bond Issues: An Analysis of the 1976–1989 Period. *Estudios de Administración, 8*(2), 41–73.

Chaplinsky, S., & Hansen, R. S. (1993). Partial Anticipation, the Flow of Information and the Economic Impact of Corporate Debt Sales. *The Review of Financial Studies, 6*(3), 709–732.

Chen, F. (2013). *Bondholder Wealth Effects surrounding Bond Offering Announcements*. Working Paper. University of Oklahoma.

Chen, L., Lesmond, D. A., & Wei, J. (2007). Corporate Yield Spreads and Bond Liquidity. *The Journal of Finance, 62*(1), 119–149.

Chen, R.-R., Fabozzi, F. J., & Sverdlove, R. (2010). Corporate Credit Default Swap Liquidity and Its Implications for Corporate Bond Spreads. *The Journal of Fixed Income, 20*(3), 31–57.

Chen, Z., Lookman, A. A., Schürhoff, N., & Seppi, D. J. (2014). Rating-Based Investment Practices and Bond Market Segmentation. *The Review of Asset Pricing Studies, 4*(2), 162–205.

Cho, D. D., Kim, H., & Shin, J. S. (2011). *The Effect of Seniority and Security Covenants on Bond Price Reactions to Credit News*. Working Paper.

Choi, S., Francis, B. B., & Hasan, I. (2010). Cross-Border Bank M&As and Risk: Evidence from the Bond Market. *Journal of Money, Credit and Banking, 42*(4), 615–645.

Chordia, T., Sarkar, A., & Subrahmanyam, A. (2005). An Empirical Analysis of Stock and Bond Market Liquidity. *The Review of Financial Studies, 18*(1).

Chow, C. W. (1983). The Impact of Accounting Regulation on Bondholder and Shareholder Wealth: The Case of the Securities Acts. *The Accounting Review, 58*(3), 485–520.

Clayton, M. J. (2011). *The Valuation Effect of IPOs: Evidence from the Bond Market*. Working Paper.

Collin-Dufresne, P., Goldstein, R. S., & Martin, J. S. (2001). The Determinants of Credit Spread Changes. *The Journal of Finance, 56*(6), 2177–2207.

Cook, D. O., & Easterwood, J. C. (1994). Poison Put Bonds: An Analysis of Their Economic Role. *The Journal of Finance, 49*(5), 1905–1920.

Cook, D. O., Easterwood, J. C., & Martin, J. D. (1992). Bondholder Wealth Effects of Management Buyouts. *Financial Management, 21*(1), 102–113.

Cornett, M. M., & Travlos, N. G. (1989). Information Effects Associated with Debt-for-Equity and Equity-for-Debt Exchange Offers. *The Journal of Finance, 44*(2), 451–468.

Cornil, A. (2009). The Impact of Accounting Restatements on a Firm's Cost of Public Debt. *Review of Business and Economics, 2*, 147–178.

Corrado, C. J. (1989). A Nonparametric Test for Abnormal Security-Price Performance in Event Studies. *Journal of Financial Economics, 23*(2), 385–395.

Corrado, C. J. (2011). Event studies: A methodology review. *Accounting & Finance 51*(1), 207–234.

Corrado, C. J., & Zivney, T. L. (1992). The Specification and Power of the Sign Test in Event Study Hypothesis Tests Using Daily Stock Returns. *The Journal of Financial and Quantitative Analysis, 27*(3), 465–478.

Cowan, A. R., & Sergeant, A. M. A. (1996). Trading frequency and event study test specification. *Journal of Banking & Finance, 20*(10), 1731–1757.

Crabbe, L. (1991). Event Risk: An Analysis of Losses to Bondholders and "Super Poison Put" Bond Covenants. *The Journal of Finance, 46*(2), 689–706.

Craney, T. A., & Surles, J. G. (2002). Model-Dependent Variance Inflation Factor Cutoff Values. *Quality Engineering, 14*(3), 391–403.

Dallocchio, M., Hubler, J., Raimbourg, P., & Salvi, A. (2006). Do Upgradings and Downgradings Convey Information? An Event Study of the French Bond Market. *Review of Banking, Finance and Monetary Economics, 35*(3), 293–317.

Daniel, K., Hirshleifer, D., & Subrahmanyam, A. (1998). Investor Psychology and Security Market Under- and Overreactions. *The Journal of Finance, 53*(6), 1839–1885.

Dann, L. Y. (1981). Common Stock Repurchases. An Analysis of Returns to Bondholders and Stockholders. *Journal of Financial Economics, 9*(2), 113–138.

Dann, L. Y., & Mikkelson, W. H. (1984). Convertible debt issuance, capital structure change and financing-related information: Some new evidence. *Journal of Financial Economics, 13*(2), 157–186.

Datta, S., & Dhillon, U. S. (1993). Bond and Stock Market Response to Unexpected Earnings Announcements. *The Journal of Financial and Quantitative Analysis, 28*(4), 565–577.

Datta, S., Iskandar-Datta, M., & Patel, A. (1997). The Pricing of Initial Public Offers of Corporate Straight Debt. *The Journal of Finance, 52*(1), 379–396.

Datta, S., Iskandar-Datta, M., & Raman, K. (2003). Value creation in corporate asset sales: The role of managerial performance and lender monitoring. *Journal of Banking & Finance, 27*(2), 351–375.

Datta, S., & Iskandar-Datta, M. E. (1995). Corporate partial acquisitions, total firm valuation and the effect of financing method. *Journal of Banking & Finance 19*(1), 97–115.

Datta, S., & Iskandar-Datta, M. E. (1996). Who Gains from Corporate Asset Sales? *The Journal of Financial Research, 19*(1), 41–58.

Datta, S., & Satten, G. A. (2005). Rank-Sum Tests for Clustered Data. *Journal of the American Statistical Association, 100*(471), 908–915.

Datta, S., & Satten, G. A. (2008). A Signed-Rank Test for Clustered Data. *Biometrics, 64*(2), 501–507.

Dbouk, W., & Kryzanowski, L. (2009). Impact of bond index revisions. *Applied Financial Economics, 19*(9), 693–702.

DeFond, M., & Zhang, J. (2008). *The Information Content of Earnings Surprises in the Corporate Bond Market*. Working Paper. University of Southern California.

DeFond, M. L., Hung, M., Carr, E., & Zhang, J. (2011). Was the Sarbanes-Oxley Act Good News for Corporate Bondholders? *Accounting Horizons, 25*(3), 465–485.

DeFond, M. L., & Zhang, J. (2014). The Timeliness of the Bond Market Reaction to Bad Earnings News. *Contemporary Accounting Research, 31*(3), 911–936.

DeFusco, R. A., Johnson, R. R., & Zorn, T. S. (1990). The Effect of Executive Stock Option Plans on Stockholders and Bond holders. *The Journal of Finance, 45*(2), 617–627.

DeJong, D. V., & Collins, D. W. (1985). Explanations for the Instability of Equity Beta: Risk-Free Rate Changes and Leverage Effects. *Journal of Financial and Quantitative Analysis, 20*(01), 73–94.

del Valle, C. L., & Ugolini, P. C. (2001). *Developing government bond markets: a handbook*: International Bank for Reconstruction and Development/The World Bank.

Dennis, D. K., & McConnell, J. J. (1986). Corporate mergers and security returns. *Journal of Financial Economics, 16*(2), 143–187.

Devaney, S., & Lizieri, C. (2004). Sale and leaseback, asset outsourcing and capital market impacts. *Journal of Corporate Real Estate, 6*(2), 118–132.

Dhillon, U. S., & Johnson, H. (1994). The Effect of Dividend Changes on Stock and Bond Prices. *The Journal of Finance, 49*(1), 281–289.

Dittmar, A. (2004). Capital Structure in Corporate Spin-Offs. *The Journal of Business, 77*(1), 9–43.

Donald, S. G., & Lang, K. (2007). Inference with Difference-in-Differences and Other Panel Data. *Review of Economics and Statistics, 89*(2), 221–233.

Drobetz, W., & Seidel, J. (2011). *Leverage, beta estimation, and the size effect*. Working Paper. University of Hamburg.

Duca, E., Dutordoir, M., Veld, C., & Verwijmeren, P. (2012). Why are convertible bond announcements associated with increasingly negative issuer stock returns? An arbitrage-based explanation. *Journal of Banking & Finance, 36*(11), 2884–2899.

Dutordoir, M., Roosenboom, P., & Vasconcelos, M. (2014). Synergy disclosures in mergers and acquisitions. *International Review of Financial Analysis, 31*(0), 88–100.

Dye, R. A. (1985). Disclosure of Nonproprietary Information. *Journal of Accounting Research, 23*(1), 123–145.

Easterwood, J. C. (1998). Divestments and financial distress in leveraged buyouts. *Journal of Banking & Finance, 22*(2), 129–159.

Eberhart, A., Maxwell, W., & Siddique, A. (2008). A Reexamination of the Tradeoff between the Future Benefit and Riskiness of R&D Increases. *Journal of Accounting Research, 46*(1), 27–52.

Eberhart, A. C., & Siddique, A. (2002). The Long-Term Performance of Corporate Bonds (And Stocks) Following Seasoned Equity Offerings. *The Review of Financial Studies, 15*(5), 1385–1406.

Eckbo, B. E. (1986). Valuation effects of corporate debt offerings. *Journal of Financial Economics, 15*(1–2), 119–151.

Eckbo, B. E., Masulis, R. W., & Norli, Ø. (2007). Chapter 6 - Security Offerings. In B. E. Eckbo (Ed.), *Handbook of Empirical Corporate Finance* (pp. 233–373). San Diego: Elsevier.

Ederington, L., Guan, W., & Yang, Z. (2012). *Bond Market Event Study Methodology*. Working Paper.

Edwards, A. K., Harris, L. E., & Piwowar, M. S. (2007). Corporate Bond Market Transaction Costs and Transparency. *The Journal of Finance, 62*(3), 1421–1451.

Eger, C. E. (1983). An Empirical Test of the Redistribution Effect in Pure Exchange Mergers. *The Journal of Financial and Quantitative Analysis, 18*(4), 547–572.

Elliott, W. B., Prevost, A. K., & Rao, R. P. (2009). The announcement impact of seasoned equity offerings on bondholder wealth. *Journal of Banking & Finance, 33*(8), 1472–1480.

Ellul, A., Jotikasthira, C., & Lundblad, C. T. (2011). Regulatory pressure and fire sales in the corporate bond market. *Journal of Financial Economics, 101*(3), 596–620.

Elton, E. J., Gruber, M. J., Agrawal, D., & Mann, C. (2001). Explaining the Rate Spread on Corporate Bonds. *The Journal of Finance, 56*(1), 247–277.

Elton, E. J., Gruber, M. J., & Blake, C. R. (1995). Fundamental Economic Variables, Expected Returns, and Bond Fund Performance. *The Journal of Finance, 50*(4), 1229–1256.

Elton, E. J., Gruber, M. J., Brown, S. J., & Goetzmann, W. N. (2011). *Modern Portfolio Theory and Investment Analysis* (8th ed.). Hoboken, NJ: John Wiley & Sons.

Fama, E. F., Fisher, L., Jensen, M. C., & Roll, R. (1969). The Adjustment of Stock Prices to New Information. *International Economic Review, 10*(1), 1–21.

Fama, E. F., & French, K. R. (1993). Common risk factors in the returns on stocks and bonds. *Journal of Financial Economics, 33*(1), 3–56.

FINRA. (2012). Trade Reporting and Compliance Engine Retrieved 10 October, 2012.

Fortin, S., Subramaniam, C., Wang, X., & Zhang, S. (2014). Incentive alignment through performance-focused shareholder proposals on management compensation. *Journal of Contemporary Accounting & Economics, 10*(2), 130–147.

Francis, B. B., Hasan, I., John, K., & Waisman, M. (2010). The effect of state antitakeover laws on the firm's bondholders. *Journal of Financial Economics, 96*(1), 127–154.

Francis, J., Schipper, K., & Vincent, L. (2002). Expanded Disclosures and the Increased Usefulness of Earnings Announcements. *The Accounting Review, 77*(3), 515–546.

Frank, K. A. (2000). Impact of a Confounding Variable on a Regression Coefficient. *Sociological Methods & Research, 29*(2), 147–194.

Fraunhoffer, R., Maul, D., & Schiereck, D. (2011). *Bondholder Wealth Effects of Voluntary Synergy Disclosure in the US Energy Sector.* Working Paper. TU Darmstadt.

Fraunhoffer, R., & Schiereck, D. (2012a). Consolidation and communication in European energy markets. *International Journal of Energy Sector Management, 6*(4), 534–557.

Fraunhoffer, R., & Schiereck, D. (2012b). Consolidation of the energy sector, potential synergies, and realized shareholder value – survey and new insights from top managers' perceptions. *Problems and Perspectives in Management, 10*(2), 68–79.

Frazzini, A. (2014). Data Library (Downloadable Files) Retrieved 11.08.2014, from http://www.econ.yale.edu/~af227/data_library.htm.

Fu, R., Kraft, A., & Zhang, H. (2012). Financial reporting frequency, information asymmetry, and the cost of equity. *Journal of Accounting and Economics, 54*(2–3), 132–149.

Galai, D., & Masulis, R. W. (1976). The option pricing model and the risk factor of stock. *Journal of Financial Economics, 3*(1–2), 53–81.

Galbraith, S., Daniel, J. A., & Vissel, B. (2010). A Study of Clustered Data and Approaches to Its Analysis. *The Journal of Neuroscience, 30*(32), 10601–10608.

Gao, Y., Liao, S., & Wang, X. (2011). *The Economic Impact of the Dodd Frank Act of 2010: Evidence from Market Reactions to Events Surrounding the Passage of the Act.* Working Paper.

Gastwirth, J. L., & Rubin, H. (1971). Effect of Dependence on the Level of Some One-Sample Tests. *Journal of the American Statistical Association, 66*(336), 816–820.

Grier, P., & Katz, S. (1976). The Differential Effects of Bond Rating Changes Among Industrial and Public Utility Bonds by Maturity. *The Journal of Business, 49*(2), 226–239.

Gropp, R., & Richards, A. J. (2001). Rating Agency Actions and the Pricing of Debt and Equity of European Banks: What Can we Infer About Private Sector Monitoring of Bank Soundness? *Review of Banking, Finance and Monetary Economics, 30*(3), 373–398.

Gupta, A., & Rosenthal, L. (1991). Ownership Structure, Leverage, and Firm Value: The Case of Leveraged Recapitalization. *Financial Management, 20*(3), 69–83.

Haleblian, J., Devers, C. E., McNamara, G., Carpenter, M. A., & Davison, R. B. (2009). Taking Stock of What We Know About Mergers and Acquisitions: A Review and Research Agenda. *Journal of Management, 35*(3), 469–502.

Hand, J. R. M., Holthausen, R. W., & Leftwich, R. W. (1992). The Effect of Bond Rating Agency Announcements on Bond and Stock Prices. *The Journal of Finance, 47*(2), 733–752.

Handa, P., & Radhakrishnan, A. R. (1991). An Empirical Investigation of Leveraged Recapitalizations with Cash Payout as Takeover Defense. *Financial Management, 20*(3), 58–68.

Handjinicolaou, G., & Kalay, A. (1984). Wealth Redistribution or Changes in Firm Value. An Analysis of Returns to Bondholders and Stockholders around Dividend Announcements. *Journal of Financial Economics, 13*(1), 35–63.

Hansen, R. S., & Crutchley, C. (1990). Corporate Earnings and Financings: An Empirical Analysis. *The Journal of Business, 63*(3), 347–371.

Healy, P. M., Hutton, A. P., & Palepu, K. G. (1999). Stock Performance and Intermediation Changes Surrounding Sustained Increases in Disclosure. *Contemporary Accounting Research, 16*(3), 485–520.

Heckman, J. J. (1979). Sample Selection Bias as a Specification Error. *Econometrica, 47*(1), 153–161.

Henderson, G. V. (1990). Problems and Solutions in Conducting Event Studies. *The Journal of Risk and Insurance, 57*(2), 282–306.

Hite, G., & Warga, A. (1997). The Effect of Bond-Rating Changes on Bond Price Performance. *Financial Analysts Journal, 53*(3), 35–51.

Hite, G. L., & Owers, J. E. (1983). Security price reactions around corporate spin-off announcements. *Journal of Financial Economics, 12*(4), 409–436.

Hong, G., & Warga, A. (2000). An Empirical Study of Bond Market Transactions. *Financial Analysts Journal, 56*(2), 32–46.

Hotchkiss, E. S., & Mooradian, R. M. (1997). Vulture investors and the market for control of distressed firms. *Journal of Financial Economics, 43*(3), 401–432.

Houston, J. F., James, C. M., & Ryngaert, M. D. (2001). Where do merger gains come from? Bank mergers from the perspective of insiders and outsiders. *Journal of Financial Economics, 60*(2–3), 285–331.

Howton, S. D., Howton, S. W., & Perfect, S. B. (1998). The Market Reaction to Straight Debt Issues: The Effect of Free Cash Flow *Journal of Financial Research, 21*(2), 219–228.

Hutton, A. P., Miller, G. S., & Skinner, D. J. (2003). The Role of Supplementary Statements with Management Earnings Forecasts. *Journal of Accounting Research, 41*(5), 867–890.

ICMA. (2013, March 12, 2015). Economic Importance of the Corporate Bond Markets, from www.icmagroup.org.

Imbierowicz, B., & Wahrenburg, M. (2013). Wealth transfer effects between stockholders and bondholders. *The Quarterly Review of Economics and Finance, 53*(1), 23–43.

Jaffe, J. F. (1974). Special Information and Insider Trading. *The Journal of Business, 47*(3), 410–428.

Jayaraman, N., & Shastri, K. (1988). The Valuation Impacts of Specially Designated Dividends. *The Journal of Financial and Quantitative Analysis, 23*(3), 301–312.

Jensen, M. C. (1986). Agency Costs of Free Cash Flow, Corporate Finance, and Takeovers. *The American Economic Review, 76*(2), 323–329.

Jensen, M. C., & Meckling, W. H. (1976). Theory of the firm: Managerial behavior, agency costs and ownership structure. *Journal of Financial Economics, 3*(4), 305–360.

Jensen, M. R. H., & Pugh, W. N. (1991). Valuation Effects of Cancelled Debt Offerings. *The Journal of Financial and Quantitative Analysis, 26*(3), 425–431.

Johnson, S. A. (1995). Dividend Payout and the Valuation Effects of Bond Announcements. *The Journal of Financial and Quantitative Analysis, 30*(3), 407–423.

Kahan, M., & Tuckman, B. (1993). Do Bondholders Lose from Junk Bond Covenant Changes. *The Journal of Business, 66*(4), 499–516.

Kahle, K. M., & Walkling, R. A. (1996). The Impact of Industry Classifications on Financial Research. *The Journal of Financial and Quantitative Analysis, 31*(3), 309–335.

Kalay, A., & Shimrat, A. (1987). Firm Value and Seasoned Equity Issues. Price Pressure, Wealth Redistribution, or Negative Information. *Journal of Financial Economics, 19*(1), 109–126.

Kapoor, A. K., & Pope, R. A. (1997). The Relationship between Corporate Debt Issuance and Changes in Systematic Risk. *Journal of Financial and Strategic Decisions, 10*(3), 13–22.

Karafiath, I. (1988). Using Dummy Variables in the Event Methodology. *Financial Review, 23*(3), 351–357.

Katz, S. (1974). The Price and Adjustment Process of Bonds to Rating Reclassifications: A Test of Bond Market Efficiency. *The Journal of Finance, 29*(2), 551–559.

Kaya, O. (2013). Corporate bond issuance in Europe: Where do we stand and where are we heading? *EU Monitor: Global financial Markets.*

Kedia, S., & Zhou, X. (2009). *Insider trading and conflicts of interest: Evidence from corporate bonds.* Working Paper. Rutgers University.

Kim, E. H., & McConnell, J. J. (1977). Corporate mergers and the co-insurance of corporate debt. *The Journal of Finance, 32*(2), 349–365.

Kim, E. H., McConnell, J. J., & Greenwood, P. R. (1977). Capital Structure Rearrangements and Me-First Rules in an Efficient Capital Market. *The Journal of Finance, 32*(3), 789–810.

Kimbrough, M. D. (2005). The Effect of Conference Calls on Analyst and Market Underreaction to Earnings Announcements. *The Accounting Review, 80*(1), 189–219.

Kimbrough, M. D., & Louis, H. (2011). Voluntary Disclosure to Influence Investor Reactions to Merger Announcements: An Examination of Conference Calls. *The Accounting Review, 86*(2), 637–667.

Kitsabunnarat-Chatjuthamard, P., Lung, P., Nishikawa, T., & Rao, R. P. (2010). Leverage-reducing exchange offers and bondholder–stockholder wealth transfers: A re-evaluation. *International Review of Economics and Finance, 19*(1), 81–94.

Klein, A., & Zur, E. (2011). The Impact of Hedge Fund Activism on the Target Firm's Existing Bondholders. *The Review of Financial Studies, 24*(5), 1736–1771.

Kliger, D., & Sarig, O. (2000). The Information Value of Bond Ratings. *The Journal of Finance, 55*(6), 2879–2902.

Kolodny, R., & Suhler, D. R. (1988). The Effects of New Debt Issues on Existing Security Holders. *Quarterly Journal of Business and Economics, 27*(2), 51–72.

Kothari, S. P., & Warner, J. B. (2005). Econometrics of Event Studies. In B. E. Eckbo (Ed.), *Handbook of Corporate Finance: Empirical Corporate Finance* (2nd ed., pp. 3–36). Amsterdam: North-Holland.

Kraft, H., & Munk, C. (2007). Bond durations: Corporates vs. Treasuries. *Journal of Banking & Finance, 31*(12), 3720–3741.

Kwan, I. P. L., & Aranda León, C. (2014). *Do Strategic Alliances Create Value for Bond Investors?* Paper presented at the Academy of Management. Annual Meeting Proceedings.

Lang, M. H., & Lundholm, R. J. (1996). Corporate Disclosure Policy and Analyst Behavior. *Accounting Review, 71*(4), 467–492.

Larcker, D. F., & Rusticus, T. O. (2010). On the use of instrumental variables in accounting research. *Journal of Accounting and Economics, 49*(3), 186–205.

Lemmon, M., Liu, L. X., Mao, M. Q., & Nini, G. (2014). Securitization and Capital Structure in Nonfinancial Firms: An Empirical Investigation. *The Journal of Finance, 69*(4), 1787–1825.

Lev, B., & Penman, S. H. (1990). Voluntary Forecast Disclosure, Nondisclosure, and Stock Prices. *Journal of Accounting Research, 28*(1), 49–76.

Lewellen, W. G. (1971). A Pure Financial Rationale for the Conglomerate Merger. *The Journal of Finance, 26*(2), 521–537.

Li, S., Madura, J., & Richie, N. (2013). Bond Market Response to the Collapse of Prominent Investment Banks. *Financial Review, 48*(4), 645–670.

Lin, H., Liu, S., & Wu, C. (2011). Dissecting Corporate Bond and CDS Spreads. *The Journal of Fixed Income, 20*(3), 7–39.

Loughran, T., & Ritter, J. R. (1995). The New Issues Puzzle. *The Journal of Finance, 50*(1), 23–51.

Loughran, T., & Ritter, J. R. (1997). The Operating Performance of Firms Conducting Seasoned Equity Offerings. *The Journal of Finance, 52*(5), 1823–1850.

MacKinlay, A. C. (1997). Event studies in economics and finance. *Journal of Economic Literature, 35*(1), 13–39.

Mahanti, S., Nashikkar, A., Subrahmanyam, M., Chacko, G., & Mallik, G. (2008). Latent liquidity: A new measure of liquidity, with an application to corporate bonds. *Journal of Financial Economics, 88*(2), 272–298.

Mandelker, G. (1974). Risk and Return: The Case of Merging Firms. *Journal of Financial Economics, 1*(4), 303–335.

Maquieira, C. P., Megginson, W. L., & Nail, L. (1998). Wealth creation versus wealth redistributions in pure stock-for-stock mergers. *Journal of Financial Economics, 48*(1), 3–33.

Marais, L., Schipper, K., & Smith, A. (1989). Wealth Effects of Going Private for Senior Securities. *Journal of Financial Economics, 23*(1), 155–191.

Marble Iii, H. (2011). Anatomy of a ratings change. *The Quarterly Review of Economics and Finance, 51*(1), 105–112.

Massa, M., & Zhang, L. (2011). *The Spillover Effects of Hurricane Katrina on Corporate Bonds and the Choice between Bank and Bond Financing.* Working Paper.

Masulis, R. W. (1980). The Effects of Capital Structure Change on Security Prices. A Study of Exchange Offers. *Journal of Financial Economics, 8*(2), 139–178.

Maxwell, W. F., & Rao, R. P. (2003). Do Spin-offs Expropriate Wealth from Bondholders? *The Journal of Finance, 58*(5), 2087–2108.

Maxwell, W. F., & Stephens, C. P. (2003). The Wealth Effects of Repurchases on Bondholders. *The Journal of Finance, 58*(2), 895–919.

May, A. D. (2010). The impact of bond rating changes on corporate bond prices: New evidence from the over-the-counter market. *Journal of Banking & Finance, 34*(11), 2822–2836.

McWilliams, A., & Siegel, D. (1997). Event Studies In Management Research: Theoretical and Empirical Issues. *Academy of Management Journal, 40*(3), 626–657.

Melicher, R. W. (1974). Financial Factors Which Influence Beta Variations within an Homogeneous Industry Environment. *Journal of Financial and Quantitative Analysis, 9*(02), 231–241.

Merton, R. C. (1974). On The Pricing of Corporate Debt: The Risk Structure of Interest Rates. *The Journal of Finance, 29*(2), 449–470.

Michayluk, D., & Zhao, R. (2010). Stock Splits and Bond Yields: Isolating the Signaling Hypothesis. *The Financial Review, 45*(2), 375–386.

Mikkelson, W. H. (1981). Convertible Calls and Security Returns. *Journal of Financial Economics, 9*(3), 237–264.

Mikkelson, W. H., & Partch, M. M. (1986). Valuation effects of security offerings and the issuance process. *Journal of Financial Economics, 15*(1–2), 31–60.

Miller, M. H., & Modigliani, F. (1961). Dividend Policy, Growth, and the Valuation of Shares. *The Journal of Business, 34*(4), 411–433.

Miller, M. H., & Rock, K. (1985). Dividend Policy under Asymmetric Information. *The Journal of Finance, 40*(4), 1031–1051.

Minnick, K., & Zhao, M. (2006). *Levered Repurchases: Who benefits?* Working Paper. Department of Finance, Bentley College.

Modigliani, F., & Miller, M. H. (1958). The Cost of Capital, Corporation Finance and the Theory of Investment. *The American Economic Review, 48*(3), 261–297.

Moeller, S. B., Schlingemann, F. P., & Stulz, R. M. (2005). Wealth Destruction on a Massive Scale? A Study of Acquiring-Firm Returns in the Recent Merger Wave. *The Journal of Finance, 60*(2), 757–782.

Moeller, S. B., Schlingemann, F. P., & Stulz, R. M. (2007). How Do Diversity of Opinion and Information Asymmetry Affect Acquirer Returns? *Review of Financial Studies, 20*(6), 2047–2078.

Morck, R., Shleifer, A., & Vishny, R. W. (1990). Do Managerial Objectives Drive Bad Acquisitions? *The Journal of Finance, 45*(1), 31–48.

Moulton, B. R. (1990). An Illustration of a Pitfall in Estimating the Effects of Aggregate Variables on Micro Units. *The Review of Economics and Statistics, 72*(2), 334–338.

Myers, S. C., & Majluf, N. S. (1984). Corporate financing and investment decisions when firms have information that investors do not have. *Journal of Financial Economics, 13*(2), 187–221.

Newberry, K., & Parthasarathy, K. (2007). *The Impact of Financial Restatements on Debt Markets*. Working Paper.

Nishikawa, T., Prevost, A. K., & Rao, R. P. (2011). Bond Market Reaction to Stock Repurchases: Is there a Wealth Transfer Effect? *The Journal of Financial Research, 34*(3), 503–522.

Nunn, K. P., Hill, J., & Schneeweis, T. (1986). Corporate Bond Price Data Sources and Return/Risk Measurement. *The Journal of Financial and Quantitative Analysis, 21*(2), 197–208.

Officer, M. S., Poulsen, A. B., & Stegemoller, M. (2009). Target-firm information asymmetry and acquirer returns. *Review of Finance, 13*(3), 467–493.

Okamoto, K., Pedersen, D., & Pedersen, N. (2011). The Price Effects of Event-Risk Protection: The Results from a Natural Experiment. *Journal of Empirical Legal Studies, 8*(4), 878–903.

Ongena, S., & Penas, M. F. (2009). Bondholders' wealth effects in domestic and cross-border bank mergers. *Journal of Financial Stability, 5*(3), 256–271.

Ongena, S., Roşcovan, V., Song, W.-L., & Werker, B. J. M. (2008). *Banks and Bonds: The Impact of Bank Loan Announcements on Bond and Equity Prices*. Working Paper.

Patell, J. M. (1976). Corporate Forecasts of Earnings Per Share and Stock Price Behavior: Empirical Test. *Journal of Accounting Research, 14*(2), 246–276.

Penas, M. F., & Unal, H. (2004). Gains in bank mergers: Evidence from the bond markets. *Journal of Financial Economics, 74*(1), 149–179.

Peterson, P. P. (1989). Event Studies: A Review of Issues and Methodology. *Quarterly Journal of Business and Economics, 28*(3), 36–66.

Plunus, S., Gillet, R., & Hübner, G. (2012). Reputational damage of operational loss on the bond market: Evidence from the financial industry. *International Review of Financial Analysis, 24*, 66–73.

Pu, N. (2012). *Impact of Shareholder Activism on Existing Bondholder Wealth: Evidence from CalPERS*. Working Paper.

Rathinasamy, R. S., Philippatos, G. C., & Shrieves, R. E. (1991). Mergers, Debt Capacity, And Stockholder-Bondholder Wealth Transfers. *The Journal of Applied Business Research, 7*(3), 92–103.

Renneboog, L., & Szilagyi, P. G. (2007). *Bondholder Wealth in Mergers and Acquisitions: Evidence on the Impact and Spillover of Governance and Legal Standards.* Working Paper.

Reviglio, E. (2012, 6th June). *Global perspectives for project financing.* Paper presented at the Presentation to the Joint EC-EIB/EPEC Private Sector Forum Brussels.

Ritter, J. R. (1991). The Long-Run Performance of initial Public Offerings. *The Journal of Finance, 46*(1), 3–27.

Rosner, B., Glynn, R. J., & Lee, M.-L. T. (2006). The Wilcoxon Signed Rank Test for Paired Comparisons of Clustered Data. *Biometrics, 62*(1), 185–192.

Ross, S. A. (1977). The Determination of Financial Structure: The Incentive-Signalling Approach. *The Bell Journal of Economics, 8*(1), 23–40.

Schlingemann, F. P., Stulz, R. M., & Walkling, R. A. (2002). Divestitures and the liquidity of the market for corporate assets. *Journal of Financial Economics, 64*(1), 117–144.

Schultz, P. (2001). Corporate Bond Trading Costs: A Peek Behind the Curtain. *The Journal of Finance, 56*(2), 677–698.

Settle, J. W., Petry, G. H., & Hsia, C.-C. (1984). Synergy, Diversification, and Incentive Effects of Corporate Merger on Bondholder Wealth: Some Evidence. *The Journal of Financial Research, 7*(4), 329–339.

Shi, C., & Zhang, S. W. (2008). *Accounting Restatements and the Cost of Debt Capital.* Working Paper.

Shin, Y. S., Han, S. H., Yi, S., & Moore, W. T. (2009). *Analysis of unsolicited and solicited credit ratings in bond markets.* Working Paper.

Shyam-Sunder, L. (1991). The Stock Price Effect of Risky Versus Safe Debt. *The Journal of Financial and Quantitative Analysis, 26*(4), 549–558.

Sirower, M. L., & Lipin, S. (2003). Investor Communications: A Message of Confidence In the Deal. *Mergers & Acquisitions: The Dealermaker's Journal, 38*(10), 21–26.

Sissine, F. (2007). Energy Independence and Security Act of 2007: a summary of major provisions: DTIC Document.

Smith Jr, C. W., & Warner, J. B. (1979). On financial contracting: An analysis of bond covenants. *Journal of Financial Economics, 7*(2), 117–161.

Stein, J. C. (1992). Convertible bonds as backdoor equity financing. *Journal of Financial Economics, 32*(1), 3–21.

Steiner, M., & Heinke, V. G. (2001). Event Study Concerning International Bond Price Effects of Credit Rating Actions. *International Journal of Finance and Economics, 6*, 139–157.

Strong, J. S., & Meyer, J. R. (1987). Asset Writedowns: Managerial Incentives and Security Returns. *The Journal of Finance, 42*(3), 643–661.

Subbaiah, P., & Xia, G. (2007). Robustness of Inference for One-sample Problem with Correlated Observations. *Journal of Applied Statistics, 34*(4), 471–486.

Tang, A. P., & Singer, R. F. (1993). Valuation Effect of Issuing Nonsubordinated versus Subordinated Debt. *Journal of Financial Research, 16*(1), 11–21.

Tendulkar, R., & Hancock, G. (2014). Corporate Bond Markets: A Global Perspective: IOSCO Research Department.

Thakar, N. (2008). The Urge to Merge: A Look at the Repeal of the Public Utility Holding Company Act of 1935. *Lewis & Clark Law Review, 12*(3), 903–942.

Van Voorhis, C. R. W., & Morgan, B. L. (2007). Understanding Power and Rules of Thumb for Determining Sample Sizes. *Tutorials in Quantitative Methods for Psychology, 3*(2), 43–50.

Veld, C., & Veld-Merkoulova, Y. V. (2008). An Empirical Analysis of the Stockholder-Bondholder Conflict in Corporate Spin-Offs. *Financial Management, 37*(1), 103–124.

Vermaelen, T. (1981). Common Stock Repurchases and Market Signalling. *Journal of Financial Economics, 9*(2), 139–183.

Verrecchia, R. E. (1990). Information quality and discretionary disclosure. *Journal of Accounting and Economics, 12*(4), 365–380.

Walker, M. M. (1994). Determinants of Bondholder Wealth Following Corporate Takeovers (1980–1988). *Quarterly Journal of Business and Economics, 33*(1), 12–29.

Wang, M., & Hussainey, K. (2013). Voluntary forward-looking statements driven by corporate governance and their value relevance. *Journal of Accounting and Public Policy, 32*(3), 26–49.

Wansley, J. W., & Clauretie, T. M. (1985). The impact of creditwatch placement on equity returns and bond prices. *The Journal of Financial Research, 8*(1), 31–42.

Wansley, J. W., Glascock, J. L., & Clauretie, T. M. (1992). Institutional bond pricing and information arrival: The case of bond rating changes. *Journal of Business Finance and Accounting, 19*(5), 733–749.

Warga, A., & Welch, I. (1993). Bondholder Losses in Leveraged Buyouts. *The Review of Financial Studies, 6*(4), 959–982.

Warga, A. D. (1998). *Fixed income data base*. University of Houston, Houston, Texas.

Warner, J. B. (1977). Bankruptcy, absolut priority, and the pricing of risky debt claims. *Journal of Financial Economics, 4*(3), 239–276.

Wei, C., & Yermack, D. (2011). Investor Reactions to CEOs' Inside Debt Incentives. *The Review of Financial Studies, 24*(11), 3813–3840.

Weil, R. L. (1973). Macaulay's Duration: An Appreciation. *The Journal of Business, 46*(4), 589–592.

Weinstein, M. (1977). The effect of a rating change announcement on bond price. *Journal of Financial Economics, 5*(3), 329–350.

White, H. (1980). A Heteroskedasticity-Consistent Covariance Matrix Estimator and a Direct Test for Heteroskedasticity. *Econometrica, 48*(4), 817–838.

Wooldridge, J. M. (2003). Cluster-Sample Methods in Applied Econometrics. *The American Economic Review, 93*(2), 133–138.

Woolridge, J. R. (1983). Dividend Changes and Security Prices. *The Journal of Finance, 38*(5), 1607–1615.

Corporate Finance and Governance

Herausgegeben von Dirk Schiereck

Band 1 Sebastian Michael Gläsner: Return Patterns of German Open-End Real Estate Funds. An Empirical Explanation of Smooth Fund Returns. 2010.

Band 2 Patrick Ams: Directors' Dealings and Insider Trading in Germany. An Empirical Analysis. 2010.

Band 3 Joachim Vogt: Value Creation within the Construction Industry. A Study of Strategic Takeovers. 2011.

Band 4 Fabian Braemisch: Underpricing, Long-Run Performance, and Valuation of Initial Public Offerings. 2011.

Band 5 Matthäus Markus Sielecki: Creating and Governing an Integrated Market for Retail Banking Services in Europe. A Conceptual-Empirical Study of the Role of Regulation in Promoting a Single Euro Payments Area. 2011.

Band 6 Arne Wilkes: Determinants of Credit Spreads. An Empirical Analysis for the European Corporate Bond Market. 2011.

Band 7 Dirk Schiereck / Martin Setzer (Hrsg.): Bankerfolg und Akquisitionen. Aktuelle Erkenntnisse zur Konsolidierung und Restrukturierung der Finanzindustrie. 2011.

Band 8 Steffen Meinshausen: M&A Activity, Divestitures and Initial Public Offerings in the Fashion Industry. 2012.

Band 9 Malte Helmut Raudszus: Financial Return Risk and the Effect on Shareholder Wealth. 2012.

Band 10 Ramit Mehta: Mergers and Acquisitions in the Global Brewing Industry. A Capital Market Perspective. 2012.

Band 11 Marcel Normann: The Influence of German Top Executives on Corporate Policy and Firm Performance. 2012.

Band 12 Christoph Böhm: Risk-Adjusted Performance and Bank Governance Structures. 2013.

Band 13 Christian Thamm: Minority Shareholder Monitoring and German Corporate Governance. Empirical Evidence and Value Effects. 2013.

Band 14 Robert M. Fraunhoffer: Mergers and Acquisitions in the Energy Sector. The Impact of Synergy Disclosures on Shareholder Wealth and Operating Performance. 2013.

Band 15 Heiko Schön: Pharma M&A versus alliances and its underlying value drivers. Are M&A or alliances the right therapy for an ailing pharmaceutical industry? A capital market perspective. 2015.

Band 16 Sascha Kolaric: Bank mergers and acquisitions in the Asia-Pacific region. An investigation of the shareholder wealth effects of the financial sector consolidation and its impact on the acquirer's cost of debt. 2015.

Band 17 Ulrich Erxleben: Value Creation of Corporate Restructuring. A Market Cycle and Industry View. 2015.

Band 18 Dennis Froneberg: Bank Governance Structures and Risk Taking. 2015.

Band 19 Michael G. Müller: Erklärungsansätze für NAV-Spreads und deren Implikationen für das Management von REITs. Auf Basis einer empirischen Untersuchung des pan-EU-REIT-Marktes. 2016.

Band 20 Daniel Maul: Analyzing Wealth Effects for Bondholders. New Insight on Major Corporate Events from the Debtholders' Perspective. 2016.

Band 21 Claudia Max: Valuation and Value Creation of Insurance Intermediaries. 2016.

www.peterlang.com